SOVIET MILITARY POWER:

AN ASSESSMENT OF THE THREAT

1988

CONTENTS

1

The Nature of the Soviet Threat

2

An Assessment of the Threat

PREFACE

Since 1981 the Secretary of Defense has published an assessment of the Soviet Union's military strength. This publication, *Soviet Military Power,* has provided the American people, our friends and allies throughout the world, and others, with a clear, concise description of Soviet military capabilities.

This year we have adopted a slightly different approach and taken a more comprehensive view of the trends and implications observed in Soviet military strength since 1981. Part 1 of this document describes the traditional components of Soviet military power. Chapter I provides an overview of Soviet military strategy, policy, organization, and doctrine. Chapter II analyzes Soviet foreign policy under General Secretary Gorbachev. Chapter III describes the resource base from which the Soviets draw their military strength. Chapter IV assesses Soviet strategic offensive, strategic defensive, and space forces. Chapter V summarizes Soviet conventional military power.

To understand fully the potential implications of Soviet military strength, however, it is necessary to examine the Soviet Union's military capabilities in relation to those of the United States and our allies. Part 2 of *Soviet Military Power 1988* places this Soviet strength in perspective by providing an assessment of the significant military power balances. Chapter VI discusses the history and current status of the balance between our strategic forces and those of the Soviet Union. Chapter VII contains our assessment of the military balances in Europe, Southwest Asia, and the Far East, as well as the maritime balance and our comparative capabilities to project military power. Because both the United States and the Soviet Union rely heavily on technology to improve their respective military capabilities, Chapter VIII provides a comparative assessment of how emerging technologies will affect our security in the not-too-distant future. Chapter IX concludes by reflecting on how we might best strengthen our collective security in light of the military threat presented by the Soviet Union, and our willingness to commit resources to deal effectively and efficiently with this threat.

As in previous issues, this year's *Soviet Military Power* also draws attention to some of the more noteworthy developments in Soviet military strength observed since the publication of *Soviet Military Power 1987,* among them:

- The Soviets' longstanding extensive program to build deep underground facilities for leadership protection during nuclear war is discussed in detail for the first time in this year's edition.
- The SS-24 rail-mobile intercontinental ballistic missile (ICBM) began its initial deployment;
- The SL-16 medium-lift space-launch vehicle became operational;
- The first launch of the SL-X-17 heavy-lift space-launch vehicle was observed;
- The SS-N-21 sea-launched cruise missile became operational;
- A fourth KIEV-Class aircraft carrier became operational;
- A third AKULA-Class nuclear-powered attack submarine was launched; and
- The Il-76/MAINSTAY airborne warning and control system aircraft became operational.

These are merely the most recent manifestations of a continuing buildup of Soviet nuclear and conventional force capabilities. Since 1981, virtually every component of Soviet military power has been expanded and modernized:

- Soviet strategic nuclear offensive forces continue to be upgraded. The decade began with the completion of fourth-generation ICBM deployment — the SS-17, SS-18, and SS-19. In 1985, the Soviets led off the introduction of a fifth generation of ICBMs with the road-mobile SS-25.
- The TYPHOON ballistic missile submarine (SSBN) carrying 20 SS-N-20 missiles was introduced, followed closely by the DELTA IV SSBN carrying the SS-N-23 missile.
- The BEAR H bomber, armed with the AS-15 long-range, nuclear-armed cruise missile, was introduced, and deployment of the new strategic bomber, the BLACKJACK, is about to begin.
- The Soviets continue modernizing their ballistic missile defense system around Moscow by converting it into a two-layer defense composed of silo-based, long-range, modified GALOSH interceptors; silo-based GAZELLE high-acceleration endoatmospheric interceptors; and associated engagement, guidance, and battle management radar systems, including the new PILL BOX large phased-array radar at Pushkino.

- The across-the-board modernization of Soviet conventional forces in the 1980s, including tanks, artillery, fighter aircraft, and surface and submarine combatants, constitutes a major improvement in Soviet military capabilities. The T-80 tank, BTR-80 armored personnel carrier, SPAA-M-1986 air defense gun, SA-12 surface-to-air missile, and SS-23 short-range ballistic missile have all become operational since 1981.
- The Su-25/FROGFOOT and the state-of-the-art Su-27/FLANKER, MiG-29/FULCRUM, and MiG-31/FOXHOUND aircraft are now all operational and widely deployed.
- In the Soviet Navy, a 65,000-ton aircraft carrier designed for ramp-assisted aircraft launch is under construction. Additionally, four new surface warship classes, two attack submarine classes, three new naval aircraft types, six new naval surface weapon systems, and six new general purpose submarine classes have been put to sea by the Soviets since 1981.

Soviet military power and the threat it represents are not, then, abstract notions. The Soviets' willingness to use military force to exact compliance through threats or even by crossing international borders in armed aggression, as they did in Afghanistan, is undeniable.

But the Soviets are now projecting a much different international image, giving rise to hopes for fundamental changes in Soviet behavior. Whether these changes, if realized, will constitute a real opportunity for more fundamental improvements in our relations with the Soviet Union remains to be seen. While recognizing the competitive and predominantly adversarial character of our relationship with the Soviet Union, it is our policy to pursue a dialogue with them in order to seize opportunities for more constructive relations. In the spirit of this policy, I recently met with the Defense Minister of the Soviet Union, General Dmitri Yazov. My purpose was to discuss a variety of security issues, including prevention of dangerous incidents. I also wanted to gain a better understanding of Soviet public declarations of a "defensive doctrine" and their concept of "reasonable sufficiency." Our discussions produced little if any specific information about whether there is indeed a new Soviet doctrine, and, if there is, whether it will mean substantive changes in Soviet force structure or military spending. I did not learn what definitive changes might take place in Soviet military posture if a truly "defensive" doctrine based on "reasonable sufficiency" were implemented.

While we continue to hope for meaningful change on the Soviets' part to less aggressive and less dangerous policies and postures, to date, we have seen no evidence of the USSR changing the offensive nature of its force structure and deployment patterns. Military output has not been reduced nor has military spending decreased. On the contrary, the Soviet military budget under General Secretary Gorbachev continues to grow at a rate of 3 percent per year at a level representing 15 to 17 percent of their GNP. Most important, the Soviet force posture and military capabilities detailed in this book are not consistent with a defensive military posture. We would all welcome a sincere Soviet effort to change their military posture, especially if it is backed up by observable reductions in forces and spending. We will continue to watch — while maintaining our vigilance.

It is my hope that this realistic portrait of the Soviet Union's military capabilities and the threat they constitute to the Free World will assist all Americans, our friends, and our allies to appreciate the tremendous size and scope of the security challenges before us. We must not be overawed by Soviet military capabilities, though they are formidable indeed. Rather, we must strengthen our resolve to preserve our freedoms and our national security, and fashion an enduring program for our collective security. Only in this way can we, our allies, and our friends secure the blessings of liberty and freedom for ourselves and our posterity in the years ahead.

Frank C. Carlucci
Secretary of Defense

1

The Nature of the Soviet Threat

- Soviet National Security Policies

- Soviet Foreign Policy Under Gorbachev

- Military Resources Allocation

- Soviet Strategic Programs and Space Forces

- Soviet Conventional Forces

Our consideration of *Soviet Military Power* begins with a detailed examination of Soviet goals and objectives. By first understanding the foundations that shape the character of Soviet military power, we can assess properly the overall threat posed by Moscow's arsenal; then, we can evaluate the balance of power between the United States and Soviet Union.

Soviet national goals and objectives, doctrine, and military capabilities are not discrete items to be examined in isolation from each other. Indeed, there is a close relationship between the Soviet Union's overarching national goals, its military doctrine, and the forces it has amassed to accomplish its political and military ends. The Kremlin's military doctrine and the forces that flow from that doctrine have become more complex over the years as the leadership refined its understanding of the nature of future war and the best methods available to employ military power. Soviet goals, however, are unchanged, for those goals are defined by the principles of the Soviet regime, and these principles have remained basically constant in the post-war period.

There is certainly a desire on the part of some to believe or wish that this were otherwise. A number of political, as well as military, changes have taken place in the Soviet Union, some quite recent. It would be a mistake, however, to regard political and military shifts as mirroring fundamental changes in the nature of the Soviet regime.

CHAPTER I

Soviet National Security Policies

The Soviets' national goals and objectives are best understood within the broader framework of their culture, politics, ideology, and history.

■ Russian civilization has not assimilated such basic Western concepts as constitutionalism, democratic government, the rights of the individual, or the free, entrepreneurial market.
■ Politically, both Tsarist and Soviet systems have been characterized by autocratic rule, a centralized bureaucracy, and control by police power.
■ Marxist-Leninist ideology teaches that the Soviets are engaged in a long-term struggle between two basically irreconcilable political, economic, and social systems. In this struggle, they believe history and time are on their side.
■ The Soviet Union and the Tsarist system that preceded it have justified their expansionist policies over the past three centuries by asserting — often falsely — that Russian history is a repetitive story of invasion and occupation.

These factors, among others, help explain the Soviet leadership's view of the world that shapes the political behavior and military actions of the Soviet Union. Culturally, they take great pride in what they believe to be the superiority of a political and economic system, buttressed by military power, that elevated the Soviet Union to superpower status. On the other hand, they experience feelings of inferiority when they are not accepted as full participants in world affairs. Thus, a fundamental goal of Soviet national strategy is to achieve the status that would guarantee "equal participation in world affairs" and freedom from any criticism of, or interference in, Soviet internal affairs.

The ideological dimension of Soviet national strategy envisages a basically adversarial relationship that is explicit in Marxist dialectic. This causes the Kremlin to engage in a continual struggle with the West. This conflict requires the total integration of political, military, economic, and subversive components of Soviet national power. Their national goals and objectives require that the Soviets expand their military power and political influence beyond their own borders to ensure their security and satisfy their imperialist urge.

These cultural, ideological, political, and historical factors help explain Soviet national security priorities. These are:

■ To strengthen the Soviet political system and preserve rule by the Communist Party of the Soviet Union.
■ To extend and enhance Soviet influence worldwide.
■ To defend the Soviet homeland and state against potential aggression.
■ To maintain dominance over the land and sea areas adjacent to Soviet borders.

Soviet behavior reveals that they would prefer to achieve these objectives by peaceful means. At the same time, the Soviets have amassed enormous military power, far in excess of what might be required for defense. Though they prefer peace to war, they are perfectly willing to advance their interests by intimidation, coercive diplomacy, or the direct use of force as in Hungary, Czechoslovakia, or Afghanistan.

SYSTEMIC TRENDS

The early 1980s marked the close of the Brezhnev era, a time of relative prosperity at home and dramatic increase in Soviet military power and political influence abroad. Despite these achievements, the final years of the Brezhnev era brought increasing difficulties in foreign and domestic affairs. The Kremlin leadership was faced with a marked slowdown in economic growth. Based on Soviet data, average annual national income declined from a growth rate of over 8 percent in the 1960s, to 5 to 6 percent in the 1970s, to 1 to 2 percent in the early 1980s. As economic growth decreased, the Soviets' objective of reducing the technology gap with Western industrial nations was jeopardized. Even the modest improvements in living standards of the 1960s and 1970s came to a halt. At the same time, events such as the Polish crisis of the early 1980s affected the Kremlin's thinking about the risks of ignoring public dissatisfaction with economic conditions and an unresponsive political system.

Meanwhile, the political leadership became increasingly entrenched. "Stability of cadres" — the implied political contract between Brezhnev and the bureau-

During the 27th Party Congress, General Secretary Gorbachev espoused a new concept of military "sufficiency" which would achieve "parity at a lower level." The General Secretary's public statements notwithstanding, Soviet military spending has increased during his tenure. Aware that Moscow's superpower status is derived from its military power, he and the Soviet leadership are fully committed to nuclear and conventional force modernization.

cratic elite — gradually took the form of a lifetime guarantee of job tenure, even for officials who were inept or corrupt. Upon Brezhnev's death in 1982, he was succeeded by Yuri Andropov, who was succeeded, when he died in 1984, by Konstantin Chernenko.

Brezhnev's last years and the abbreviated tenures of his two ailing successors were years of malaise. The foreign policy successes of the 1970s were not sustained. More assertive Western policies and military developments in the 1980s often put Moscow on the defensive. The Soviets were unable to block the West's deployment of intermediate-range nuclear weapons in Europe, which were a response to Soviet deployments of SS-20 missiles arrayed against targets in NATO countries. Beleaguered Soviet clients in Africa faced insurgent movements, while Soviet military efforts in Afghanistan

bogged down after the December 1979 invasion.

By the mid-1980s, as the 70th anniversary of the October Revolution approached, a consensus emerged within the Kremlin on the need for policies to reverse these adverse trends. The main spokesman for this consensus was Mikhail Gorbachev, who succeeded Konstantin Chernenko as General Secretary in March 1985.

Although Soviet goals and objectives had not changed, Gorbachev and his allies realized that new policies were needed to restructure the Soviet system. They were determined to revitalize the political and economic system and overhaul the party leadership's domestic and international image by presenting themselves as representatives of a new, younger, more dynamic, and capable generation of Soviet leaders. They presented their outline for a restructured Soviet system called "perestroika."

To promote the image of a revitalized political system, the leadership renewed the crackdown on official corruption. The new leaders also initiated a sweeping shakeup of the Soviet bureaucracy designed to replace Brezhnev-era holdovers with new managers more technically competent and attuned to Gorbachev's domestic programs.

Gorbachev and his allies also endorsed a policy of "democratization," which called for a selective expansion of work force participation in enterprise decisionmaking, and permitted the popular election of its managers. The goal was to give workers a greater stake in the management of their own factories, thereby increasing the pressure on the managers to be more efficient. The new leadership also introduced multi-candidate elections to some government and party posts. Additionally, they established procedures to expand channels to air grievances against officials and opened opportunities for nationwide discussion of policies under consideration by the leadership. These measures were designed to project a populist, progressive image and to enlist the Soviet public in the effort to make a lethargic Soviet bureaucracy more efficient and productive.

To increase pressure on bureaucrats to accept the new program objectives and style of management, the Gorbachev leadership adopted a policy of "glasnost." Although "glasnost" is interpreted by some in the West to mean "openness," it is used by the Soviets to connote "publicity" or officially managed perceptions. Under this policy, while maintaining control over the media, the regime has selectively allowed more complete reporting of "negative" domestic news and foreign policy issues previously suppressed by Soviet censors. There has also been significant loosening of the strictures on cultural expression, with a much wider range of themes — including some that are politically sensitive — tolerated in literature, film, theater, and art. The Gorbachev leadership has continued to enforce a crackdown on alcohol and drug abuse and other manifestations of what Gorbachev calls "social corrosion." Nevertheless, public debate on certain topics — such as the primacy of the party in national life, the KGB, and some human rights abuses — is still prohibited.

To address the most pressing domestic problem — revitalizing the stagnating economy — Gorbachev and his allies have adopted a multi-faceted strategy. Among other things, this strategy will increase investment allocations to civilian machine building industries and will promote programs to increase work force discipline

and improve management. A key component of Gorbachev's program to reinvigorate the economy is the "new economic mechanism," an attempt to overcome the braking effect of the over-centralized command economy by expanding entrepreneurial autonomy and increasing the role of incentives. Simultaneously, the day-to-day role of central economic agencies is being reduced. The enterprise's own ability to determine the size and wage scale of its labor force is being increased, as is its ability to set its own prices or negotiate prices with its customers. Also envisioned is expanded enterprise control over its supply arrangements, previously dominated by centrally decreed distribution plans. At the same time, enterprises are expected to become less dependent on the state for subsidies and investment funds, and more self-sufficient financially as the result of profitable operations. Although Gorbachev's "new economic mechanism" is clearly a compromise between those who advocate more far-reaching changes and those who favor more modest shifts in the management apparatus, it nevertheless moves well beyond previous management efforts at reform.

What has not changed is the reliance of the Soviet Union on military power to undergird its political policies and the continued willingness of the Soviet leadership to provide the resources necessary to sustain its military power.

SOVIET MILITARY DOCTRINE AND STRATEGY

Soviet military doctrine, the military policy of the Communist Party of the Soviet Union, is concerned with the nature of a possible future war and the preparation of the country and its armed forces for conducting such a war. Military strategy deals with defining the strategic tasks of the armed forces: carrying out measures to prepare the armed forces, the economy, and the population for war; assessing the military potential of its adversaries; and determining the size and composition of military forces necessary to wage war. The actual practice of preparing armed forces for war, as well as training troops for strategic, operational, and tactical combat, is encompassed in Soviet military art — the effective application of military power to achieve the USSR's political goals.

Although the Soviet leadership appears to recognize the devastating consequences of nuclear war, Soviet military doctrine calls for the ability to achieve victory across the entire spectrum of conflict, from limited conventional to strategic nuclear war. Soviet military doctrine views war as an extension of politics and emphasizes offensive operations. The Soviet military leadership has identified these principles as essential if

The accuracy and survivability of the recently deployed rail-mobile SS-24 Mod 1 will significantly increase the lethality of the USSR's ICBM force. The missile can be deployed throughout the Soviet Union.

armed conflict is to be decided in its favor. For the Soviets, victory in either a conventional or a nuclear war would entail the defeat or neutralization of the United States and NATO and the survival of the party-dominated politico-economic structure at home.

Soviet military doctrine, strategy, and tactics have become more sophisticated in response to technological advances and changes in the political environment. Some tenets of doctrine have remained constant over the years, while others have been modified to reflect changes in the Soviet calculation of the "correlation of forces" — the quantitative and qualitative calculus they use to evaluate the current and projected status of the East-West competition. Until late 1964, the party leadership expected that the next world war would begin with a nuclear exchange. They acknowledged that conventional forces would be used to exploit the success of nuclear strikes and to seize and occupy enemy territory. Beginning in the mid-1960s, however, Soviet doctrinal statements began discussing the growing possibility of a brief conventional phase of armed conflict. Accordingly, the Soviets, in addition to their nuclear arms buildup, undertook a wide-ranging modernization of their conventional forces to ensure their capability to fight effectively on either a nuclear or a nonnuclear battlefield.

Beginning in the late 1970s, due to an acknowledged condition of nuclear parity, the Soviets began contemplating the possibility of an extended conventional war, and even the possibility that war between the superpowers might not become nuclear. This doctrinal shift was due in part to technological developments in advanced conventional weaponry, in part as a reaction to NATO's strategy of flexible response. This greater emphasis on conventional war has been reflected in force modernization and training, which stress a longer conventional phase. Soviet military doctrine now recognizes that neither strategic nuclear nor conventional forces are by themselves "decisive," but that they only achieve their maximum effectiveness in concert. The Soviets have spent great resources to modernize and expand their conventional forces, while continuing to expand their strategic nuclear offensive and defensive forces, stressing their ability to fight under both nuclear and nonnuclear conditions.

Soviet military writings during this same period continued to emphasize the initial period of war. Marshal Nikolai Ogarkov wrote in 1984, "There is a sharp expansion in the zone of possible combat operations, and the role and significance of the initial period of war and its initial operations become incomparably greater." This emphasis is also discussed in the 1984 book, *M.V. Frunze — Military Theorist*, by Colonel General M.A. Gareyev, a deputy chief of the General Staff. Gareyev stresses that "the main role of the initial period of war will increase further and this may be the main and decisive period which largely predetermines the outcome of the entire war."

During the 1980s, the Soviets have also begun to incorporate defensive operations into an overall offensive strategy. They have done so in response to what they perceive as NATO's offensive concepts of Follow-on Forces Attack, and AirLand Battle, as well as NATO's improved conventional forces. The Soviets have always accepted the idea that, for a limited time during a future war, they may have to engage in defensive operations in certain areas within an overall theater of operations. Their objective in training, however, is to move as quickly as possible to the counteroffensive.

The Gorbachev leadership continues to adhere to this military doctrine, with its emphasis on victory in any conflict contingency. Soviet training, for example, still stresses the conventional (but nuclear-threatened) battlefield and a protracted period of conventional combat. At the same time, it reflects a continuing concern with developing forces and a strategy capable of emerging victorious in all phases of warfare, including a protracted nuclear war.

GORBACHEV'S IMPACT ON MILITARY DOCTRINE

Further refinements in certain aspects of Soviet military doctrine may be in the offing. During his 27th Party Congress speech in February 1986, Gorbachev mentioned without elaboration the concept of "reasonable sufficiency." Since that speech, there have been numerous references to achieving "parity at a lower level,"

as well as other leadership statements on sufficiency. For example, in his speech to the International Forum for a Nuclear-Free World in February 1987, Gorbachev emphasized reducing conventional and nuclear forces in a way that ensures a constantly declining "balance of reasonable sufficiency." In a late May meeting of the Warsaw Pact Political Consultative Committee, these concepts were presented in what was labeled as a "Warsaw Pact statement on military doctrine." Although Soviet commentators later described the announcement as embodying a "new" Soviet military doctrine, most of the tenets in the declaration had appeared in earlier Warsaw Pact statements.

Soviet spokesmen claim — as they have for three decades — that Pact military doctrine has not changed and is defensive in nature because it is designed to maintain only those forces necessary for defense against a NATO attack. According to the Soviets, by having an exclusively defensive posture, neither the Warsaw Pact nor NATO would have the capability to launch an attack. Soviet military writings suggest that military "sufficiency" — which the Soviets have yet to define precisely — could lessen international tensions while maintaining military parity. Minister of Defense Dmitri Yazov, in his recent book *On Guard for Socialism and Peace* implies, however, that military sufficiency means force levels capable of repelling an enemy attack *and* conducting successful offensive operations to destroy the enemy. The Soviets' war-fighting strategy has consistently stipulated the requirement for sufficient military forces to achieve their strategic objectives in wartime, central among which is the destruction of the enemy forces.

To date, there is no reason to conclude that "reasonable sufficiency" represents a renunciation or even an alteration of the inherently offensive Soviet military strategy. Gorbachev and his allies are as keenly aware as their predecessors that the Soviet Union's superpower status and its ability to achieve its strategic objectives derive from its military power. Indeed, the Soviet Union's commitment to modernizing both its nuclear and conventional forces has continued under Gorbachev. Yet one cannot rule out the possibility that the announcement of the new concept may be an indication of future changes in the Warsaw Pact armed forces. If meaningful changes do occur, they could affect levels of readiness, force structure, sustainability, training, and operations. Should such changes begin to occur, the result could just as easily be a smaller and yet even more capable offensive force structure — one sufficient by any standard to pursue Soviet political and military objectives that have not really changed. In addition, the concept of "reasonable sufficiency" is consistent with Soviet long-standing objectives of dividing NATO, slowing US and NATO force modernization, derailing the US Strategic Defense Initiative program through arms control, and allowing time for Soviet economic, technological, and industrial initiatives to take effect. Thus, the West must not only listen to Soviet pronouncements but also observe Soviet actions. Rhetoric notwithstanding, Soviet defense spending has risen, not diminished, under Gorbachev's aegis.

SOVIET ARMED FORCES STRUCTURE

Supreme leadership of the Soviet Armed Forces, as in any other sector of Soviet society, is vested in the Communist Party of the Soviet Union (CPSU), notably the Politburo and the Defense Council. Direct control and administration of the daily activities of the armed forces is entrusted to the Ministry of Defense (MOD), headed by General of the Army Dmitri Yazov. As Minister of Defense, Yazov is charged with maintaining the readiness of the armed forces and overseeing their development. Yazov is also responsible, in conjunction with organizations in the Party-state hierarchy, for the comprehensive Soviet civil defense program. Party control of the armed forces is assured by its decisionmaking power, its control over personnel appointments, and by the KGB's Third Chief Directorate and the MOD's Main Political Directorate.

The MOD Collegium functions as a key consultative body and policy review board. Chaired by the Minister of Defense, the Collegium resolves issues related to the development of the armed forces, their readiness, and the effectiveness of military and political training. Its members include the three first deputy defense ministers, the 11 deputy ministers, and the Chief of the Main Political Administration.

Five of the 11 deputy ministers are Commanders in Chief (CINCs) of the five services — Strategic Rocket Forces, Ground Forces, Navy, Air Defense Forces, and Air Forces. The five service CINCs are responsible for peacetime force administration, management, and training. The remaining six deputy defense ministers oversee civil defense, rear services, the main inspectorate, construction and billeting, personnel, and armaments.

The most important element in the MOD for both peacetime and wartime force management and control is the General Staff, headed by Marshal of the Soviet Union Sergey Akhromeyev. As the central military staff organ, the General Staff exercises operational control over the armed forces. It is responsible for coordinating planning by the service main staffs and the staffs of the four high commands of forces, 16 military districts, four

groups of forces in Eastern Europe, four fleets, rear services, civil defense, and the directorates of the MOD. The General Staff also advises the Defense Council and MOD Collegium on military policy and develops positions on questions of military strategy for Defense Council approval. Its major peacetime functions are to develop integrated war plans for strategic operations and to ensure that the armed forces are ready to conduct such operations at all times.

Territorially, the USSR is divided into 16 military districts (MDs). An MD is a high-level element of military administration with subordinate military units, training institutions, recruitment and mobilization offices, and other military establishments. Aside from supervising combat training, the MD commander is responsible for overseeing draftee registration and induction, mobilization planning, civil defense, and premilitary and reserve training.

Soviet units stationed in Poland, East Germany, Czechoslovakia, and Hungary are organized into four groups of forces. The four groups and most military districts are subordinate to one of four permanent regional high commands. These high commands of forces control the ground, air, and naval forces that would conduct operations in the Western, Southwestern, Southern, and Far Eastern Theaters of Military Operations (TVDs). Acting as regional extensions of the Supreme High Command and General Staff, the four high commands are designed to centralize General Staff control over wartime theater operations.

In peacetime, non-Soviet Warsaw Pact (NSWP) forces are subordinate to their respective national commands. In wartime, however, NSWP forces would come under Soviet command under the High Commands of Forces in the Western and Southwestern TVDs. Their war plans, training, tactics, force structure, and readiness are dictated by the concerns of the Soviet military establishment. This command structure reflects the fact that the national interests of the Warsaw Pact's East European members are routinely subordinated to those of the USSR.

East European reliability and the military capabilities of Moscow's allies are matters of considerable concern to the Kremlin. NSWP forces can probably be counted on to support Soviet-determined Pact objectives during the initial stages of a conflict. Soviet control mechanisms and the caliber of training and discipline among most NSWP forces should ensure reliable response to alert and mobilization orders and the conduct of initial operations. Reliability becomes increasingly doubtful after the initial stages of hostilities. The circumstances

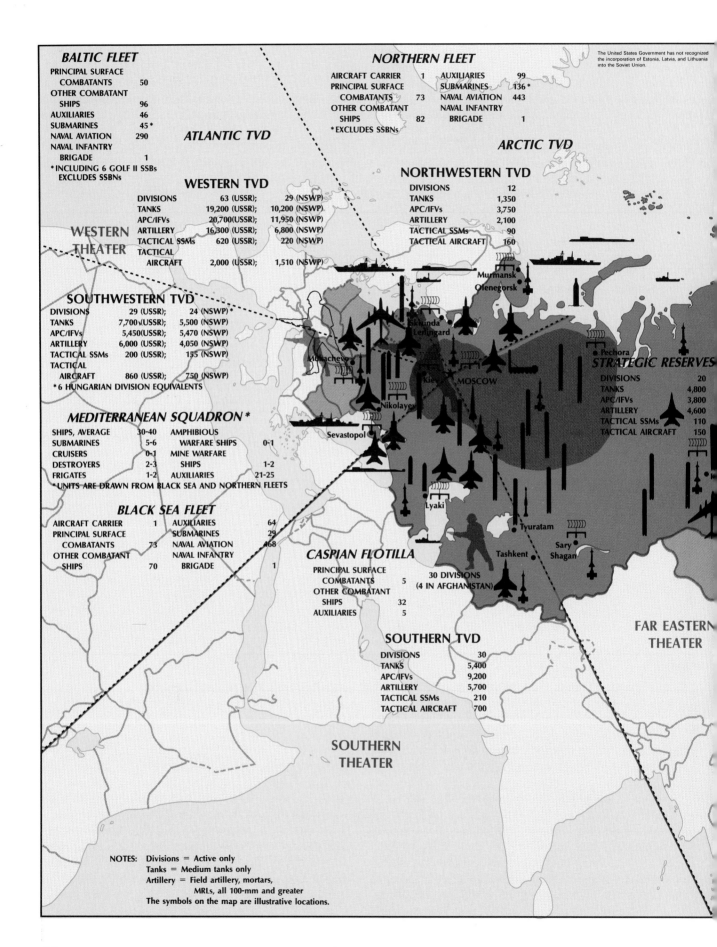

BALTIC FLEET

PRINCIPAL SURFACE COMBATANTS	50
OTHER COMBATANT SHIPS	96
AUXILIARIES	46
SUBMARINES	45 *
NAVAL AVIATION	290
NAVAL INFANTRY BRIGADE	1

*INCLUDING 6 GOLF II SSBs
EXCLUDES SSBNs

ATLANTIC TVD

NORTHERN FLEET

AIRCRAFT CARRIER	1	AUXILIARIES	99
PRINCIPAL SURFACE COMBATANTS	73	SUBMARINES	136 *
		NAVAL AVIATION	443
OTHER COMBATANT SHIPS	82	NAVAL INFANTRY BRIGADE	1

*EXCLUDES SSBNs

The United States Government has not recognized the incorporation of Estonia, Latvia, and Lithuania into the Soviet Union.

ARCTIC TVD

NORTHWESTERN TVD

DIVISIONS	12
TANKS	1,350
APC/IFVs	3,750
ARTILLERY	2,100
TACTICAL SSMs	90
TACTICAL AIRCRAFT	160

WESTERN THEATER

WESTERN TVD

DIVISIONS	63 (USSR);	29 (NSWP)
TANKS	19,200 (USSR);	10,200 (NSWP)
APC/IFVs	20,700 (USSR);	11,950 (NSWP)
ARTILLERY	16,300 (USSR);	6,800 (NSWP)
TACTICAL SSMs	620 (USSR);	220 (NSWP)
TACTICAL AIRCRAFT	2,000 (USSR);	1,510 (NSWP)

SOUTHWESTERN TVD

DIVISIONS	29 (USSR);	24 (NSWP) *
TANKS	7,700 (USSR);	5,500 (NSWP)
APC/IFVs	5,450 (USSR);	5,470 (NSWP)
ARTILLERY	6,000 (USSR);	4,050 (NSWP)
TACTICAL SSMs	200 (USSR);	135 (NSWP)
TACTICAL AIRCRAFT	860 (USSR);	750 (NSWP)

*6 HUNGARIAN DIVISION EQUIVALENTS

MEDITERRANEAN SQUADRON *

SHIPS, AVERAGE	30-40	AMPHIBIOUS WARFARE SHIPS	0-1
SUBMARINES	5-6	MINE WARFARE SHIPS	1-2
CRUISERS	0-1		
DESTROYERS	2-3		
FRIGATES	1-2	AUXILIARIES	21-25

*UNITS ARE DRAWN FROM BLACK SEA AND NORTHERN FLEETS

BLACK SEA FLEET

AIRCRAFT CARRIER	1	AUXILIARIES	64
PRINCIPAL SURFACE COMBATANTS	73	SUBMARINES	29
		NAVAL AVIATION	468
OTHER COMBATANT SHIPS	70	NAVAL INFANTRY BRIGADE	1

CASPIAN FLOTILLA

PRINCIPAL SURFACE COMBATANTS	5
OTHER COMBATANT SHIPS	32
AUXILIARIES	5

30 DIVISIONS
(4 IN AFGHANISTAN)

STRATEGIC RESERVES

DIVISIONS	20
TANKS	4,800
APC/IFVs	3,800
ARTILLERY	4,600
TACTICAL SSMs	110
TACTICAL AIRCRAFT	150

SOUTHERN TVD

DIVISIONS	30
TANKS	5,400
APC/IFVs	9,200
ARTILLERY	5,700
TACTICAL SSMs	210
TACTICAL AIRCRAFT	700

SOUTHERN THEATER

FAR EASTERN THEATER

NOTES: Divisions = Active only
Tanks = Medium tanks only
Artillery = Field artillery, mortars, MRLs, all 100-mm and greater
The symbols on the map are illustrative locations.

14

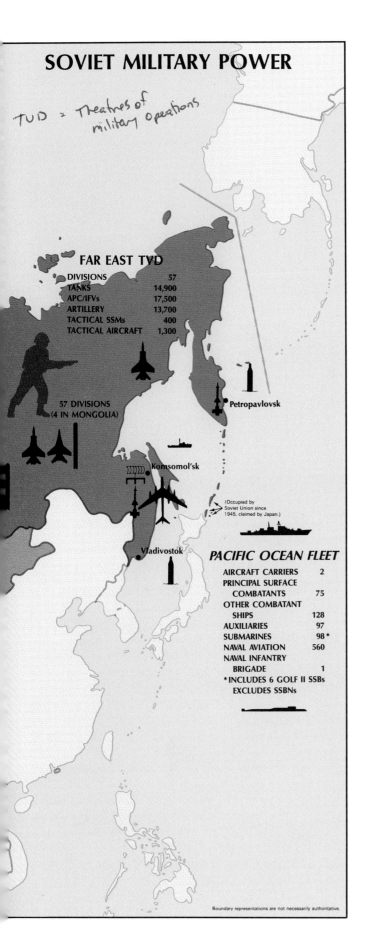

SOVIET MILITARY POWER

TUD = Theatres of military operations

FAR EAST TVD

DIVISIONS	57
TANKS	14,900
APC/IFVs	17,500
ARTILLERY	13,700
TACTICAL SSMs	400
TACTICAL AIRCRAFT	1,300

57 DIVISIONS
(4 IN MONGOLIA)

Petropavlovsk

Komsomol'sk

(Occupied by Soviet Union since 1945, claimed by Japan.)

Vladivostok

PACIFIC OCEAN FLEET

AIRCRAFT CARRIERS	2
PRINCIPAL SURFACE	
COMBATANTS	75
OTHER COMBATANT	
SHIPS	128
AUXILIARIES	97
SUBMARINES	98 *
NAVAL AVIATION	560
NAVAL INFANTRY	
BRIGADE	1
*INCLUDES 6 GOLF II SSBs	
EXCLUDES SSBNs	

Boundary representations are not necessarily authoritative.

NUCLEAR FORCES

FIXED AND MOBILE ICBMs

SS-11	420
SS-13	60
SS-17	138
SS-18	308
SS-19	350
SS-25	About 100
SS-24 (MOD 1)	About 10

LRINF

SS-4	52
SS-20	441[1]

SLBMs

SS-N-5	36
SS-N-6	256
SS-N-8	286
SS-N-17	12
SS-N-18	224
SS-N-20	100
SS-N-23	64

BOMBERS [2]

BACKFIRE	321
BEAR	160
BADGER	272
BLINDER	135

TACTICAL AIRCRAFT

TACTICAL AIRCRAFT	5,170

GROUND FORCES [3]

MOTORIZED RIFLE DIVISIONS	150
TANK DIVISIONS	52
AIRBORNE DIVISIONS	7
STATIC DEFENSE DIVISIONS	2

NAVAL FORCES

AIRCRAFT CARRIERS	4
PRINCIPAL SURFACE	
COMBATANTS	276
OTHER COMBATANT	
SHIPS	408
COMBATANT CRAFT	765
AUXILIARIES	311
SUBMARINES	308
NAVAL AVIATION	1,761

STRATEGIC DEFENSE FORCES

ABM/BMEW RADAR	
INTERCEPTORS	2,250
ASAT	
SAM [4] LAUNCHERS	9,000 +
ABM LAUNCHERS	100

[1] 405 at fixed sites; 441 includes 36 taken off line but counted for threat assessment purposes.
[2] Includes 143 BACKFIRE in Soviet Naval Aviation (SNA). Excludes some 120 SNA BADGER Cs. 11 BLACKJACK in advanced flight testing.
[3] Totals exclude Soviet and NSWP mobilization divisions and 2 Soviet New Army Corps.
[4] In USSR only — does not include Soviet strategic SAMs (SA-2/3/5) in Mongolia or with Groups of Forces.

Although public statements by Soviet leaders in 1987 indicated a change in emphasis away from the military, the USSR continued to fund the modernization of all Soviet forces.

surrounding the outbreak of war, the extent of the Pact's battlefield success, and the personal motivations of the NSWP leadership would all affect Pact reliability. These factors may be complicated by NATO initiatives to disrupt Pact unity.

WARTIME COMMAND AND CONTROL

In the Soviet view, modern war demands a system of strategic leadership capable of making a rapid transition to wartime conditions and structured to provide central direction to the entire war effort. To this end, peacetime national security decisionmaking bodies have been established that constitute the nucleus of the highest-level organs of Soviet wartime strategic leadership. These peacetime organizations can shift to their wartime structure and function with minimal disruption and little increase in membership. They have available wartime command post complexes equipped with life support systems and relatively survivable communications designed to enable the leadership to manage operations throughout a nuclear war, as reported in Chapter IV.

As the readiness of the armed forces rises during a crisis, the Defense Council probably will be expanded to include several additional party and state leaders. In wartime, it will fulfill the same functions as the World War II State Defense Committee: to ensure that all aspects of the Soviet war effort are centrally directed. The General Secretary will chair the wartime Defense Council and will, as Supreme Commander in Chief, head the General Headquarters (*Stavka*) of the Supreme High Command (*Verkhovnoye Glavnokomandovaniye or VGK*). The VGK Stavka is the highest leadership body for the armed forces in wartime, planning strategic operations, and overseeing the wartime development of the armed forces. The MOD Collegium will probably provide the foundation for the VGK Stavka. In addition to the CPSU General Secretary, it will include the Minister of Defense, the Chief of the General Staff and other first deputy defense ministers, the Chief of the Main Political Directorate, and the five service CINCs.

The General Staff will provide the VGK Stavka with

staff support and act as its executive agent. Working with the staffs of each of the services, the Main Operations Directorate of the General Staff will draft for the Stavka detailed plans for strategic operations. Once approved, these plans will be issued to operational commanders as VGK directives. Since these directives will necessarily be affected by the uncertainties of combat, they will be reevaluated and refined continually. Thus, the General Staff and VGK Stavka representatives will ensure the timely execution and oversee precise evaluation of VGK directives. This command structure ensures Party control over and direct participation in Soviet military combat planning and execution.

The Soviet Armed Forces have been structured to perform three basic strategic missions: strikes by strategic nuclear forces against targets in adjacent theaters and distant continents; strategic defensive operations to defeat enemy air and missile attack and to ensure the stability of the national war management system; and offensive strategic operations by combined forces in key theaters on the periphery of the USSR. The Soviet strategic nuclear forces — land- and sea-based strategic missile and air forces — are assigned nuclear strike missions against targets in North America, Europe, the Far East, and elsewhere. These forces will be controlled directly by the VGK Stavka. Soviet and Warsaw Pact ground, air, air defense, naval, and civil defense forces will conduct operations to limit damage to the USSR and to defeat enemy forces.

The General Staff's planners view a multi-theater war as their worst-case contingency. As a result, Soviet forces designated for operations in Europe, the Far East, and Southwest Asia are large enough to function independently. With the formation of high commands for controlling the ground, air, and naval forces in each of the theaters on the Soviet periphery, campaigns in several widely separated regions can be conducted simultaneously. Each of the four high commands will act to centralize and integrate effectively General Staff control over theater-wide offensive operations. The bulk of the forces that each high command would control in wartime consists of fronts generated by border military districts in the USSR, Soviet Groups of Forces, and NSWP forces. Inside the USSR, military districts will continue to perform territorial administration, military support, and recovery management.

Since the late 1970s, the Soviets have introduced and institutionalized measures aimed at modernizing the Warsaw Pact's unified wartime command structure. These measures are designed to ensure that NSWP forces are quickly subordinated to the Soviet high commands that now exist for Western and Southwestern

TVD forces. As they are in peacetime, these commands will be headed by senior Soviet officers in war.

The Soviets have established a comprehensive, redundant set of both fixed and mobile command facilities throughout the USSR to direct their strategic nuclear and theater general purpose forces. Each significant military command element is provided at least one exurban wartime command post. These wartime command posts are mostly near-surface bunkers but include deep-underground complexes for the highest civilian and military leadership. Having undergone several periods of expansion and renovation, Soviet deep-underground command facilities today are, in some cases, hundreds of meters deep and can accommodate thousands of people for an extended period.

PROSPECTS

The Soviets' active public relations campaign to change Western perceptions of the USSR has demonstrated their keen understanding of the influence of Western mass media. The Soviets have not likely changed their long-standing ambition to become the dominant global power. During the next 10 years, the Soviets can be expected to press domestic initiatives to reinvigorate their economy, modernize their industrial base, and acquire the technologies to maintain a powerful military force for the full spectrum of conflict.

The Soviets will continue to adhere to the concept that the defense of the USSR must be built upon a force capable of seizing the offensive and destroying the enemy's means of waging war. This concept holds that their forces must be prepared to fight and prevail at all levels of conflict. In the past decade, the economic costs to acquire large nuclear forces, strategic and tactical defensive forces, modern general purpose forces, and a command, control, and communications structure, as well as to provide deep-underground shelters for leadership protection cannot be ignored or taken lightly. While the Soviets have been on a steady course of expanding their military capabilities to underwrite their political ambitions, they have realized that high-technology programs underway in the West, if fielded, could widen the gap in advanced military capabilities, hamper all their recent gains, and impede plans for the future. Thus, they have embarked on broad-based political, economic, and active-measures programs to slow the West's efforts and gain time to acquire a more modern industrial base and vigorous economy, so as to be even more competitive in the future. While clearly intending to change Western perceptions of the USSR, they have as yet shown no tangible evidence of changing their long-term goals.

CHAPTER II

Soviet Foreign Policy Under Gorbachev

Soviet foreign policy has not abandoned its traditional long-term objective of shifting "the correlation of forces" in its favor. Under Gorbachev, the Soviets intend to protect earlier gains by involving themselves in more creative ways in world political and economic affairs. The USSR may be expected to continue to challenge Western interests through diplomacy, military and economic aid, and the support of proxies, regimes, and movements opposed to Western policies. The Soviets will also continue to develop and deploy their own powerful armed forces. The basic Soviet conviction that conflict is normal in foreign affairs, and that they must exploit opportunities to enhance their power and reduce Western influence, remain unchanged. Nonetheless, the Soviets have begun to use more sophisticated tactics in the international arena. Gorbachev apparently perceives that long-term efforts to spread Soviet influence may fail if the USSR's economy continues to stagnate and if Soviet technology and industry remain inferior to that of the industrialized West.

The Soviets have relied largely on military assistance to client regimes such as Cuba and Vietnam, and to leftist revolutionaries as the primary means of extending their influence in the Third World. This approach has often yielded promising short-term, but limited long-term, results. Traditional ties to a few key clients such as Afghanistan, Vietnam, and Syria have inhibited Moscow's ability to deal with other regional powers. Furthermore, the Soviet style of communism has been increasingly seen as a failure, in large part because of endemic economic shortcomings. These failures have detracted from the political component of Soviet foreign policy. In those Third World countries where communism has taken root, economic disaster has become the norm, and the Soviets have been unwilling or unable to provide meaningful assistance.

General Secretary Gorbachev is seeking to make the USSR a more adept competitor in the international arena by improving Soviet domestic and international economic performance and by expanding political ties to Third World countries previously assumed to be in the "Western camp." These efforts are part of a long-term strategy designed to exploit opportunities that would have eluded the Soviets under earlier, more rigid foreign policies, which were heavily influenced by former Foreign Minister Andrei Gromyko. The Soviets are not likely to reduce military assistance or political support for their traditional clients, but they are not likely to increase economic aid either.

The most apparent changes in Soviet activities have been the expansion of contacts to a greater variety of countries, while counseling their traditional clients to be less confrontational. The Soviets intend to increase their influence in regional affairs and to change the perception of the USSR as a one-dimensional power dependent solely upon military strength as its major instrument of foreign policy. Gorbachev's foreign policy will seek to portray the Soviet Union as a power intent on fostering political and economic solutions to regional and global problems.

To implement these new strategies, Gorbachev has made major changes in the Foreign Ministry and the International Department of the Central Committee. He has replaced Gromyko as Foreign Minister with Eduard Shevardnadze and Boris Ponamarev as Head of the International Department with Anatoliy Dobrynin. The Soviet leadership has begun to emphasize the necessity of "new thinking" in world affairs, in particular, on the issues of war and peace and concepts of international security. At the 27th Party Congress in 1986, Gorbachev affirmed that changes in the contemporary world were so profound as to require "new approaches, methods, and forms of relations between different social systems, states, and regions." According to Gorbachev, these purported changes are forcing all countries to readjust their foreign and security policies in accordance with the Soviet perspective that security no longer can be assured solely by military means. In reality, the profound change in the contemporary world that has necessitated "new thinking" was probably in part the realization by the Soviets that their economic, technological, and industrial infrastructure would have great difficulty supporting their military establishment in the competition with the West in the future. As a result, the Soviets have initiated a number of programs designed to ensure that they will be militarily competitive with, if not superior to, the West in the next century. Soviet foreign policy under Gorbachev underwrites these objectives.

TASS TIME MAGAZINE

The Soviet leadership has promoted "new thinking" in world affairs, but military power remains the predominant element which asserts Moscow's influence in world affairs.

The stated objectives of Soviet foreign policy reveal that "new thinking" does not alter the fundamental tenets of communism. The 1986 Soviet Communist Party Program reiterated that socialism and capitalism are engaged in a historic competition in which the final victory of socialism is inevitable. The Program depicted the United States in the traditional manner as a dying but dangerous enemy.

The disparity between the "new thinking" and current actions is also evident in Soviet policy toward the Third World. Gorbachev, in his speech on the 70th Anniversary of the Russian Revolution, described the international communist movement as the "carrier of the alternative to capitalism" and as the movement of the bravest fighters for "peace, and for the independence and progress of their countries." His statement confirmed that support for revolutionary movements and wars of "national liberation" is consistent with

both the "new thinking" in foreign policy and with the declared Soviet goal of "peaceful coexistence." Moreover, Gorbachev's book, *Perestroika,* defines peaceful coexistence in almost the same terms as did Khrushchev and Brezhnev; namely, as the "peaceful form of the struggle between opposing social systems in the political, economic, and ideological spheres."

Under Gorbachev, Soviet foreign policy has begun to emphasize more sophisticated understanding of the Soviet-American relationship. Its objectives still include:

- attempting to use the arms control process to protect planned Soviet force modernization and development;
- fragmenting the NATO Alliance and decoupling the United States from Europe;
- continuing to secure access to Western technology and financial credits; and
- undermining Western military programs, especially

Comparison of US and Soviet Military Deliveries by Region 1980-1987

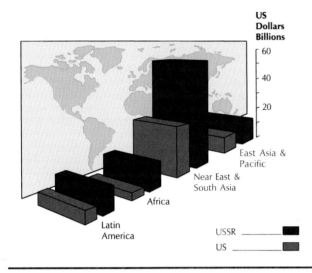

the US Strategic Defense Initiative (SDI) and US and NATO force modernization.

Since the 1979 NATO decision to deploy Pershing II and ground-launched cruise missiles in Western Europe to counter the Soviet SS-20 and the President's announcement of the SDI program in 1983, the Soviets have shown a renewed interest in arms control. They seek, through arms control, to eliminate those US forces that undermine their counterforce and damage-limiting doctrine and strategy, while maximizing prospects for a continuation of strategic trends favorable to them.

SOVIET REGIONAL POLICIES

Western Europe

The basic political-military objectives of Soviet policy toward Western Europe have not changed in the 1980s. Under Gorbachev, the Soviet Union's long-standing policy of seeking to drive a wedge between the United States and NATO by, among other things, generating concern within Western Europe over US defense programs has been given new impetus. The basic Soviet goal remains the transformation of the political *status quo* in Europe to favor the USSR. To achieve this, the Soviets seek to: preserve their considerable conventional and theater nuclear military advantage over NATO; weaken or dissolve US political and military ties to Western Europe; expand Soviet access to West European credits, technology, and trade; and encourage neutralist elements in Western Europe through a selective policy of assisting and manipulating "progres-

sive" elements, with special emphasis on the antinuclear labor and socialist parties and the various peace movements. Moscow's new tactics toward Western Europe have largely resulted from a number of setbacks the Soviets suffered before Gorbachev took power. These include:

- US deployments of intermediate-range nuclear forces (INF) on schedule;
- the failure of Soviet attempts to exploit the West European peace movement on the INF issue;
- the fact that many socialist and conservative governments in the West remained oriented toward the United States and initiated stronger defense policies;
- the breaking off of arms control negotiations; and
- President Reagan's announcement of the SDI and other efforts to enhance US defense capabilities.

Although the Soviet Union changed its tactics in 1983 and 1984 following these developments, Moscow:

- continued to carry out a range of propaganda activities and active measures designed to exacerbate political tensions within NATO and between Europe and the United States;
- attempted to break down the domestic consensus in key countries such as West Germany and Denmark regarding security policy toward the Soviet Union;
- nourished public opinion in favor of neutralism and accommodation with the newly emergent "westernized" USSR; and
- launched new "peace initiatives" for NATO flank areas designed to undermine support for a US naval presence there.

In this period, steps taken by the Soviet leadership to improve its position included attempts to forge links with Western Europe based on geography (Europe is our "common home"), reviving the prospects of a new detente, and undertaking an ambitious diplomatic campaign that included a wide range of familiar disarmament initiatives. In 1987, Gorbachev's negotiating strategy in the INF talks was designed to a large extent to support Soviet efforts to decouple Western Europe from its alliance with the United States and to generate opposition to SDI and other US strategic programs which threaten to nullify many improvements to the Soviet nuclear arsenal. With the signing of the INF Treaty in December 1987, Moscow continued to believe that its policy toward Western Europe will serve traditional Soviet objectives and increase Soviet influence in the region. For example, the Soviets continue to seek to include theater nuclear platforms in the new negotiations on conventional forces. They have also proposed limitations on naval activity that would

The MIDAS tanker aircraft, which became operational in 1987, will be used to support strategic bombers such as the BEAR H and possibly tactical and air defense aircraft. In peacetime, in-flight refueling extends the Soviets' reach farther from their homeland.

curtail deployment of US naval systems in support of NATO's northern and southern regions. These proposals demonstrate that Soviet policy aims with regard to Western Europe remain intact.

Eastern Europe

Gorbachev's endorsement of the legitimacy of different paths to socialism does not imply that Soviet control over Eastern Europe will slacken. His clear message is that results rather than process are what count and that Eastern European regimes are expected to improve their economic performance, while continuing to follow Moscow's lead on foreign and defense policies. Gorbachev has concentrated on improving alliance cohesion through the Council for Economic Mutual Assistance, and the Warsaw Pact. He has also emphasized the need for closer bilateral economic cooperation and for some limited diversity and restructuring within the narrow parameters of "national conditions" in each member state.

Although Gorbachev has outwardly assured non-Soviet Warsaw Pact (NSWP) leaders that he does not expect them to copy Soviet "restructuring" and "openness," these Soviet initiatives have created internal pressures within the orthodox regimes of Eastern Europe. Gorbachev's demands for controlled changes in Soviet political, economic, and social life have made some leaders uneasy, particularly in Romania, East Germany, Czechoslovakia, and Bulgaria. The old-guard rulers of the nations genuinely fear Gorbachev's initiatives because they may threaten their positions and policies, and create social unrest. In fact, Gorbachev's domestic policies have already raised popular expectations for change in Eastern Europe. These rising expectations, coupled with declining living standards, have created conditions for unrest.

The NSWP allies are experiencing little economic growth, rising foreign debt, and in some cases, low-key social unrest fostered by rising prices and austerity measures. Without the resources or effective policies to carry out their own economic modernization, the NSWP members are having trouble meeting Gorbachev's simultaneous demands for more and better exports to the USSR as well as higher defense budgets.

Moscow is not reducing its commitment to strengthen its security interests in Eastern Europe and to maintain firm control over the Warsaw Pact. Gorbachev, however, favors innovation and flexibility in order to make communism work more effectively. In dealing with the East Europeans, he has shown greater flexibility on a wider range of issues than his predecessors: more sensitivity to regional diversity; greater concentration on improving Soviet-Polish relations; hinting at Soviet force reductions; and permitting more inter-German relations. Whether or not Gorbachev's flexibility translates into genuine improvements in the region's social and economic conditions remains to be seen. The General Secretary is, however, unlikely to alter traditional relationships that retain the non-Soviet Warsaw Pact nations firmly under Soviet dominance.

Moscow's attempts to improve the Warsaw Pact's political and economic cohesion have been motivated, at least in part, by Gorbachev's desire to project a more positive image in Western Europe. Under Gorbachev's leadership, Moscow is making greater use of the East Europeans in an attempt to exploit NATO's divergent views on security issues as well as to acquire sensitive technology from the West. Gorbachev is further using the East Europeans as frontmen to help keep the United States and NATO off balance by introducing a variety of attractive arms control initiatives and other foreign policy proposals.

The Middle East

Gorbachev's policies toward the Middle East typify his efforts to re-energize Soviet foreign policy. The Soviet Union's fundamental objectives in the Middle East remain unchanged. In particular, Moscow hopes to gain acceptance in the region as a legitimate arbiter of regional disputes and as a nonthreatening guarantor of security. Ultimately, however, the Soviet Union is striving to become the dominant superpower in the region. But while fundamental objectives remain the same, there have been some changes evident in Moscow's Middle East strategy. The most obvious differences reflect a shift away from the heavy-handed actions and dogmatic policies of Leonid Brezhnev. Moscow now appears to

Major Soviet Equipment Delivered to the Third World 1982-1987*

	Near East and South Asia	Sub-Saharan Africa	Latin America	East Asia and Pacific	Total
Tanks/Self-propelled Guns	3,335	635	610	190	4,770
Light Armor	7,650	1,160	470	450	9,730
Artillery	5,800	2,880	975	625	10,280
Major Surface Combatants	24	3	3	7	37
Minor Surface Combatants	28	22	38	36	124
Submarines	9	0	1	0	10
Missile Attack Boats	9	6	4	0	19
Supersonic Aircraft	945	320	85	210	1,560
Subsonic Aircraft	120	5	0	1	126
Helicopters	645	230	140	45	1,060
Other Aircraft	300	65	50	45	460
Surface-to-Air Missiles	12,900	4,920	1,400	1,000	20,220

*Revised to reflect current information

favor a solution to the Iran-Iraq war, but it has so far been unwilling to support sanctions against Iran. It is concerned that the war will jeopardize larger Soviet objectives in the region. In pursuing Middle East peace on its own terms, Moscow hopes to gain acceptance by regional states as a legitimate, if not the predominant, world actor in Middle East politics.

Moscow has moved from sole reliance on ties to radical Arab states toward improving ties with the more moderate Arab states such as Egypt, Oman, the United Arab Emirates (UAE), Kuwait, Saudi Arabia, and Jordan. The Soviets are also paying greater attention to key international and regional organizations — the Organization of Petroleum Exporting Countries, the Arab League, and the Organization of the Islamic Conference. Oman and the UAE established diplomatic relations with Moscow in late 1985 — a significant advance for the Soviet Union in the Persian Gulf. Additional Soviet diplomatic gains in the region will probably come more slowly, however.

The recent rescheduling of Egypt's decade-old military debt to the Soviet Union, estimated at almost $4 billion, opened yet another door for the Soviets. Although Moscow probably realizes that a return to the USSR's former dominant position with Egypt is unlikely, even a modest advance with Cairo could return significant dividends to the Kremlin's efforts to influence the peace process. The debt issue has wider implications for Soviet policy as well. Recognizing that a number of Arab debtor nations probably will be unable to repay their outstanding loans, Gorbachev may seek to gain the political benefits of renegotiating terms on capital investments Moscow likely would never recover anyway, making a virtue of necessity.

The extended Soviet consular visit to Israel, which began in 1987, is another element in Moscow's strategy. The Soviets probably believe that hints at improvements in the rate of emigration of Soviet Jews could pay dividends in Israel, and there appears to be a greater Israeli receptivity to a possible Soviet role in the peace process.

Arms sales remain a key instrument of Soviet policy, but the Kremlin is now more selective in its application, mainly for economic reasons. Only a few key recipients, such as Iraq, can count on continued massive military support. Most sales are now for hard currency. Oil barter agreements are accepted as partial payment when necessary, as with Libya. Concessionary terms are reserved for protecting a special relationship or developing a promising new one. Moscow offered Jordan the MiG-29/FULCRUM, for example, with very

favorable financing terms, but Amman eventually chose to purchase the French Mirage 2000. Kuwait is another moderate Arab state that has turned to the Soviet market for some critical weapon systems, particularly air defense missiles.

Elsewhere in the Middle East, Soviet desires for increased influence have been frustrated. The change with the most adverse implications for Soviet prospects in the Middle East has been the shift toward the West by a number of Arab states which had previously been firmly in the Soviet camp. Algeria, for example, has pursued a course aimed at strict nonalignment since the early 1980s and has approached the West for economic and military assistance. North Yemen's President Salih, often dissatisfied with the level and quality of Soviet assistance, has clearly signaled a desire for closer ties to the West. Iraq, concerned by Soviet overtures to Iran and anticipating post-war needs, is also seeking closer ties to the West.

Soviet advances in the Middle East remain constrained by several other liabilities:

- The USSR has no formal and very limited informal relations with Israel;
- Arab states are concerned over Soviet intentions in the region and object to the continued Soviet occupation of Afghanistan, Moscow's role in the coup in South Yemen in 1986, and Soviet efforts to improve ties to Iran;
- The Islamic societies of the Middle East reject the USSR's atheism and object to Moscow's treatment of Soviet Muslims;
- Moscow has little to offer economically, and the Soviet system has proven a poor model for economic development in the Arab world;
- There is a perception in several Arab capitals that Moscow has provided them only half-hearted support during crises. Critics point to the relatively muted Soviet reaction to the US-Libyan confrontation in April 1986;
- The reputation of Soviet arms has suffered in the Middle East. The quality of Soviet training and maintenance is not well regarded by most Arab states, due principally to the poor performance of Soviet equipment when employed in combat against Western equipment.

While these liabilities do not constitute any overwhelming obstacles to Soviet policies in the Middle East, they serve to limit the extent to which many regional states are willing to accept a greater Soviet role in the area that would convey to the Soviets the status they desire.

Despite the Soviet Union's largely cosmetic withdrawal of forces in 1986, more than 115,000 Soviet troops remain in Afghanistan.

Southwest Asia

Afghanistan

The March-April 1988 round of UN-sponsored talks in Geneva, Switzerland, between Pakistan and Afghanistan resolved the last outstanding issues in these six-year-old negotiations. The Soviets and their Afghan clients agreed to a nine-month timetable for a complete Soviet troop withdrawal from Afghanistan (Moscow has publicly indicated that it expects the withdrawal to be completed by the end of 1988). The Soviets also agreed to withdraw 50 percent of their troops in the first three months of the timetable, and informally indicated that Soviet forces in Afghanistan would engage only in defensive actions during the withdrawal period.

One final stumbling block to an Afghan settlement was removed when the US and Soviet Union reached an understanding on the central question of "symmetry" in their respective rights to supply arms to factions inside Afghanistan. Given a Soviet assertion that it would remain free to continue military aid to the Kabul regime while the Geneva Accords were being implemented, the US asserted its own right to continue supplying the Afghan resistance. The US indicated its preference for a moratorium on such supplies by both sides, but made clear at the time the Accords were signed that under any circumstances it would insist on a balanced, symmetrical outcome.

Pakistan and Afghanistan signed the Geneva Accords on April 14, 1988. The US and USSR also signed in their capacity as "guarantors" to the Accords, with Moscow additionally taking on the obligation to remove all its troops by February 15, 1989. Soviet troop withdrawals were to begin on May 15, just prior to the Moscow Summit between President Reagan and General Secretary Gorbachev. The Geneva Accords call for the prompt return of the more than five million Afghan refugees, mostly in Pakistan and Iran, and provide for a UN monitoring force to ensure compliance with the agreement.

Moscow had seriously miscalculated in December, 1979, when it made the decision to send its troops into Afghanistan:

- It assumed that its client government in Kabul could establish sufficient domestic support to sustain its power and eventually take on the military burden of defending itself.
- It expected US and worldwide condemnation for the Soviet invasion to subside quickly.
- It miscalculated the ability of the Afghan nationalist resistance to defend its country against both the unpopular Kabul regime of the People's Democratic Party of Afghanistan (PDPA) and its Soviet benefactors.

The persistence and valor of the Afghan resistance over the past eight years has been instrumental in

The acquisition of handheld surface-to-air missiles by the resistance has had a major effect on Soviet air operations in Afghanistan.

convincing the Soviet Union of its mistake in invading its southern neighbor. The US has maintained its steadfast support for the Afghan resistance's cause in that period. Along with the rest of the international community, Washington has made clear to the Soviet Union the unacceptability of its attempt to dictate to another sovereign nation through the introduction of Soviet troops. The US has also worked together closely with Pakistan to obtain common goals of prompt and complete Soviet troop withdrawal from Afghanistan, restoration of independence and the return home with safety and honor of the Afghan refugees. The completion of the Geneva Accords, with their written, signed political commitment by the Soviet Union to completely withdraw their forces from Afghanistan on a short timetable, satisfied the first of these goals and created the primary precondition for fulfillment of the other two.

While the signing of the Geneva Accords marks an historical event, the Afghan saga is not over. The US and others will be carefully monitoring to ensure that Moscow meets all of its obligations under the Accords. The question of forming an acceptable Afghan interim government was not addressed in the agreement, but all the parties to Geneva have agreed to continue working on this question under UN auspices. The process of genuine Afghan self-determination should be given impetus by the withdrawal of Soviet troops. The massive movement back home of millions of displaced Afghans will require tremendous financial input from both the West and, hopefully, the Soviet Union. Finally the

Afghan economy, never very robust, has been crippled by over eight years of warfare. International support for economic reconstruction will be badly needed.

The Soviet Union undoubtedly is counting on its close geographical proximity to Afghanistan and the complex web of economic ties which it has built up with its southern neighbor over recent years to sustain a close relationship once its troops have withdraw. But the future state of Afghan-Soviet relations will be up to the Afghan people to decide, once Soviet troop withdrawal has opened the way to Afghan self-determination, free of the shadow of foreign troops. The PDPA regime will have difficulty sustaining itself in power without Soviet military backing. The hope is that the political future of Afghanistan can be peacefully resolved, bringing to an early end the long suffering of the Afghan people.

Pakistan

In December 1979, the Soviet invasion of Afghanistan opened a new era in relations between the Soviet Union and Pakistan. Previously, Soviet objectives and activities in Pakistan were secondary to Moscow's considerably more important objectives in Afghanistan and India. Since 1979, however, Islamabad's support for the Mujahideen has been instrumental in frustrating the consolidation of Soviet control in Afghanistan. Moscow has sought to alter Islamabad's policy of support to the Mujahideen by employing a dual approach to cajole and intimidate Islamabad simultaneously. Soviet military

In early 1988, Moscow leased to the Indian Navy a cruise-missile-equipped CHARLIE I-Class nuclear attack submarine — a key step in India's efforts to build a blue-water Navy.

pressure along the Afghan-Pakistani border increased in 1987. Frustrated with Islamabad's policy of support for the Mujahideen, the Soviet military command, with obvious support and direction from Moscow, stepped up Soviet-Afghan airspace violations, bombings, and artillery "bombardments" into Pakistan. The Afghan secret police, the KhAD, also expanded its sabotage and bombing campaign in a concerted effort to fan local Pakistani resentment toward the presence of Afghan refugees.

The Soviet Union also seeks to influence Pakistani policy through economic inducements. Soviet economic aid to Pakistan is modest by Western standards and is focused on showcase projects. For example, Moscow has sought to exploit Islamabad's need for expertise in developing the Pakistani steel industry. Moscow regularly proffers the prospect of increased aid but makes it conditional on Pakistan's adopting a "more realistic" position regarding Afghanistan.

India

Moscow pursues its relationship with India as a means of countering Chinese and American influence in the region and securing the support of a respected and influential member of the Nonaligned Movement. India abstains on UN resolutions, for example, condemning Soviet behavior in Afghanistan, and the 1986 Rajiv Gandhi-Gorbachev joint statement on global disarmament opposed the SDI.

This bond is based in large measure on Moscow's 25-year record as a dependable and predictable arms supplier to India. Although India is attempting to

become self-sufficient in arms production, the Soviet Union remains New Delhi's primary source for weapons. The Indian Air Force is one of the few that operates the MiG-29/FULCRUM, a top-of-the-line Soviet fighter. India has also received T-72 tanks, An-32/CLINE and Il-76/CANDID transport aircraft, and SS-N-2C surface-to-surface missiles. Earlier this year, the Soviets leased to the Indian Navy a CHARLIE I-Class guided-missile nuclear attack submarine — the first time that any country has transferred a nuclear-powered warship to another. India attached considerable importance to this acquisition, which underscores Moscow's desire to maintain its position as New Delhi's principal arms supplier. India also has eight 1960s-vintage Soviet FOXTROT-Class and three modern KILO-Class diesel submarines.

East Asia

The Soviet Union has accorded East Asia increased priority in its global policy during the 1980s for three reasons. First, as regional economic development accelerated, Moscow noted the growing importance of the region in the world's economy. Second, the Soviets realized that their own economic development, particularly in Siberia and the Far East, required far greater trade with Asian nations. Third, the Soviets were concerned with the strategic importance of the region, especially as the GNPs of China, Japan, and South Korea increased. This increased emphasis was reflected in Gorbachev's July 1986 address at Vladivostok, in his July, 1987 interview in the Indonesian newspaper *Merdeka* and in Foreign Minister Shevardnadze's March 1987 tour of Thailand, Indonesia, Australia, and the Indochinese communist states.

China

Since 1982, Moscow has had some success in improving its relations with China, particularly in trade and economic cooperation. Since October 1982, Moscow and Beijing have held biannual consultations on normalizing political relations. Although 11 rounds have taken place, little progress has been made. China continues to insist that full normalization requires progress in removing the "three obstacles": Soviet support for Vietnam's occupation of Cambodia; the presence of Soviet forces in Afghanistan; and Moscow's military deployments along the Sino-Soviet frontier and in Mongolia.

Nevertheless, Sino-Soviet contacts in a variety of areas have expanded: Gorbachev met with then-Deputy Premier Li Peng (currently Premier) in 1985; then-planning head Nikolay Talyzin institutionalized contacts with China's planning organization in September 1986; and both sides exchanged visits by parliamentary delegations, reestablished trade union ties, and began a modest dialogue regarding economic reform. Following US practice, the Soviets have also begun to brief the PRC on US-Soviet arms control discussions. In addition, then-acting General Secretary Zhao Ziyang's July 1987 tour of Eastern Europe reestablished Party ties between China and Moscow's East European allies.

In his Vladivostok speech, Gorbachev made several gestures toward China. His offer to compromise on the Amur River boundary led to a resumption of border negotiations in February 1987. Furthermore, during the spring 1987 troop rotation, the Kremlin redeployed the personnel from a motorized-rifle division from Mongolia into the Soviet Union, but the unit exchanged its modern equipment for the older weapons of a division which remained behind. Gorbachev reinforced his previous efforts to encourage significant Sino-Soviet political relations by calling for a summit of Chinese and Soviet leaders in late 1987 and again in early 1988. Gorbachev used an unusual interview with the Chinese journal *Liaowang* — the first such interview of a top Soviet official in a Chinese journal in decades — to issue his early January call for a summit. China, however, continued to reject both resumption of Party ties and a summit until Moscow pressures Vietnam to pull out of Cambodia.

Economic relations have progressed farther than political accommodation. In December 1984, First Deputy Chairman Ivan Arkhipov met Vice Premier Yao Yilin in Beijing, where they agreed to establish a Joint Commission of Economic, Trade, and Scientific-Technical Cooperation. Yao met Arkhipov again in July 1985 and signed a five-year economic agreement designed to increase reciprocal trade to $3.5 billion by 1990. In addition, the Soviets agreed to build seven new Chinese enterprises and to renovate 17 others. Border trade, which resumed in 1982 and 1983, has grown rapidly.

Japan

Soviet relations with Japan have been strained throughout the 1980s. The principal sources of tension remain the Soviet Union's occupation of the Northern Territories and its deployment of enhanced military forces, including MiG-23/FLOGGERs, to the disputed islands. Trade relations also have suffered. Total trade volume peaked in 1982 at about $5 billion, and then fell sharply to about $3.6 billion in 1984. By 1986, the volume of trade again exceeded $4.5 billion, but Japanese restrictions imposed in the wake of the Toshiba technology-transfer case reduced the figure to $4.4 billion in 1987.

After taking power, Gorbachev attempted to improve Soviet-Japanese relations in order to gain advanced technology for his industrial modernization program and to enhance the Soviet Union's diplomatic position in Northeast Asia. Foreign Ministers Shevardnadze and Shintaro Abe exchanged visits in 1986, ending an eight-year hiatus in such contacts. At least four factors, however, led to renewed strains in 1987. First, Moscow continued to criticize Japan's interest in SDI research and refused to set a date for Gorbachev to visit Japan. Second, when Japan increased restrictions on the export of high technology in response to the Toshiba technology-transfer case, the Kremlin charged Japan with mounting an anti-Soviet campaign. Third, Soviet espionage in Japan resulted in an exchange of personnel expulsions, which further poisoned the atmosphere between the two countries. Fourth, in December 1987 a Soviet reconnaissance aircraft overflew Okinawa and was challenged by a Japan Air Self-Defense Force aircraft. Although the USSR officially apologized and called the overflight accidental, it increased Japanese mistrust of the Soviets.

North Korea

The Soviet Union's ties to North Korea have improved markedly since 1984. Kim Il-song's May 1984 and October 1986 visits to Moscow highlighted the warming trend. In May 1985, Moscow began delivering 46 MiG-23/FLOGGER aircraft to North Korea. The Soviets also supplied sufficient equipment for North Korea to deploy several SA-3/GOA battalions and to update some older North Korean SA-2/GUIDELINE systems. In 1987, Moscow reportedly provided Pyong-

Soviet MiG-23/FLOGGER aircraft based at Cam Ranh Bay would escort Tu-16/BADGER bombers on antiship attack missions.

yang with two new items, the ZSU-23-4 self-propelled antiaircraft gun and the long-range SA-5/GAMMON surface-to-air missile launcher.

Combined naval exercises, symbolic port visits and aircraft exchanges, and cooperation in intelligence gathering also characterized Soviet-North Korean relations. Since December 1984, Soviet aircraft have overflown North Korea while conducting intelligence collection flights against US, South Korean, Japanese, and Chinese forces. Overflight operations have included Tu-16/BADGER bombers, Tu-95/BEAR D naval reconnaissance collectors, and Tu-95/BEAR G strike aircraft. These aircraft have used several different flight routes during their missions over Korea. Since 1986, the Soviets have overflown North Korea during transit to Cam Ranh Bay, Vietnam. The frequency of overflights, however, declined in 1987.

Vietnam

Between 1982 and 1986, Moscow delivered almost $7 billion in military aid to Vietnam — over 40 percent of total Soviet military assistance provided to Hanoi since 1954. Items of equipment include MiG-21/FISHBEDs, Su-22/FITTERs, An-26/CURL transports, Mi-24/HIND helicopters, PETYA II-Class frigates, T-55 tanks, and SA-3/GOA surface-to-air missiles. In 1987, Hanoi received for the first time SONYA and YEVGENYA-Class minesweepers. More than 2,700 Soviet military advisers and technicians are present in Vietnam. Despite the complaints of China and the Association of Southeast Asian Nations (ASEAN), the Soviets continue to provide the military and financial support necessary to sustain Vietnam's occupation of Cambodia.

The Soviet Union also supplies the economic support needed to sustain Vietnam's faltering economy. In 1986, Moscow pledged to double economic assistance to Hanoi during the next five years. Soviet aid is currently $1.5 to $2 billion annually. In return for this economic and military aid and implicit protection from China, Hanoi has allowed Moscow to develop Cam Ranh Bay into the largest Soviet naval deployment base outside of the USSR. Access to Cam Ranh Bay has enabled the Soviets to establish a continuous naval presence in the South China Sea and to support naval operations in the Indian Ocean more efficiently. Cam Ranh Bay also extends the Soviet wartime reach over East Asia's sea lines of communication in the South China Sea and poses a challenge as well to the US military presence in the Philippines. Ten of the Soviets' 16 BADGER aircraft normally stationed in Vietnam are strike variants capable of carrying antiship cruise missiles. To provide air defense and fighter escort, the Soviets have maintained a squadron of 14 MiG-23/FLOGGERs at Cam Ranh Bay since 1984. In addition to deploying naval and naval air forces, Moscow has established regional communications and intelligence-gathering sites.

South Pacific

Two fishing agreements highlight the Soviet Union's growing desire for increased access in the South Pacific. In August 1985, Moscow signed a one-year accord with the island state of Kiribati. Although this treaty was not renewed, in early 1987 the Soviets signed an agreement with Vanuatu that allows them port access. The Soviets have also sought to exploit regional anti-nuclear sentiments by acceding to the protocols of the 1986 Treaty of Rarotonga, which established the South Pacific Nuclear-Free Zone.

Latin America

While Latin America is of less immediate concern to Soviet policy than Europe, Asia, and the Middle East, Moscow recognizes that political instability in America's backyard furthers Soviet interests. Therefore, Soviet interest in the region remains strong. Since March 1985, the Soviet Union has stepped up diplomatic contacts with the region's noncommunist nations. Shevardnadze visited Mexico in October 1986 and in 1987 toured Brazil, Argentina, and Uruguay. These visits were the first by a Soviet Foreign Minister to Latin American countries other than Cuba. Furthermore, in 1987 Moscow hosted visits by the Brazilian, Argentine, and Uruguayan Foreign Ministers and by President Raul Alfonsin of Argentina. The Soviets' diplomatic activism has extended to Central America, where they have obtained Aeroflot landing rights in Panama and are attempting to reestablish diplomatic relations with Guatemala.

While Moscow works to improve its relations with the region's noncommunist nations, it has not abandoned its traditional clients in the region, Cuba and Nicaragua.

Cuba

The scale of Soviet arms deliveries to Cuba reflects that country's importance to the Soviet Union: over 60 percent of the total value of arms deliveries to the Cubans since 1960 has been delivered in this decade. These deliveries have made possible the continuing modernization of Cuba's Armed Forces. Major items of equipment received include: FLOGGER and FISHBED fighter aircraft; HIND, Mi-14/HAZE A, and HIP H helicopters; FOXTROT-Class submarines; KONI-Class frigates; ZHUK-Class patrol boats; T-54/55 and T-62 tanks; BTR-60P armored personnel carriers; BM-21 rocket launchers; GOA, SA-9/GASKIN, and SA-13/GOPHER surface-to-air missiles; and various radar and electronic warfare equipment. The Soviets continue to support Cuba's military with 2,800 military advisers, a 2,800-man Soviet brigade, and with 2,100 Soviet personnel to man the signals intelligence (SIGINT) site at Lourdes. The USSR furnishes large quantities of economic aid in the form of trade, development, and technical services, and trade subsidies for sugar, petroleum, and nickel. Work also proceeds on the Cienfuegos nuclear power station. Soviet economic assistance averages $4.5 billion annually and involves 5,000 civilian Soviet advisers/technicians. Hard currency shortages, however, continue to plague the Cubans. Although they have re-exported Soviet petroleum imports for hard currency, declining oil prices make it impossible to maintain previous earnings levels.

Soviet assistance to Cuba makes possible a union of Soviet aims and Cuban ambitions. The Soviet Union has gained Cuban assistance in supporting Soviet-backed movements in Angola, Nicaragua, and Ethiopia. In early 1988, the Cubans admitted in public statements that they had 40,000 military personnel in Angola. There are also 3,000 Cuban troops and advisers in Ethiopia and about 1,500 Cuban military advisers in Nicaragua. Cuba also provides the Soviets with valuable military and intelligence collection support. Since 1981, there have been more than 60 deployments of BEAR D naval reconnaissance aircraft and over 20 deployments of BEAR F antisubmarine warfare aircraft to Cuba. The Soviet SIGINT site at Lourdes, near Havana, continues to monitor US military, space, and

domestic communications. In addition, the Soviets have deployed naval task forces to the Caribbean six times this decade. Activity during those deployments included joint exercises with the Cubans and participation in national celebrations.

Despite the close cooperation, several disagreements continue to plague relations between Moscow and Havana, the most persistent being Soviet contentions that Castro is mismanaging the Cuban economy and wasting Soviet aid. Nevertheless, the two countries cooperate closely to achieve commonly held goals, such as support to Nicaragua.

Nicaragua

Soviet assistance to the Sandinista regime in Nicaragua serves several purposes, all aimed at creating a new strategic pressure point against the United States. The Soviet role as superpower sponsor for the Sandinista regime's consolidation of power gives the USSR vital influence and the promise of a strategic foothold on the American continent, 1,400 miles south of the US border and 350 miles north of the Panama Canal. Ports and airfields now being constructed under Soviet supervision could prove important assets in time of crisis or conflict. In addition, Sandinista-sponsored subversion will continue to be a real threat to neighboring nations, raising the prospect of greater region-wide instability.

As the principal supplier of the Sandinista regime, the Soviet Union has supported Managua's consolidation of power through the delivery of significant amounts of military and economic assistance. Since 1980, the USSR and its allies have supplied Nicaragua with more than 120,000 metric tons of military and military-related equipment, worth approximately $2.3 billion. Since 1984, Managua has received over 80,000 metric tons of military supplies worth an estimated $1.8 billion.

With a deteriorating economy, Nicaragua requires increasing economic assistance. During 1987, this aid included more than $300 million from the Soviets, which is up from $200 million in 1985. Moreover, Moscow maintains 250 advisers and technicians in-country to oversee its investment and to ensure the survival of the Sandinista government.

Recent revelations made by Major Roger Miranda Bengoechea, a high-level Sandinista defector (many of which were confirmed by public statements by the Sandinista Minister of Defense, Humberto Ortega), demonstrate that the USSR and its allies not only intend to guarantee the survival of Nicaragua's Sandinista regime but also underwrite its military supremacy in

The tonnage of Soviet military equipment delivered to Nicaragua, which included the heavily armed HIP (above) and HIND attack helicopters, reached a record high in 1987.

Central America. Miranda revealed that the Sandinistas have asked the Soviet Union to supply additional tanks, armored vehicles, trucks, aircraft, including 12 Mi-24/HIND gunships and 12 MiG-21/FISHBED supersonic fighters, and the equipment necessary to allow the Sandinistas to field a 600,000-man army by 1995.

Peru

Peru is noteworthy among South American countries for purchasing Soviet military equipment in large quantities. For Moscow, these deliveries serve to improve prospects for increased Soviet influence in this country. Arms deliveries from the Soviet Union during the 1980s amounted to an annual average of almost $70 million and have helped Peru modernize its armed forces at discount prices. Currently, there are approximately 50 to 60 Soviet military advisers stationed with the Peruvian Army and Air Force. Peru continues to support the Soviet fishing fleet and plans to construct a number of commercial vessels for the USSR in exchange for debt relief. Additionally, Peru acts as a port of entry in South America for Aeroflot, the Soviet state airline. Soviet trade elsewhere in South America remains strictly non-military.

Africa/Indian Ocean

In comparison with the second half of the 1970s, which witnessed a dramatic expansion of Soviet power into sub-Saharan Africa, the 1980s have seen the Soviets trying to consolidate their gains. This consolidation has been hampered, however, by the insurgency of the National Union for the Total Independence of Angola (UNITA) against the regime in Angola and by Mozambique's gradual turn toward the West. The quarter-century-old Eritrean insurgency against the Marxist Ethiopian government also has persisted. These rebellions pose a military challenge to the regimes and also enable Moscow to increase its influence in the target countries by serving as their primary source of military assistance.

The most important instrument for the spread of Soviet influence in sub-Saharan Africa remains the provision of military equipment and advisers. The continuing use of proxy forces — especially Cuban — has facilitated Soviet inroads without risking the escalation of a regional African conflict into a superpower confrontation. During the period 1980 through 1987, the USSR has delivered about $15 billion worth of increasingly sophisticated weapons to sub-Saharan

The Soviets export SA-6 surface-to-air missile systems, with a range of 30 kilometers, to a number of Third World clients, including this Libyan unit captured by Chadian forces.

Africa. Moreover, Soviet military advisers have adopted an increasingly active role in Africa. Angola is a case in point. Although the 1,200 Soviet advisers there continue to avoid direct combat against the UNITA freedom fighters, a Soviet general reportedly was responsible for planning and directing the Luanda regime's 1987 offensive, in conjunction with Soviet military advisers assigned to each Angolan army battle group. Several advisers apparently were killed during the offensive.

In exchange for military assistance to African governments, the USSR has sought access to ports and airfields for its West African naval patrol ships and long-range reconnaissance aircraft. Although the Soviets lost access to the excellent Somali deep-water harbor at Berbera, they have retained other valuable privileges. These include the use of Dahlak Island, Ethiopia, to support the operations of the Soviet Indian Ocean Squadron and access to Al-Anad Airfield in South Yemen to support naval reconnaissance flights in the Gulf of Aden and the Indian Ocean. In addition, Moscow is eyeing other possible staging points, notably the airfield and port at Antsiranana in Madagascar; naval and air basing rights in the Seychelles; and access to facilities in Djibouti.

In the past, the USSR sought to support and ride the coattails of charismatic African leaders such as Kwame Nkrumah in Ghana, Modibo Keita in Mali, and Sekou Toure in Guinea to advance its interests in the region. During the 1980s, it has sought to institutionalize Marxist revolutions to ensure continued Soviet influence irrespective of the death or political demise of a favorite ally. One of Moscow's successes in this regard was the establishment in 1984 of the Workers' Party of Ethiopia (WPE), a vanguard-style Communist Party that supplanted the military council as the main ruling body of the country. Although the military retains a majority in the new party's Politburo and all key government positions, the Soviets evidently hope that the party-to-party ties between the CPSU and the WPE will provide Moscow with a secure channel of influence in Addis Ababa.

While the Soviets continue to create and exploit targets of opportunity to extend their presence in sub-Saharan Africa, an equally important objective is undermining the West's influence in the region. By obtaining naval and air access privileges, the USSR could be in a position to interdict sea lines of communication in the event of a global crisis or outbreak of hostilities. Moscow also is positioning itself to play a dominant role in southern Africa in a transition (whether peaceful or violent) from the apartheid regime to black majority rule in South Africa. Moscow's efforts to cultivate the regime of President Robert Mugabe in Zimbabwe indicate that it is striving for closer links with southern African countries that are nonaligned or have historical ties to the West. The consummation of a Soviet-Zimbabwean arms deal — the first ever between the two countries — would bring about a boost to stagnant Soviet fortunes in the region, even if it does not immediately endanger the influence of the West or the dominant regional position of South Africa. The Soviet Union, which already is providing substantial political and propaganda support and some indirect military assistance to the African National Congress, probably would raise the ante further if a "war of national liberation" erupts. The ascension to power of a pro-Soviet regime in South Africa remains Moscow's principal long-term objective.

Moscow's continuous probing for advantage in sub-Saharan Africa suggests that Gorbachev's concentration on domestic economic reform in the Soviet Union does not preclude an active foreign policy, even in areas such as southern Africa, that are of peripheral strategic concern to the Kremlin. This probing can be expected to continue.

PROSPECTS

Gorbachev's "new thinking" primarily reflects a change in style, while his diplomatic initiatives embody new tactics. By cultivating a less threatening international image, Moscow aims to deflect attention away from Soviet militarism and adventurism in its foreign policy. In Moscow's view, the consequent international climate will improve Soviet prospects for maintaining an advantageous "correlation of forces" worldwide, especially in an era of economic stagnation. At the same time, Moscow will aim to expand its power and influence; reduce external pressure on its client states; broaden opportunities for East-West trade; acquire Western technology; and rejuvenate the Soviet economy. On balance it is too early to determine whether changes in the style of Soviet foreign policy will eventually affect Moscow's fundamental goals. Ultimately, the USSR may intend to use the improved position it hopes will result from internal reform to compete more effectively with the West politically, militarily, and economically.

CHAPTER III

Military Resources Allocation

A fundamental Marxist-Leninist maxim — that military power depends on the strength of the economy — has taken on renewed importance under General Secretary Gorbachev, who clearly recognizes that the major challenge facing the Communist Party is to revitalize the Soviet economy and ensure its ability to support military requirements. To appreciate fully the basis of Soviet military power and its potential for future development requires an examination of the underlying human and material resources and the mechanisms by which they are translated into the instruments of war. Consequently, this chapter analyzes the military dimensions of the Soviet economy, the production of materiel by the Soviet military-industrial complex, and the manpower and demographic trends in the USSR.

Soviet military power growth is dependent upon the defense industry's priority access to raw materials, key intermediate subcomponents, scientists and engineers, and skilled labor. This has led to the development of the world's largest military-industrial complex. The economic cost of Soviet military power has been, and remains immense. High levels of defense spending have been a major contributor to progressively slower Soviet economic growth rates, as the most productive resources were channeled to the military at the expense of living standards and investment in industries essential for civilian economic growth. The neglect of the civilian industrial sector has contributed to economic problems such as low productivity, transportation and supply bottlenecks, inefficient use of resources, and slow technological development. The Soviet defense burden increased from about 14 to 16 percent of Soviet gross national product (GNP) in 1980 to about 15 to 17 percent in 1987 — roughly two and one-half times that of the United States. Even more telling, Soviet defense industrial ministries now account for almost 60 percent of total production of the vital machine building/metal working (MBMW) branch of industry. The MBMW branch is the source for military weapons and equipment, the machinery and equipment employed by all industries, as well as consumer durables. While these defense industrial ministries manufacture some important goods for the civilian sector, they concentrate primarily on the military production that has driven their rapid growth over the past 20 years.

Over the last decade, the magnitude of the Soviet military effort greatly exceeded that of the United States. Based on a dollar cost comparison of cumulative US and USSR military programs for the past 10 years, the total Soviet military effort was almost 20 percent greater than that of the United States. In 1987, as a result of the continued growth of US outlays, primarily for procurement, the annual difference in the cost of the military programs was virtually eliminated. Nevertheless, cumulative Soviet military procurement for the decade was higher than that of the United States. Furthermore, Soviet defense allocations are expected to remain at levels high enough to allow for the continued modernization of the armed forces.

THE MILITARY DIMENSIONS OF THE SOVIET ECONOMY

The Soviet system of centralized planning and management facilitates the direction of resources to meet military requirements, especially in heavy industry. The Politburo, in conjunction with the Defense Council, is responsible for all aspects of military and national security decisionmaking in the Soviet Union. At all lower levels of party and government decisionmaking there exist institutional mechanisms to enforce defense production priorities. This system extends down to the level of defense plants, where specially trained officers are responsible for quality control over weapons production and possess the authority to reject any item that does not meet military specifications.

Several factors complement the economic planning and management system in the maintenance of military priorities. The military's five-year and long-term defense plans are prepared before national economic plans are formulated, ensuring that the military is given priority over other sectors, and that military resource requirements are incorporated into national plans. The long administrative tenure of many managers throughout the military-industrial complex promotes stability and continuity in weapons development and production. The high priority accorded the military in the planning process and the secrecy with which this process is conducted prevent the diversion of resources

Over the past 10 years, the value of the Soviet military procurement budget was greater than that of the US, allowing the Soviets to deploy significantly more weapons to its forces in the field.

to competing civilian economic needs. Weapon systems are approved at the highest levels of the party and government, and funding is typically authorized for a system's entire production cycle. This process enables the Soviets to select weapons for priority development while avoiding the uncertainties of annual budgetary reviews and funding adjustments that occur in the United States.

The Soviet leadership is obviously disturbed by the current state of the economy, which threatens to compromise future military requirements. While the economy has expanded over the last 15 years, growth has slowed progressively, reaching a postwar low in the early 1980s. The leadership views current economic growth as inadequate to maintain military capabilities and living standards at desired levels while simultaneously providing enough resources to invest in future economic and military growth.

The problem of reduced economic growth poses a predicament for the Soviet Union's ability to match the West in some key advanced technologies. To bring the Soviet Union to the forefront of military and civilian technology, Gorbachev has proposed an economic program to modernize rapidly the country's machinery-producing sector. Through huge investments, Moscow intends to accelerate the production of new and advanced machinery and equipment with which to renovate the country's obsolete industrial base. Priority is being given to the high-technology fields of microelectronics, computers, robotics, advanced machine tools, instruments, and biotechnology.

Soviet leaders apparently have concluded that, in addition to a massive investment program, "perestroika" is also required for economic revitalization to succeed. The June 1987 Central Committee Plenum represented a potential watershed in Soviet economic history. At the Plenum, Gorbachev characterized his early attempts to effect change, and those of his predecessors, as mere "piecemeal" efforts that could not by themselves sustain accelerated economic growth. "The system of management that has taken shape," Gorbachev said, "has, with the passing years, come into increasingly acute conflict with the conditions and needs of economic development." Long-term Soviet economic revitalization requires fundamental economic reforms and a thorough technological modernization of the country's aging and inefficient industrial base.

At the June Plenum, Gorbachev outlined a program, dubbed the "new economic mechanism," for radical economic reform and a timetable for its implementation. This program contains a series of potentially far-reaching changes in the centralized economic system, including a major expansion of the rights of enterprises to manage their own funds, labor, and supplies. There will be closer linkage between performance and pay; reduction in the size of central ministries; and curtailment of their detailed management of enterprise activity in favor of concentration on strategic, long-range economic planning. The Soviets have scheduled, as well, an overhaul of the banking, finance, credit, supply, and price mechanisms in the economy.

There appears to be a consensus among the leadership on the *need* for economic reform, yet some disagreement over the *pace* and kind of change — especially in sensitive political areas. There is also growing resistance from members of the bureaucracy who stand to lose power and privilege, while workers are concerned that the reforms will bring higher consumer prices, pressures to work harder, and even layoffs in some inefficient firms. The military leadership realizes, however, that the technologically sophisticated future generations of weapon systems needed to compete effectively with the West can only be provided through a strong, advanced economy founded upon a modern industrial base.

Gorbachev has made it clear that economic revitalization is a long-term effort that will require at least 10 to 15 years, if not a generation. It will demand innumerable short-term adjustments, many of which may be disruptive and confusing. Consequently, the initial rate of growth could be low for several years as the economy passes through the necessary transitions. Low growth rates, however, would not necessarily indicate that the program is faltering. Slow economic growth over the short term may be the price the Soviets will have to pay as increased product quality and technical progress replace the previous emphasis on simple quantity.

NATO and Warsaw Pact Procurement of Major Weapon Systems 1978-1987*

	US	NUSN	NATO:PACT Ratio	NSWP	USSR
Tanks	7,600	4,100	1:1.7	4,800	25,300
Other Armored Vehicles**	10,800	9,300	1:2.7	7,600	46,000
Artillery, Mortars, and MRLs (≥ 100-mm)	3,200	2,900	1:5.4	5,700	27,300
Long- and Int.-Range Bombers	81	0	1:4.8	0	390
Fighter/Attack Aircraft	3,600	3,000	1:1.4	1,300	7,700
Military Helicopters	2,100	1,900	1:1.3	700	4,400
Major Surface Warships (≥ 900 tons)	87	101	1:0.6	25	83
Submarines***	41	30	1:1.2	2	82
ICBMs and SLBMs	700	100	1:3.7	0	3,000
IRBMs and MRBMs	250	50	1:3.3	0	1,000
Surface-to-Air Missiles****	18,000	37,000	1:2.4	10,000	120,000

*That portion of military production for own armed forces, to include imports, but excluding exports
**Excludes combat service support vehicles
***Includes SSBNs and attack submarines
****Includes naval SAMs

Economic reform and industrial modernization are unlikely to affect military production in the near term. Military industry is well situated through huge previous investments to produce the current generation of weapon systems. During the 12th Five-Year Plan (1986-1990), military industry has been assured continued growth. With the high priority accorded the industrial modernization program, there could be increased competition between the military and civil sectors for resources and materials. To date, however, there is

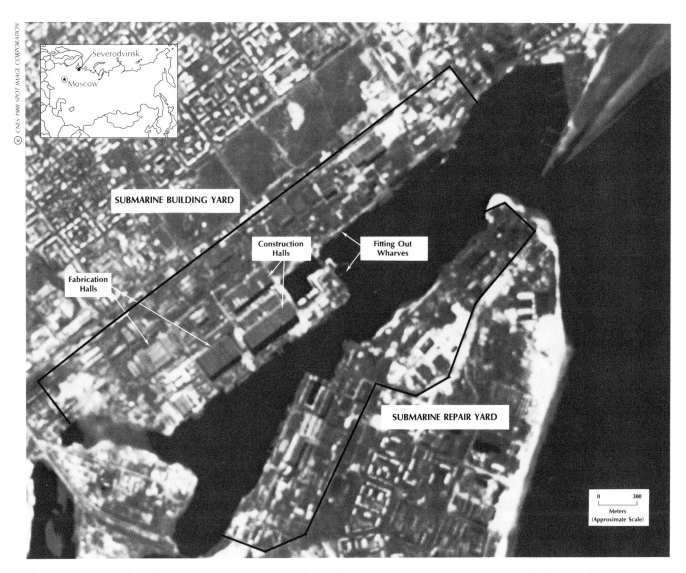

SUBMARINE BUILDING YARD

Construction Halls

Fitting Out Wharves

Fabrication Halls

SUBMARINE REPAIR YARD

0   300
Meters
(Approximate Scale)

The Soviets are building three classes of nuclear-powered attack submarines, TYPHOON and DELTA IV ballistic missile submarines, as well as modifying the YANKEE ballistic missile submarine, at the naval shipyard at Severodvinsk on the White Sea.

no indication that the industrial modernization program has been at the expense of the military industry's growth.

To the extent that the new economic reforms are successful, they will, in the long run, benefit the military by providing a modernized production capacity and a reliable supply of high-quality raw materials, subcomponents, and other products necessary for advanced weapon systems. A number of Soviet military writers have stressed the importance of a modernized economy to maintaining future military capabilities.

Gorbachev, more than his predecessors, has openly addressed the high cost of the long-term military buildup and its impact on the economy. He has described the immense resources devoted to the military as "a burden on the economy," and he continues to call for

military industry to provide greater assistance to the civil economy by increasing the quantity and improving the quality of civilian output and by making more efficient use of resources. While there have been some instances of increased cooperation with civilian industry, there is no evidence to date of a significant increase in the share of civilian output within the defense industry, despite the General Secretary's exhortations.

A transfer of expertise from the Soviet military production sector might help raise civilian quality control and management, but it cannot ensure that next-generation production techniques will be applied extensively. The Soviets therefore may need to moderate the growth of their military spending and to funnel additional resources to the civilian sector to help sustain the momentum of industrial modernization. If they do,

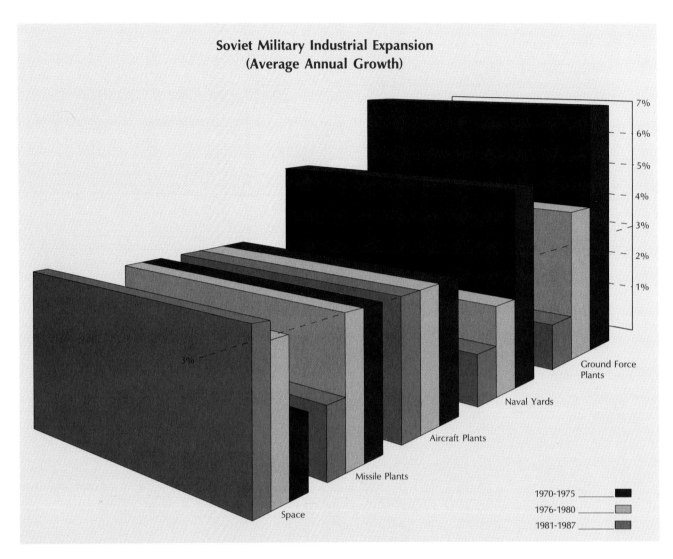

Soviet Military Industrial Expansion
(Average Annual Growth)

7%
6%
5%
4%
3%
2%
1%

Ground Force Plants

Naval Yards

Aircraft Plants

3%

Missile Plants

Space

1970-1975
1976-1980
1981-1987

some weapons procurement programs may be stretched out, some lower priority military activities may be reduced, or both may happen. Nevertheless, Soviet defense spending has continued to rise annually even through Gorbachev's tenure, and defense allocations will remain at levels high enough to allow for continued modernization of the USSR's military forces.

MILITARY PRODUCTION

By 1982, Soviet military industry had experienced a decade of expansion and was better equipped to produce larger amounts of advanced equipment than ever before. Now the Soviets are focusing on producing technologically advanced weaponry and providing their military with new systems that challenge the West in other arenas, such as space. Meanwhile, the ability to produce large quantities of materiel has been maintained.

This new emphasis on producing advanced weaponry is reflected in the ways the Soviets have enhanced their

industrial base. Their major expansion of space-related industries, begun in the late 1970s, continues. While other military industrial sectors have not been expanded equally, nearly all have been modernized or re-equipped. For some light arms, trainer aircraft, and naval ship production, the Soviets use the industries of their Warsaw Pact allies. This practice frees Soviet factories to make newer models of more advanced weapons.

Some floorspace expansion for ground force materiel production was achieved by expanding existing Soviet plants, converting civilian equipment producers to military systems producers and, when necessary, building entirely new plants. For example, since the early 1970s, the rate of aircraft plant floorspace expansion has remained constant, while a major new facility has been essentially completed at Ulyanovsk. Other airframe plants almost certainly have been modernized or retooled to produce newer models of Soviet fighters and other types of aircraft. The rate of overall missile industry growth has tailed off, but expansion of floorspace for strategic

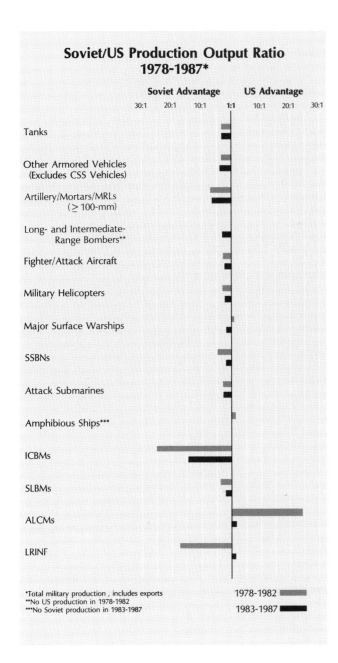

Soviet/US Production Output Ratio
1978-1987*

	Soviet Advantage				US Advantage		
	30:1	20:1	10:1	1:1	10:1	20:1	30:1

Tanks

Other Armored Vehicles (Excludes CSS Vehicles)

Artillery/Mortars/MRLs (≥ 100-mm)

Long- and Intermediate-Range Bombers**

Fighter/Attack Aircraft

Military Helicopters

Major Surface Warships

SSBNs

Attack Submarines

Amphibious Ships***

ICBMs

SLBMs

ALCMs

LRINF

*Total military production, includes exports
**No US production in 1978-1982
***No Soviet production in 1983-1987

1978-1982
1983-1987

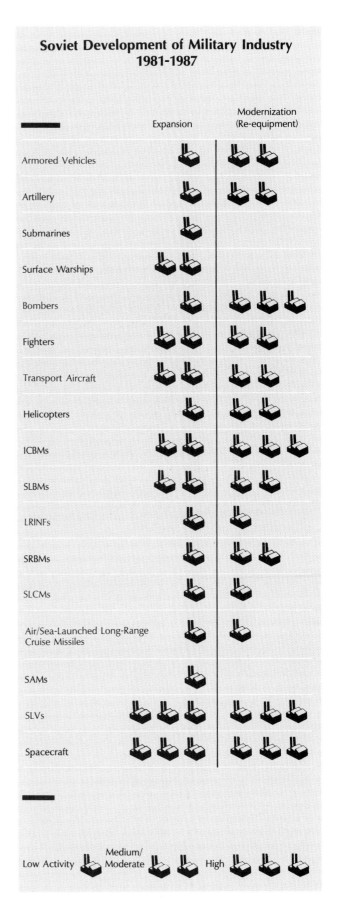

Soviet Development of Military Industry
1981-1987

	Expansion	Modernization (Re-equipment)
Armored Vehicles		
Artillery		
Submarines		
Surface Warships		
Bombers		
Fighters		
Transport Aircraft		
Helicopters		
ICBMs		
SLBMs		
LRINFs		
SRBMs		
SLCMs		
Air/Sea-Launched Long-Range Cruise Missiles		
SAMs		
SLVs		
Spacecraft		

Low Activity   Medium/Moderate   High

systems continues in preparation for production of new models of intercontinental ballistic missiles (ICBMs) and submarine-launched ballistic missiles (SLBMs).

Overall Soviet production of military equipment has remained at a high level since 1980. The Soviet Union accounts for nearly one-half of the world's output of military materiel, turning out three-quarters of the world's ballistic and surface-to-air missiles; more than one-half of its tanks and bombers; and better than a third of its artillery, submarines, fighters, cruise missiles, light armor, and military helicopters. While this lead has been reduced slightly by increased US weapons production, the Soviets still outproduce the West in most types by a ratio of better than two to one.

While current output levels are high, before 1980 they were even higher in nearly every production category. These earlier output rates reflect production of larger numbers of far less sophisticated systems. Current industrial modernization and plant growth indicate that higher output rates can probably be achieved again. In some industrial sectors, such as those supporting space, the Soviets have already built the required industrial infrastructure to support a demand for far higher production rates of spacecraft and space launch vehicles, as is discussed in the next chapter.

Ground Forces Production

The USSR's four major tank complexes have produced more than 40,000 modern tanks, including the T-64, T-72, and T-80, for the Soviet military, the Warsaw Pact, and the armies of client states. The output of ground force systems has remained generally stable, but production of some systems such as tanks and self-propelled field artillery has increased. In fact, production of the latter is at an all-time high. Soviet industry has the capacity to increase current tank output by a factor of five in the event of war. The T-80, some T-64s, and T-72s are now equipped with new technology, including reactive armor, laser rangefinders, and improved tank guns that significantly improve their capabilities.

Naval Production

The trend in Soviet naval production since 1981 has been to construct fewer, but much more capable surface warships, submarines, and auxiliary ships. This trend reflects not only the expense of naval construction programs but also the importance of maritime power in broadening the range of military and political options available to Moscow across the entire spectrum of conflict.

The Soviets are building two classes of nuclear-powered ballistic missile submarines (SSBN) — the TYPHOON and the DELTA IV. They are also producing the OSCAR II-Class nuclear-powered cruise missile attack submarine (SSGN); three classes of nuclear-powered attack submarine (SSN) — the SIERRA, the AKULA, and the VICTOR III; and the KILO-Class diesel-powered attack submarine (SS).

Soviet shipyards have eight classes of surface warships under series production. The first unit of a new class of aircraft carrier displacing 65,000 metric tons, approaching the size of US carriers, is being outfitted before sea trials. A second carrier of this class is under construction at Nikolayev.

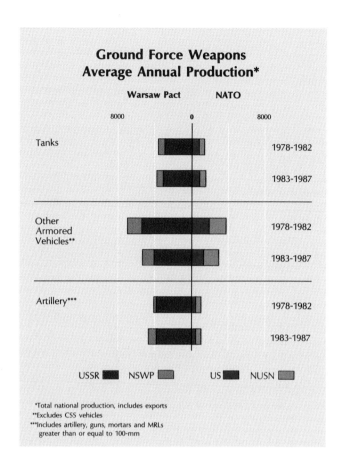

**Ground Force Weapons
Average Annual Production***

Warsaw Pact   NATO

Tanks — 1978-1982 / 1983-1987

Other Armored Vehicles** — 1978-1982 / 1983-1987

Artillery*** — 1978-1982 / 1983-1987

USSR ■   NSWP ▢   US ■   NUSN ▢

*Total national production, includes exports
**Excludes CSS vehicles
***Includes artillery, guns, mortars and MRLs greater than or equal to 100-mm

Aircraft Production

The Soviets are making strenuous efforts to increase aircraft quality and to concentrate on advanced models. While their new aircraft are more costly, more difficult to develop, and will take longer to produce than the older models, their superior quality will enable the Soviet Air Force and Air Defense Forces to meet their requirements more effectively, even though in some instances they may replace existing aircraft on less than a one-for-one basis. While the Soviets have shown renewed interest in the development of strategic aviation assets, they continue to invest heavily in modernizing their tactical assets.

In the early 1980s, two new Soviet bomber programs emerged, marking an important step in modernizing the Soviet strategic long-range bomber force. The first, the BEAR H cruise missile carrier, accounts for the greatest percentage of bomber production in this decade, with over 70 built. The second program involves the more versatile and capable BLACKJACK, whose operational deployment is imminent. BLACKJACK will not be produced in significant numbers, however, until the end of this decade or the early 1990s.

Since the early 1980s, there has been a decline in

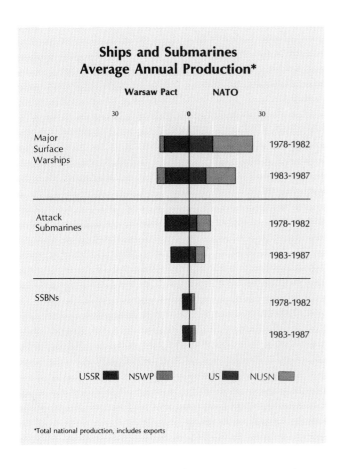

**Ships and Submarines
Average Annual Production***

Warsaw Pact   NATO

Major Surface Warships — 1978-1982, 1983-1987

Attack Submarines — 1978-1982, 1983-1987

SSBNs — 1978-1982, 1983-1987

USSR ■   NSWP ▨   US ■   NUSN ▨

*Total national production, includes exports

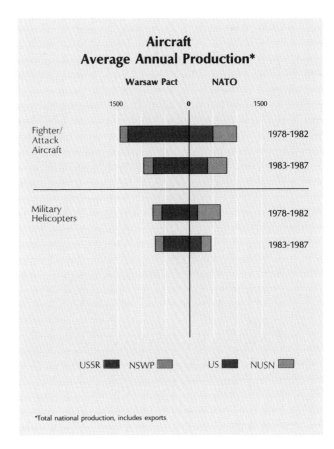

**Aircraft
Average Annual Production***

Warsaw Pact   NATO

Fighter/Attack Aircraft — 1978-1982, 1983-1987

Military Helicopters — 1978-1982, 1983-1987

USSR ■   NSWP ▨   US ■   NUSN ▨

*Total national production, includes exports

the output of tactical aircraft for the Soviets' forces. This decline is principally a result of the rapid phase-down of the older, long-running, and less sophisticated fighter programs, which have yet to be offset by newer, more technologically advanced fighter programs. The Soviets were producing five tactical fighter aircraft for their own forces at the beginning of the 1980s — FOXBAT, FLOGGER, FITTER, FORGER, and the FROGFOOT (a dedicated ground support fighter). A new counterair fighter, the FULCRUM, was in the late stages of development when the new FOXHOUND entered production. The FULCRUM, along with the FLANKER, entered series production in the mid-1980s, as production of the FOXBAT and FLOGGER for Soviet tactical air forces ended, while production of FITTER and FORGER began to decline. Output from both of these latter programs has been cut drastically over the past several years.

In the near term, the Soviets will likely focus on producing fighter aircraft for strategic defense and tactical operations. It is also probable that additional plants will begin producing these modern fighters.

Helicopter production has declined only slightly, due primarily to the beginning of the phase-down of the long-running HIP and HIND helicopter programs. As

with other systems, the emphasis in the 1980s has been on producing fewer, more technologically advanced, more capable models, and on improving and expanding the roles of the existing line of Soviet helicopters. Two new helicopters, HAVOC and HOKUM, are expected to enter serial production soon.

Since 1977, the overall number of Soviet transport aircraft produced has fallen by more than one-half, as the Soviets moved to larger, more capable models. Output of their primary long-range military transport, the Il-76/CANDID, continues at over 50 annually. Series production of two new military transports — the An-124/CONDOR and An-72/COALER — has begun.

Missile Production

The strategic ballistic missile industry is accorded a high priority in the Soviet military program. It is engaged in continuous expansion and modernization. The Soviets are now manufacturing a number of solid-propellant ICBMs. Since 1981, the USSR has completed series production of its fourth-generation ICBM force and has produced significant numbers of fifth-generation systems. Follow-on systems to both the fourth- and fifth-generation missiles are being developed, with production expected to begin soon. Emphasis

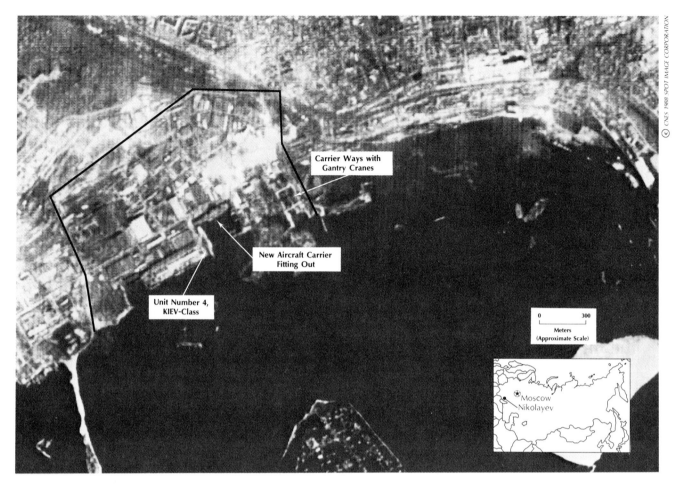

Carrier Ways with
Gantry Cranes

New Aircraft Carrier
Fitting Out

Unit Number 4,
KIEV-Class

0   300
Meters
(Approximate Scale)

Moscow
Nikolayev

The Nikolayev Shipyard is the only Soviet shipyard to build aircraft carriers. Sea trials for the first of a new class of aircraft carrier are anticipated in 1989. A second carrier of this class is under construction.

has been on designing a significantly more flexible, survivable, and effective ICBM force.

The lower level of SLBM production since the early 1980s is due primarily to the production phase-out of older missiles and to the slower production of two new missiles. This lower missile output reflects the low output of SSBNs. New SLBM systems incorporate modern technologies and have enhanced the capabilities of the strategic offensive forces.

Since January 1981, the Soviet Union has been developing nuclear-armed long-range cruise missiles (LR-CMs) to enhance the capabilities of its strategic forces. One, the AS-15, arms the BEAR H strategic bomber. The other, the SS-NX-24, is likely to be deployed on a specially configured YANKEE-Class SSGN.

The follow-on to the SS-18 ICBM should enter series production soon, as has the SS-24 rail-mobile, solid-propellant ICBM. New SLBMs should be well into developmental flight testing before 1990.

The Soviet industrial base for space launch vehicles (SLV) and spacecraft has grown to support the world's largest military space program. As a result of expansion of space-related industrial plants and launch facilities, the Soviets soon will be able to increase their space launch capability by one-third. With the production of the SL-16 and Saturn V-Class SL-X-17 SLVs (with payload capacities of over 15,000 and over 100,000 kilograms, respectively) the Soviets will double their payload weight capability in the next few years.

Due to the industrial modernization program requirements introduced by General Secretary Gorbachev, the Soviet government may be forced to make more difficult decisions on resource allocation over the next few years, particularly in preparation for the 13th Five-Year Plan (1991-1995). It is possible that short-term military production will be reduced or that planned advances will be completely cancelled to assure long-term progress. Additionally, significant amounts of military equipment are already in the production pipeline and would likely be unaffected by any long-term allocation decisions.

The US Navy has taken fixed-wing aircraft to sea since the early 1920s. The Soviets are now developing the aircraft for their future carriers. FULCRUM and other aircraft are being evaluated for ramp-assisted takeoff at Saki naval airfield on the Crimean Peninsula.

DEMOGRAPHY AND THE SOVIET MILITARY

Just as the allocation of military resources will play a critical role in future Soviet military capabilities, so will the size and ethnic makeup of its population. Low birth rates and declining longevity have constrained population growth and affected the nation's overall ethnic composition, the available labor force, and the military manpower pool. During the decade of the 1970s, the population growth in the USSR was marked by wide regional variations: low in the European republics, but very high in the Central Asian republics. These regional variances in population growth changed the population's ethnic balance. The Russians, once a strong majority, now comprise only 51 percent of the total population. Nonetheless, they will remain the single dominant Soviet nationality well into the future, comprising more than 40 percent of the total population as late as 2010. The Soviets consider the other Slavic nationalities (Ukrainians and Belorussians) to be fully integrated in their political and military leadership structures. When taken as a whole, the Slavic

nationalities will comprise a majority through 2050. Thus, while Central Asian nationalities will account for more than half the total population growth through 2010, and nearly two-thirds by 2050, Slavic dominance is assured for the foreseeable future.

Overall, birth rates have risen since the adoption of a set of child-bearing incentives by the 26th Party Congress in 1981. Soviet attempts to alter regional discrepancies in population growth are yielding small but measurable results. Birth rates in the European republics have risen to levels that will ensure modest Slavic population growth in the future, while the higher fertility rates of the Central Asian nationalities have begun to level off. Despite these reversals, the imbalances in population growth and shifts in ethnic composition will persist into the next century.

Soviet military capabilities have been affected by both slow population growth in the European republics and the resulting changes in the population's ethnic composition. The single most important factor affecting

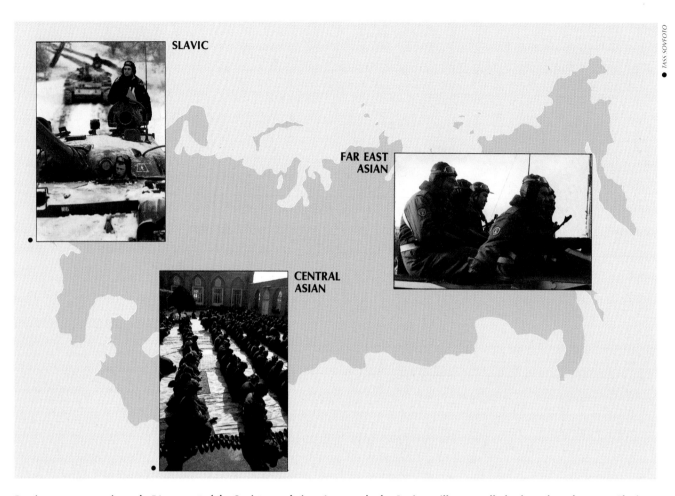

TASS SOVFOTO

Russians now comprise only 51 percent of the Soviet population. As a result, the Soviets will eventually be forced to place non-Slavic minorities into some leadership positions usually reserved for Slavs.

Soviet military manpower is conscript availability. Because military manpower requirements compete with the civilian labor force for recruits, the size of the conscript pool is critical. The Soviet conscript pool began to shrink in the early 1980s and reached a low point in 1987. The child-bearing incentives initiated in 1981, however, will produce a slightly larger manpower pool by 1999. In addition, recent tightening of deferments by the Soviet draft authorities will also slightly increase the conscript levels.

The changing ethnic composition of the Soviet military has the potential to degrade its capabilities. Based on current birth rates and other demographic trends, Central Asian nationalities will comprise an increasing share of conscripts, rising from the current 16 percent to 22 percent by 2010 and increasing thereafter. Military training has been hampered, to some degree, by the increasing percentage of conscripts not fluent in Russian. The language barrier creates communication problems between officers and enlisted personnel, and exacerbates existing discipline and morale problems in multinational

military units. Soviet concern over this situation has been demonstrated by the introduction of expanded pre-induction Russian-language training in the secondary school curriculum in Central Asia. Ultimately, an increased proportion of Central Asian conscripts, whose native language is not Russian, will force the Soviets to place non-Slavic minorities into some leadership positions in the military traditionally reserved for Slavs. On the other hand, greater involvement of Central Asians in the military leadership might improve morale and enhance minority reliability. Whether an increased number of Central Asians within the officer corps will improve or destabilize the cohesiveness of multinational Soviet military units remains uncertain.

Arriving at solutions to the demographic problems of population growth and ethnic composition of the population will challenge the Soviet Union for the foreseeable future. Under Gorbachev's "perestroika" campaign, the problems are likely to be given serious attention since human resources will be a critical factor in the success or failure of the Soviet economy.

The significant decline in output of Soviet tactical aircraft has been offset by the production of technologically sophisticated aircraft such as the Su-27/FLANKER.

PROSPECTS

Clearly, the Soviets recognize that they are at a crossroads. They know that military power — the single most important measure of their current superpower status — will diminish relative to the West if their economy continues to falter.

The Soviets realize that while their current economic and industrial infrastructure could probably support the future needs of the nation, it will not close the technological gap with the West. In the highly technical world of the future, even small, newly industrialized nations employing modern methods of production will outproduce them in some areas, as well as provide better quality products for both their people and the international market.

Although the Soviets acknowledge that future superpowers must have viable economies and technologically advanced industries, they will not sacrifice what they consider to be their security requirements. Though the military has been directed to support the civil sector in its restructuring attempts, the primary mandate of the military sector remains to produce more efficiently and equip the Soviet Armed Forces with the most advanced weapon systems possible.

As a result, the Soviets are likely to continue the production trends begun at the beginning of this decade to complete their current force modernization. They believe, however, that with some systems, such as aircraft, high output rates for technologically advanced weapons are both costly and unnecessary because qualitative advantages compensate for quantity.

Even if Gorbachev's modernization program falters, national security will remain the prime imperative, and the Soviets will, as necessary, continue to pursue new military programs at the expense of the civilian economy. Should Gorbachev's programs be successful, however, the West will be facing a substantially stronger Soviet Union, economically, politically, technologically and militarily in the 21st century.

CHAPTER IV

Soviet Strategic Programs and Space Forces

During the past decade, the Soviets allocated resources equivalent to approximately $400 billion to both strategic offensive and defensive programs in almost equal amounts — roughly $20 billion per year for each program. Space programs during this same period approached $80 billion.

Since 1981, Soviet strategic nuclear offensive forces have been upgraded as deployment of a fourth-generation of intercontinental ballistic missiles (ICBMs) (the SS-17, SS-18, and SS-19) was completed. In 1985, the Soviets introduced the road-mobile SS-25, and in 1987 they began deployment of the rail-mobile SS-24 ICBM. In the Soviet ballistic missile submarine fleet the TYPHOON, carrying 20 SS-N-20 MIRVed (multiple, independently-targetable reentry vehicles) missiles, was introduced, followed closely by the new DELTA IV carrying the even more capable SS-N-23. Soviet long-range bomber capabilities were enhanced by the introduction of the BEAR H carrying the AS-15 nuclear-armed cruise missile. Deployment of the new long-range strategic bomber, the BLACKJACK, is imminent.

In the area of strategic defense, the Soviets are modernizing the ballistic missile defense system around Moscow by replacing 64 old, reloadable above-ground GALOSH launchers with a two-layer defense composed of silo-based, long-range, modified GALOSH interceptor missiles; silo-based GAZELLE high-acceleration endoatmospheric interceptor missiles; and associated engagement, guidance, and battle management radar systems, including the new PILL BOX phased-array radar near Moscow at Pushkino. This phase of the modernization program should be completed in the late 1980s.

In space developments, the Soviets have orbited their MIR space station, established new endurance records for men in space, flight-tested a subscale model of what appears will become their space plane, and deployed a new medium-lift launcher, the SL-16. In addition, the Soviets launched their heavy-lift SL-X-17, capable of carrying payloads in excess of 100,000 kilograms. The SL-X-17 will also be used to launch the Soviet version of the space shuttle, which the Soviets acknowledge has undergone flight testing under its own power.

These are but a few examples of the trends in Soviet strategic programs. In this chapter, these and other trends, as well as future prospects, are discussed.

STRATEGIC FORCES

Missions and Operations

The Strategic Rocket Forces (SRF) constitute the Soviets' premier military service. Created in 1959 to control all long-range, land-based missiles with a range exceeding 1,000 kilometers, the SRF plays the dominant role in the Soviet strategic forces, controlling over 6,000 of the Soviets' 10,000 strategic warheads.

In a nuclear conflict, SRF missiles would attack:

- Enemy nuclear forces, including silos, missile sites, airfields, naval bases, weapons depots, and nuclear command-and-control facilities;
- Enemy power-projection assets, including military forces, ports, and transportation links; and
- Enemy civilian and military industrial facilities.

Soviet military planners anticipate having to launch their nuclear forces under a variety of circumstances. Thus, they have conducted training and built assets to support the following operations:

Preemption — To achieve the capability to execute this preferred option, the Soviets have emphasized the collection and processing of strategic intelligence concerning their potential enemies' intentions. If convinced that the time for nuclear preemption has come, the Supreme High Command would order a strategic strike. To ensure that the SRF will be ready, the Soviets conduct numerous test missile launches throughout the year, many of them from operational bases.

Launch on warning — The comprehensive Soviet planning for a nuclear war includes preparing their forces to perform their missions under the most adverse conditions. In the event the Soviets fail to execute their preemptive option, they will depend on their early warning networks to provide them with sufficient response time. This network comprises launch detection

The PILL BOX, a large four-faced phased-array radar, is located north of Moscow near Pushkino. This radar for the Moscow ballistic missile defense system will track incoming warheads and guide interceptor missiles toward their targets.

satellites and over-the-horizon radars that can ascertain the general direction of an attack and provide up to 30 minutes warning. Eleven HEN HOUSE radars located around the USSR, which will be augmented in the mid-1990s by nine new large phased-array radars, can confirm the attack and begin missile tracking. Once notified, the SRF would have to launch its missiles before enemy warheads hit. To ensure that it can do so, the SRF exercises the procedures involved in such a response.

Launch after attack — Should the SRF not launch some or most of its missiles before an enemy attack, the Soviets have made provisions to help them survive the attack and conduct strikes in response. Their silos and launch control facilities, as well as their command, control, and communications links to the Supreme High Command, are hardened and highly survivable.

Command and communications entities also have mobile back-up units. To enhance survivability further, the Soviets have included both rail- and road-mobile missiles in their newest generation of ICBMs. Provisions have been made to refurbish and reload SRF silos, thereby enabling the Soviets to fire additional strategic missiles. These techniques will also be used after both sides' initial strikes during the period of prolonged nuclear conflict envisioned in Soviet doctrine.

ICBM Force Developments

The period 1980 to 1988 witnessed the rapid modernization and sophistication of the Soviet ICBM arsenal. Soviet missiles have been upgraded or replaced with new models of greater accuracy and survivability. After 30 years of sustained growth and improvement, the Soviet Strategic Rocket Forces are extremely capable

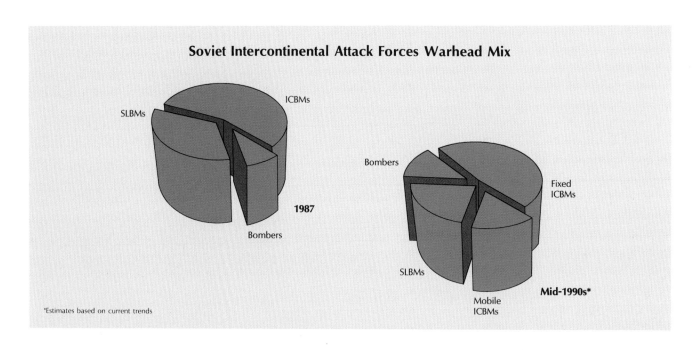

Soviet Intercontinental Attack Forces Warhead Mix

SLBMs

ICBMs

1987

Bombers

Bombers

Fixed ICBMs

SLBMs

Mobile ICBMs

Mid-1990s*

*Estimates based on current trends

US and Soviet ICBM Launcher and Reentry Vehicle (RV) Deployment 1981-1988

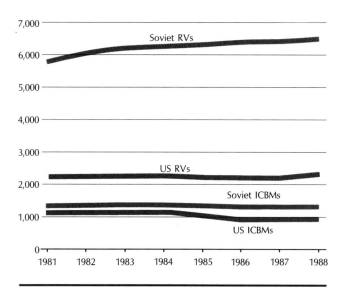

of conducting global nuclear strikes. Yet improvements to this force continue unabated. By the mid-1990s, the Soviets will be fielding a completely new generation of increasingly accurate missiles, many of them mobile, posing a heightened threat to US strategic forces.

The Soviets maintain numerous SS-11 and SS-13 third-generation ICBMs. While these missiles are not capable of destroying hardened targets, they are fully capable of destroying unhardened targets.

The centerpiece of the current Soviet SRF arsenal is the SS-18 heavy ICBM, designed to destroy hardened targets such as ICBM silos and command facilities. This missile, larger than the US PEACEKEEPER, has been modernized over the last seven years. The majority of the current force consists of SS-18 Mod 4s, which carry 10 MIRVed warheads. The SS-18 force alone could destroy 65 to 80 percent of all US ICBM silos using two warheads per target, and still have 1,000 warheads remaining. The total SS-18 force has about 3,000 warheads.

The Soviets have also modernized their other two fourth-generation ICBMs, the SS-17 and SS-19. The SS-19 Mod 3 carries six MIRVed warheads and is roughly comparable in size to the US PEACEKEEPER. The SS-17 Mod 3, while less accurate than the SS-18, carries four warheads and can destroy any unhardened targets. Both the SS-17 and SS-19 are capable of flexible targeting: they can hit Eurasian as well as transoceanic targets with a total of about 2,700 warheads, thereby facilitating the Soviet Union's ability to adjust to the situation created by the Intermediate-range Nuclear Forces (INF) Treaty.

The Soviets have invested enormous effort and resources in increasing the survivability of their strategic systems against nuclear attack. To make their fourth-generation missiles survivable, for instance, the Soviets placed them in rebuilt, very hard silos. Of the Soviet inventory of 1,400 operational ballistic missile silos, 818 have been rebuilt since 1972. Fully one-half of these silos have been totally reconstructed and hardened since 1980.

The road-mobile SS-25 ICBM continues to be fielded in remote areas of the Soviet Union. The mobility of such systems increases the survivability of the Soviet land-based intercontinental missile force.

The Soviets have begun operating fifth-generation ICBMs, missiles with great throw-weight and accuracy. They use solid-fuel propellants (which provide longer life and require less maintenance), and are fully mobile, and hence highly survivable. The SS-24, currently in the initial stages of deployment, is comparable in size to the US PEACEKEEPER. It carries 10 warheads and is designed for both rail and silo deployment. The SS-25 is a road-mobile, single-warhead, three-stage system. It can fire from field deployment sites or through the sliding roof garage it occupies at its base. The missile's mobility makes it inherently survivable and capable of reload/refire operations. The SS-25 joined operational Soviet SRF regiments in 1985.

By the 1990s, assuming the continuation of the current modernization tempo, the Soviets will be in a position to field over 15,000 warheads. Additionally, these weapons would be placed on newer, more capable and survivable strategic delivery systems during the next decade. It is likely that by the mid-1990s, the Soviets will have completely phased out their third-generation missiles, while the fourth-generation will be undergoing replacement by systems currently in development and testing. The SS-18 Follow-On, a more accurate version than its predecessor, has been tested recently; preparations for deployment of this missile are already under way. In October 1987, the US protested the apparent Soviet intention to test the SS-18 Follow-On in such a manner as to have its reentry vehicles land in the Pacific extremely close to the major populated islands of Hawaii. Mobile, solid-fueled SS-24s and SS-25s will be fully operational and will themselves be replaced by follow-on systems in the next decade. These advances will ensure that the Soviet ICBM force will remain the world's largest and most modern strategic missile force.

Submarine-Launched Ballistic Missile Force Developments

The Soviet Navy operates the world's largest strategic missile submarine force. Although it includes some older submarines, the majority of the nuclear-powered ballistic missile submarine (SSBN) force consists of more

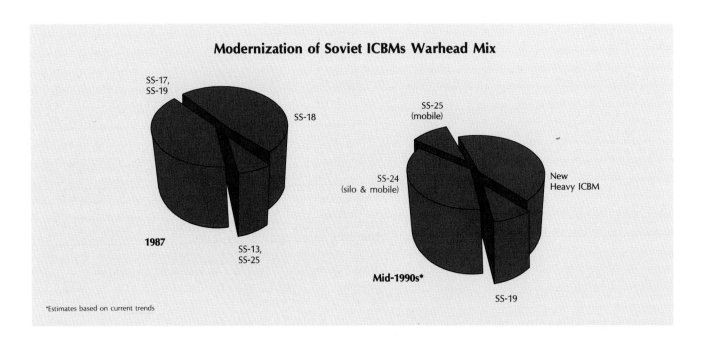

Modernization of Soviet ICBMs Warhead Mix

SS-17,
SS-19

SS-18

1987

SS-13,
SS-25

SS-25
(mobile)

SS-24
(silo & mobile)

New
Heavy ICBM

Mid-1990s*

SS-19

*Estimates based on current trends

modern DELTA I, II, and III submarines armed with intercontinental-range missiles that can reach North America from Soviet ports and coastal waters.

Within the last seven years, the Soviets have introduced the TYPHOON and the DELTA IV, both equipped with more accurate, longer range MIRVed intercontinental missiles. The introduction of these systems has enabled the Soviets to increase their SLBM weapons delivery capabilities by nearly 30 percent without increasing the overall size of their SSBN force. At the same time, submarine survivability was being significantly enhanced.

Based in the Pacific Ocean and Northern Fleet areas, the Soviet ballistic missile submarine force is equipped with over 3,000 warheads on submarine-launched ballistic missiles (SLBMs). In wartime, a portion of these forces is expected to serve as a survivable nuclear reserve. In the last decade, the deployment of multiple-warhead SLBMs with ranges sufficient to reach the United States from waters near the USSR has allowed the Soviets to plan to operate the majority of their SSBNs in protected "bastions," or havens, near the Soviet Union. Mixed groups of naval air, surface, and submarine assets, along with fixed sensors and mine-fields, will operate in wartime to protect these SSBN bastion areas against US/NATO antisubmarine forces.

Additionally, within the last several years the Soviet Navy has increased greatly its interest in the Arctic as an area of military operations, particularly for its SSBNs. The Soviets think that SSBN operations in the Arctic ice zone could increase submarine survivability, based on

Modern SSBN Force Levels

US
8 OHIO

US
27 LAFAYETTE
BEN. FRANKLIN
JAMES MADISON

USSR
24 DELTA
9 YANKEE
5 TYPHOON

USSR
16 DELTA
8 YANKEE

Boundary representations are not necessarily authoritative. The United States Government has not recognized the incorporation of Estonia, Latvia, and Lithuania into the Soviet Union.

their belief that operations under and near the Arctic ice pack might provide their deployed SSBNs with greater security and protection than in more exposed waters.

To ensure that they can communicate with their SSBN/SLBM assets, the Soviets have recently improved their submarine command, control, and communications (C^3) systems by deploying an extremely low frequency (ELF) communications system. Newly deployed BEAR J aircraft offer an additional means of effective SSBN communication redundancy by providing very low frequency (VLF) communication transmissions to SSBNs on patrol.

The Soviets may begin at-sea flight testing of a modified version of the SS-N-20 missile sometime this year. A modified version of the SS-N-23 missile will probably complete testing in 1988. Improved accuracy of the Soviets' latest SLBM systems, as well as possible efforts to increase SLBM reentry vehicle size and warhead yield, would confirm Moscow's plans to

Modernization of Soviet SLBMs Warhead Mix

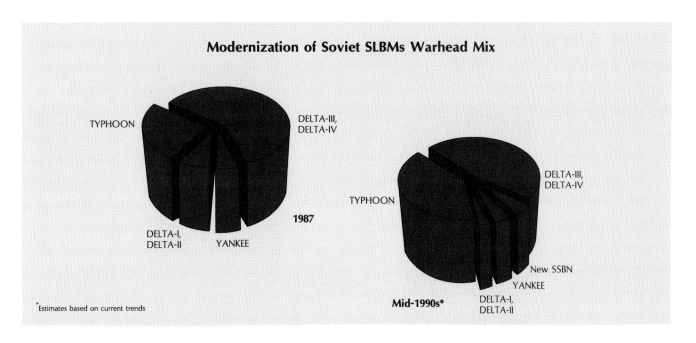

TYPHOON

DELTA-III,
DELTA-IV

1987

DELTA-I,
DELTA-II

YANKEE

TYPHOON

DELTA-III,
DELTA-IV

New SSBN

YANKEE

DELTA-I,
DELTA-II

Mid-1990s*

*Estimates based on current trends

As illustrated in the 1987 edition of *Soviet Military Power*, (middle right), the ALEXANDER BRYKIN is specially designed to reload Soviet SSBNs away from their homeports, thereby increasing SSBN survivability and enhancing Soviet wartime capabilities. The lead unit of this new class of missile support ship was photographed last year, providing a detailed view of SLBM storage and handling areas.

As newer classes of nuclear-powered ballistic missile submarines are deployed, existing platforms may be converted to cruise missile carriers, such as the YANKEE shown here, which has been modified to carry the SS-N-21 sea-launched cruise missile.

US and Soviet SLBM Launcher and Reentry Vehicle (RV) Deployment 1981-1988

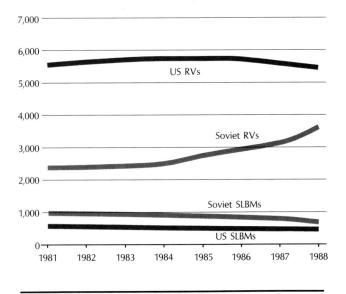

develop a hard-target-kill capability for its SLBM force. The new missile support ship class, the ALEXANDER BRYKIN, is designed to reload SSBNs with these modern missiles. This capability will allow Soviet SSBNs to hold additional targets at risk.

Soviet Strategic Aviation Developments

The Soviet intercontinental bomber force has historically lagged behind the SRF and navy in systems development. Recent Soviet efforts in strategic aviation, however, particularly with the BEAR H and BLACK-JACK long-range bombers, signal heightened interest in a manned-bomber attack force to diversify the character of their strategic forces.

The BLACKJACK is the world's largest and heaviest bomber. Designed to carry bombs and air-launched cruise missiles (ALCMs), the BLACKJACK can cruise subsonically over long ranges, perform high-altitude supersonic dash, and attack utilizing low-altitude, high-subsonic penetration maneuvers. As with the B-1, the BLACKJACK has a blended wing-body design with a variable-sweep wing and a single vertical stabilizer. It has an unrefueled combat radius of about 7,300 kilometers and a maximum speed of Mach 2.0. Eleven BLACKJACK bombers have been produced, and the first BLACKJACK regiment should begin forming this year. The backbone of the modern Soviet intercontinental bomber force of the 1980s, however, will remain the BEAR H, armed with the AS-15/KENT ALCM. The Soviets also have in their inventory about 100 other BEAR bombers and air-to-surface missile carriers. The BEAR was first produced in the late 1950s, but some of these aircraft have been updated in subsequent years with new technology.

The BEAR H bomber can launch AS-15 nuclear-armed cruise missiles as far as 3,000 kilometers from their targets. These bombers often practice strike missions against North America and are routinely intercepted by North American Aerospace Defense Command fighters.

Soviet strategic aviation capabilities are enhanced through training and exercises. BEAR H bombers are regularly observed simulating attacks against North America. When operational, the BLACKJACK can be expected to engage in similar operations. Additionally, older BEAR bombers carrying the AS-3 air-to-surface missile (ASM) are being rejuvenated through a modification program that upgrades them to carry the newer AS-4 supersonic ASM. More than 45 of these reconfigured aircraft, designated BEAR Gs, are now operational.

The current Soviet intercontinental bomber force is more flexible and survivable than it has ever been. Prior to the recent introduction of longer range cruise missiles, Soviet bombers would have had to penetrate Canadian or US airspace to launch their attacks. Now the BEAR H can launch its long-range AS-15 cruise missiles from well offshore and still hit targets in North America. The BLACKJACK will be able to conduct both standoff and penetration attacks using a variety of nuclear missiles and bombs.

Until recently, the Soviets had only aging BISON tankers for aerial refueling support of BISON and BEAR aircraft. In 1987, the first unit of new MIDAS tankers entered operational service. While the BISON tankers remain in service, they are expected to be replaced as sufficient numbers of MIDAS tankers become available.

US and Soviet Intercontinental-Capable Bombers*

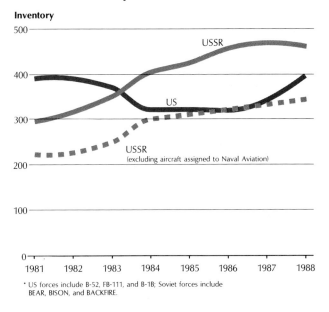

Inventory

* US forces include B-52, FB-111, and B-1B; Soviet forces include BEAR, BISON, and BACKFIRE.

Cruise Missile Developments

The Soviets are on the verge of deploying a variety of sophisticated cruise missile systems. At sea, the Soviets have tested the SS-N-21 sea-launched cruise missile

Modernization of Soviet Heavy Bombers Weapons Mix

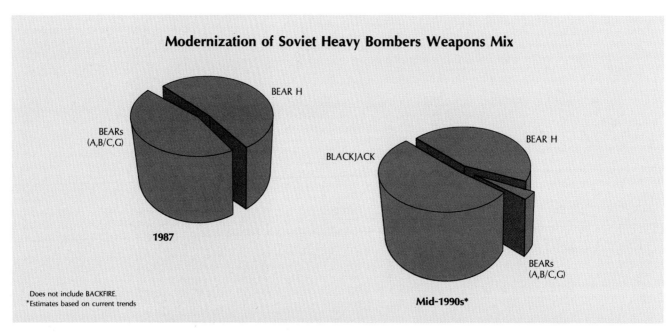

BEAR H

BEARs
(A,B/C,G)

1987

BLACKJACK

BEAR H

BEARs
(A,B/C,G)

Mid-1990s*

Does not include BACKFIRE.
*Estimates based on current trends

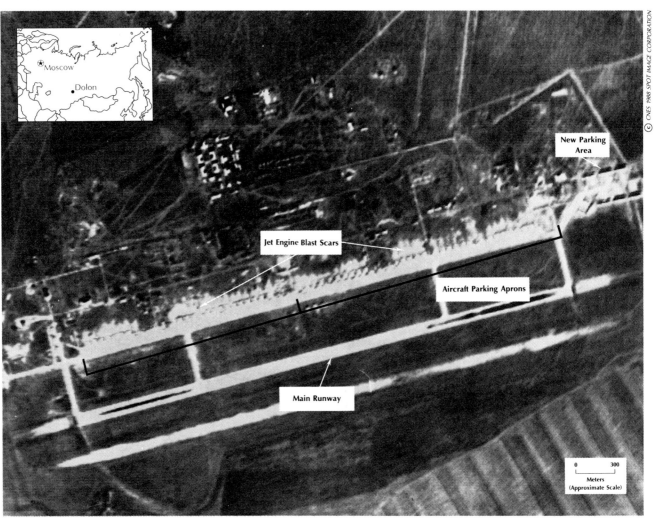

New Parking
Area

Jet Engine Blast Scars

Aircraft Parking Aprons

Main Runway

Moscow

Dolon

0   300
Meters
(Approximate Scale)

© CNES 1988 SPOT IMAGE CORPORATION

Dolon Airfield is the main operating base for the Soviets' BEAR H intercontinental bomber. The new BLACKJACK strategic bomber will probably also be based there when it is operationally deployed later this year.

The Soviets have developed a full family of cruise missiles — including air-, sea-, and ground-launched systems. Depicted here are the transporter-erector-launcher and, in the insert, the SSC-X-4 GLCM it carries.

(SLCM). A variety of Soviet general purpose attack submarines such as VICTORs, AKULAs, or SIERRAs could carry and launch the SS-N-21. Additionally, a YANKEE-Class nuclear submarine has been converted to carry SS-N-21 missiles. Targets in either Eurasian or North American theaters could be attacked by these accurate missiles, which are fitted with nuclear warheads. The larger SS-NX-24 missile, which could be carried from specialized submarine platforms such as a modified YANKEE, is expected to be operational in the next few years.

The Soviets have deployed an air-launched long-range cruise missile — the AS-15/KENT — with their intercontinental-range BEAR H force. Armed with this standoff weapon, the BEARs pose a much greater threat to Eurasian and US targets. Work on a new bomber-launched cruise missile is underway.

The Soviets had developed and were preparing to deploy a ground-launched cruise missile (GLCM) — the SSC-X-4 — which is a version of the SS-N-21/AS-15 system. A GLCM-variant of the larger SS-NX-24 was also a possibility as a theater strike weapon. Both GLCM systems are banned by the INF Treaty.

INTERMEDIATE-RANGE NUCLEAR FORCES

In addition to ICBMs, the SRF is responsible for intermediate-range (IRBM) and medium-range (MRBM) ballistic missiles — the latter two being longer range intermediate-range nuclear forces. The INF Treaty will

eliminate these Soviet systems. Until the treaty enters into force and the missiles are destroyed as required over a three-year period, INF systems, such as the SS-20, will continue to pose a threat to Eurasian targets.

The last seven years have seen the full expansion and deployment of the Soviet SS-20 IRBM force, from approximately 250 SS-20s in 1980 to a high of 441. The less capable SS-4 MRBM force has been reduced in size during this period, and now numbers approximately 50 missile launchers.

The SS-20 is a remarkably capable IRBM system which first became operational in 1977. The missile carries three highly accurate MIRVed warheads and can deliver them out to a range of about 5,000 kilometers. It has a reliable solid-fuel propellant system and is fully mobile, making countertargeting efforts extremely difficult. It can fire either from sliding-roof garages at regimental bases or from field-deployed sites. The Soviets have the capability to reload and refire SS-20s. The older SS-4 system is still maintained at the theater level. This liquid-fueled system is located at soft launching sites. The missile can deliver one warhead out to a range of 2,000 kilometers.

These missile forces can be augmented or replaced by a variety of other nuclear delivery systems. The Soviets retain 12 older GOLF II diesel-powered ballistic missile submarines, six of which are assigned to the Baltic Fleet. Each GOLF can deliver three SS-N-5 missiles on Eurasian targets. Additionally, Soviet aviation

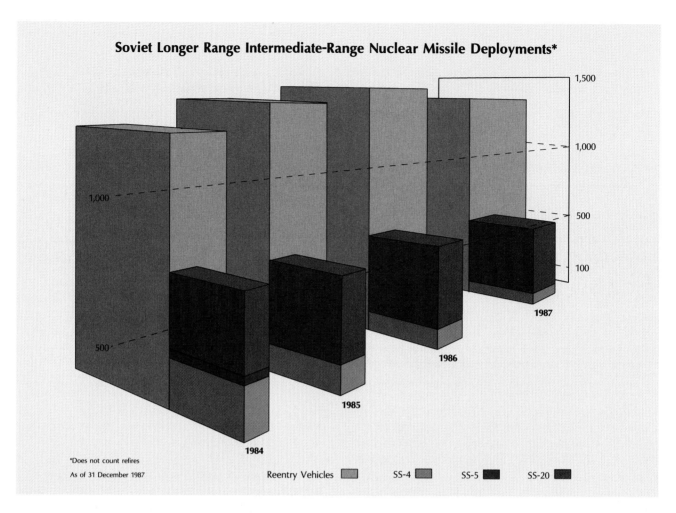

Soviet Longer Range Intermediate-Range Nuclear Missile Deployments*

*Does not count refires
As of 31 December 1987

Reentry Vehicles ▢   SS-4 ▢   SS-5 ▮   SS-20 ▮

assets, particularly the BACKFIRE and FENCER, can conduct theater nuclear operations.

The role of Soviet INF missiles will likely be redistributed to other systems in light of the recent INF Treaty. The treaty requires the destruction without replacement of all existing missiles and launchers over a three-year period, including the SS-20, SS-4, and SS-5 ballistic missiles, as well as the SSC-X-4 cruise missile, which was tested but not deployed. After the agreement takes effect, however, the Soviets may be able to turn to other strategic ballistic missiles (ICBMs and SLBMs), aircraft, and perhaps sea-launched cruise missiles to fulfill their strategic theater requirements in Eurasia.

SHORT-RANGE NUCLEAR FORCES

The Soviet military also deploys a wide variety of nuclear delivery systems with a range less than 1,000 kilometers. These include shorter range intermediate-range nuclear forces (SRINF) missiles, which are covered by the INF Treaty. Specifically, the SCALEBOARD and SS-23/SPIDER will be eliminated within 18 months after the treaty enters into force. The INF Treaty does not cover short-range nuclear missiles with a range less than 500 kilometers, dual-capable aircraft, and artillery pieces. Thus, while the INF Treaty eliminates the most threatening Soviet nuclear systems, the Soviets will retain a more than adequate capability to provide tactical nuclear support for their ground forces.

The SRINF systems eliminated by the INF Treaty had posed new challenges to NATO during the 1980s. At the theater- and front-level, the older SCALE-BOARD had been replaced by a modernized version. The modification significantly improved the missile's accuracy while maintaining its 900-kilometer range. Until 1983, the SCALEBOARD had not been deployed outside the USSR. In 1984, one brigade was deployed in Czechoslovakia, and two brigades were deployed in East Germany. SCALEBOARD units are also located in the western Soviet Union, and in the Central Asian and the Far Eastern USSR. Over 100 SCALEBOARD missiles remain in the inventory.

At the front- and army-levels, the SS-23/SPIDER was designed as the successor to the 1960's vintage SCUD. Over 75 are now in the inventory. With improvements

The Soviet SS-20 IRBM system, shown in these photos provided by the Soviets under the terms of the INF Treaty, was the first mobile MIRVed nuclear ballistic missile deployed into European and Asian theaters.

in accuracy, responsiveness, and range, the SS-23 poses a greater threat to time-critical targets such as NATO nuclear missile units, airfields, and air defense sites. The SPIDER has been deployed since 1985 in several locations within the USSR and was recently introduced into East Germany. Over 600 SCUD missiles, however, remain deployed. Although SCALEBOARDs, SPIDERs, and SCUDs could be deployed with chemical or conventional high-explosive warheads, their principal role is to serve as the ground force's primary nuclear fire support means.

The Soviet military also operates tactical nuclear missile and artillery systems deployed at front level. At the division-level, nuclear fire support is provided by 660 free-rocket-over-ground (FROG) missiles, deployed in battalions of four launchers (one in each division). In 1981, the SS-21, a guided missile (providing improvement in both range and accuracy), began replacing the FROG in forward-deployed divisions, and 140 are now deployed. Division-level SS-21 battalions are being consolidated into brigades in Soviet armies in East Germany.

Soviet nuclear-capable artillery and mortars underwent qualitative improvements in the 1980s, with the replacement of older, towed-artillery pieces with self-propelled (SP) versions. These SP weapons, including the 152-mm howitzer 2S3, the 152-mm gun 2S5, the 203-mm gun 2S7, and the 240-mm 2S4 mortar, enable the Soviets to provide more responsive nuclear support for their ground maneuver units.

STRATEGIC DEFENSES

In a dramatic departure from past assertions that only the United States is working to "militarize" space, General Secretary Gorbachev acknowledged on 30 November 1987 that the USSR is involved in strategic defense research. He stated, "The Soviet Union is doing all that the United States is doing, and I guess we are engaged in research, basic research, which relates to these aspects which are covered by the SDI of the United States." But the Soviet effort into all aspects of strategic defense has been consistently far more vigorous than that of the United States.

Ballistic Missile Defense

The Soviets maintain the world's only operational ABM system, and a nearly completed construction program begun during the 1980s will yield an expanded and upgraded system comprising a two-layer defense of 100 launchers. When fully operational around 1989, the system will defend selected leadership and strategic facilities in the Moscow area.

The new Moscow ABM system includes two interceptor missiles: a long-range modified GALOSH ABM that is intended to engage ballistic missile reentry vehicles (RVs) outside the atmosphere; and the GAZELLE, a shorter range, high-acceleration missile that, like the

PRAVDA

When the Soviets published this photo of their space-tracking facility at Dushanbe, they maintained that its purpose is to track satellites. The amount of power supplied by a nearby hydroelectric dam, however, exceeds that needed solely for satellite tracking. It may in fact be used to generate high-energy laser beams for antisatellite missions.

now-defunct US SPRINT system, is designed to engage RVs after they have reentered the Earth's atmosphere. New, hardened silos have been constructed for the new interceptor missiles. The modified GALOSH and GAZELLE are expected to become operational in 1988 or 1989.

A large multifunction phased-array radar nearing completion at Pushkino is also an integral part of the new Moscow ABM system. The radar, which has 360-degree coverage, will provide support for the new interceptor systems. It is expected to reach full operational capability around 1989.

In the aggregate, the Soviet Union's ABM and ABM-related actions suggest that the USSR may be preparing an ABM defense of its national territory. These actions include radar construction, concurrent testing, SAM upgrade, ABM rapid reload, ABM mobility, and deployment of ABM components to Gomel.

The Soviets began building a large phased-array radar (LPAR) network in the 1970s, and since 1981 the number of LPARs under construction has more than doubled. There are now nine LPARs in varying stages of completion, forming a nearly complete ring of ballistic missile detection coverage for the Soviet landmass. They duplicate and augment coverage provided by the older HEN HOUSE ballistic missile early warning radars, but also could provide the detailed detection and tracking

data which would be required for a nationwide ABM system. Since these radars take a long time to construct, the entire network probably would not be operational until the mid-1990s.

The Soviets have deployed and tested components required for an ABM system that could be deployed to a site in months rather than years. Recent Soviet activities with respect to moving a FLAT TWIN ABM radar and a PAWN SHOP van, both components of an ABM system, from a test range and initiating deployment at a location outside an ABM deployment area or ABM test range, constitute a violation of the ABM Treaty. Moreover, the SA-10/SAM system already in the air defense forces may have the potential to intercept some types of ballistic missiles, as may the SA-X-12B/GIANT when it is deployed.

One of the principal concerns regarding Soviet non-compliance with the ABM Treaty is the Krasnoyarsk radar, which is in clear violation of the treaty. The only permitted functions for an LPAR with Krasnoyarsk's location and orientation would be space-tracking and National Technical Means (NTM) of verification. Conclusive evidence suggests, however, that this radar is primarily designed for ballistic missile detection and tracking, not for space-tracking and NTM as the Soviets claim. Moreover, the coverage of the Krasnoyarsk radar closes a major gap in the coverage of the Soviet ballistic missile detection, warning, and tracking screen. The

The PILL BOX radar associated with the Moscow ABM system will be completed around 1989. A potential ability to integrate target tracking with ABM intercept would result in a genuine battle management capability.

The 30-story Krasnoyarsk large phased-array radar receiver and the 18-story transmitter are positioned in violation of the ABM Treaty. They are neither on the periphery of the Soviet Union nor pointed outward, as the treaty requires.

Soviet ABM/Space Defense Programs

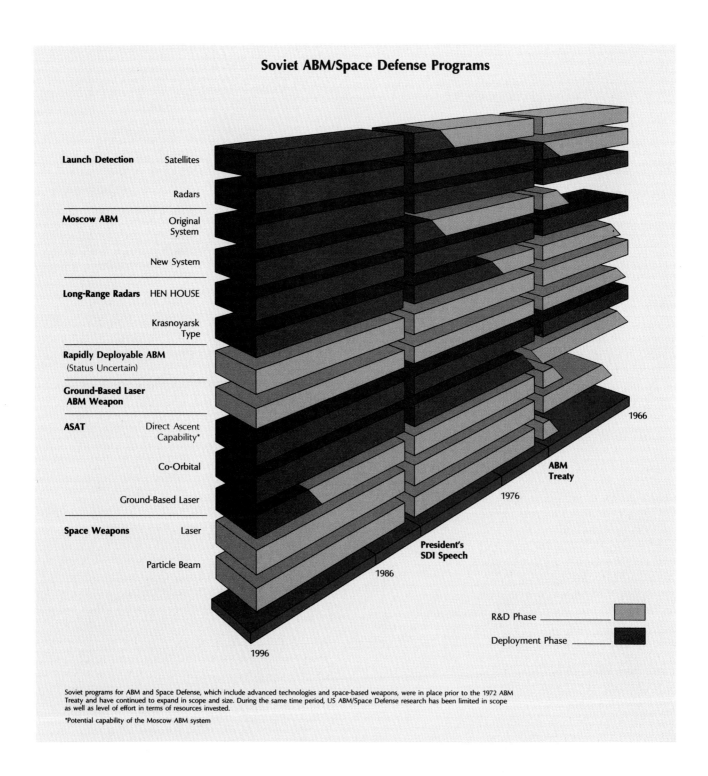

Launch Detection — Satellites, Radars

Moscow ABM — Original System, New System

Long-Range Radars — HEN HOUSE, Krasnoyarsk Type

Rapidly Deployable ABM (Status Uncertain)

Ground-Based Laser ABM Weapon

ASAT — Direct Ascent Capability*, Co-Orbital, Ground-Based Laser

Space Weapons — Laser, Particle Beam

1966 — ABM Treaty — 1976 — President's SDI Speech — 1986 — 1996

R&D Phase
Deployment Phase

Soviet programs for ABM and Space Defense, which include advanced technologies and space-based weapons, were in place prior to the 1972 ABM Treaty and have continued to expand in scope and size. During the same time period, US ABM/Space Defense research has been limited in scope as well as level of effort in terms of resources invested.

*Potential capability of the Moscow ABM system

location of the Krasnoyarsk radar allows it to provide warning of a ballistic missile attack, to acquire attack characterization data that will enable the Soviet strategic forces to respond in a timely manner, and to aid in the battle management of Soviet strategic defensive forces. All LPARs, including the Krasnoyarsk radar, have the inherent capability to track large numbers of objects accurately. Thus, they not only could perform as ballistic missile detection, warning, and tracking radars, but also have an inherent technical potential, depending on location and orientation, of contributing to ABM battle management. A US Congressional delegation visited the Krasnoyarsk LPAR facility on 5 September 1987 and was allowed to view selected areas of both the transmitter and receiver facilities. No information derived from this visit, however, changed the assessment that the radar is designed for ballistic missile detection and tracking.

Advanced Strategic Defense Technologies

Since the 1960s, the Soviets have been conducting a substantial research program to develop a defense against ballistic missiles. As noted by General Secretary Gorbachev, this effort covers many of the same technologies currently being explored by the US SDI. The Soviet effort, however, involves a much greater investment of plant space, capital, and manpower.

For example, the Soviet laser research program, with ballistic missile defense applicability, has historically been much larger than its US counterpart. At Sary Shagan, one of a half-dozen major R&D facilities involved in laser research, the Soviets are believed to be developing several lasers for strategic applications such as air defense or a terminal ABM, and at least one laser believed capable of an antisatellite mission.

Moscow hopes that its huge investment to design and build high-energy lasers will provide it with laser systems for strategic air defense, space-based antisatellite missions and, conceivably, defense against ballistic missiles. The first prototype systems, some with limited operational capability, might be seen before the end of the decade, but except for air defense, full-scale, fully operational defensive systems are not expected until the late 1990s at the earliest.

In some areas of ballistic missile defense-related technology, the USSR has progressed beyond technology research. It has ground-based lasers with some capability to attack US satellites, and it could have a space-based antisatellite laser prototype within the next several years. The Soviets also could have ground-based laser prototypes for ballistic missile defense in the early 1990s, and they could begin testing a limited-scale deployment system in the late 1990s.

Moscow is exploring several other advanced technologies for use in ballistic missile defense. Since the late 1960s, for instance, the Soviets have explored the use of particle beam and kinetic energy weapons for antisatellite (ASAT) and ballistic missile defense missions. Although the Soviets may be able to test a prototype particle beam ASAT weapon in the mid-to-late 1990s, operational systems that could destroy satellites or incoming ballistic missiles will not exist until the 21st century.

Long-range, space-based kinetic energy weapons for defense against ballistic missiles probably could not be developed until at least the mid-1990s. The Soviets could, however, deploy a short-range, space-based system for space station defense or close-in attack by a maneuvering satellite in the near future.

The USSR has also conducted research in the use of radio-frequency weapons to interfere with or destroy the electronic components of ballistic missile warheads or satellites. A ground-based version of such a weapon could be tested in the 1990s. Free-electron lasers, which generate intense microwave and millimeter-wave pulses, have been developed by the Soviets, possibly for use in radio-frequency weapons.

Passive Defense

The Soviet passive defense program is a comprehensive system of measures designed to inhibit the effects of a nuclear attack on the Soviet Union. The main objectives of the passive defense program in effect today are: ensuring the survival and continuity of the Soviet leadership; planning for efficient wartime mobilization of manpower and the economy; protecting the industrial base and essential workers; and providing a credible reconstitution capability. Integral to the Soviet passive defense program are thousands of hardened facilities.

Deep Underground Facilities

For 40 years, the Soviet Union has had a vast program underway to ensure the survival of the leadership in the event of nuclear war. This multifaceted program has involved the construction of deep underground bunkers, tunnels, secret subway lines, and other facilities beneath Moscow, other major Soviet cities, and the sites of major military commands. This program is designed solely to protect the senior Soviet leadership from the effects of nuclear war. These deep underground facilities today are, in some cases, hundreds of meters deep and can accommodate thousands of people. As nuclear arsenals on both sides have become larger and more potent, these facilities have been expanded and have reached greater depths.

Neither changes in the Soviets' leadership nor the restructuring of the strategic balance and the refinements in military doctrine that accompanied these changes appear to have diminished their commitment to the program. Over the program's history, its purpose has remained unchanged — leadership survival so that it can maintain internal control and ensure that Soviet military power can be centrally directed throughout all phases of a world war. The secrecy of the program and the uncertainty about the extent and nature of these facilities are major causes for concern.

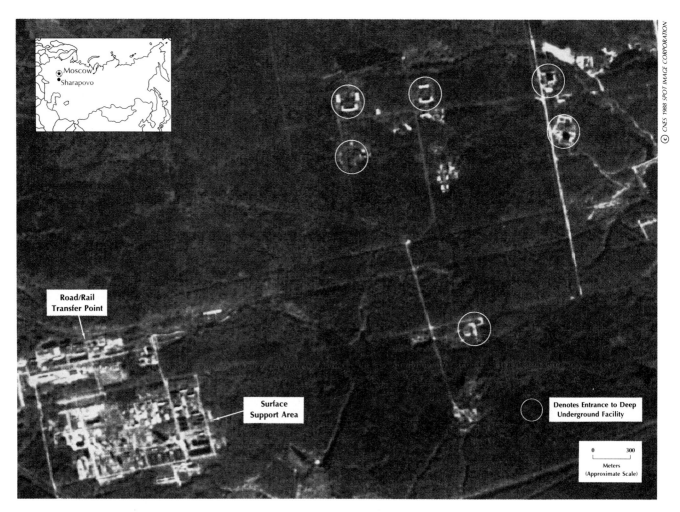

Road/Rail Transfer Point

Surface Support Area

Denotes Entrance to Deep Underground Facility

0   300
Meters
(Approximate Scale)

Some underground facilities designed to protect the Soviet leadership are relatively shallow and can accommodate thousands of people. This deep underground facility is a wartime relocation center for the Soviet National Command Authority.

The deep underground program, which rivals Soviet offensive strategic weapons programs both in scale and level of commitment, remained undiminished even as the Soviets agreed to limit their defenses against ballistic missiles in the ABM Treaty. Indeed, a major augmentation of the original activities was started about the time the ABM Treaty was being concluded. Yet another round of construction on these complexes began in the early 1980s, when Soviet leaders were publicly emphasizing that a nuclear war would be so catastrophic that attempts to achieve victory or even seriously limit damage in such a war no longer made sense. The latest round of construction coincided with intensified Soviet preparations for the possibility that a nuclear war could be protracted.

The deep underground facilities beneath the city of Moscow are directly associated with the main centers of state power. They provide the leaders of the various organs of state control the opportunity to move from their peacetime offices through concealed entryways down to protective quarters below the city, in some cases, hundreds of meters down. Once there, the Politburo, the Central Committee, the Ministry of Defense, the KGB, and the apparatuses of the many other state ministries can remain sheltered while the USSR converts to a wartime posture. The fruits of this 40-year construction program now offer the Soviet wartime leadership the option of remaining beneath Moscow or, at some point, boarding secret subway lines connecting these deep underground facilities. From there the Soviets can make their way to nearby underground complexes outside Moscow where they plan to survive nuclear strikes and to direct the war effort. The support infrastructure for these facilities is substantial. A highly redundant communications system, consisting of both on-site and remote elements, supports these complexes and permits the leadership to send orders and receive reports through the wartime management structure.

These installations also have highly effective life support systems capable of protecting their occupants

Soviet leaders in Moscow can move to protective quarters hundreds of meters below the city if hostilities seem imminent. Additionally some deep underground complexes are located far outside urban areas.

against chemical and biological attack. Such arrangements may enable independent operations to be carried out from these facilities for many months. The top leadership of the USSR also has the option of going by secret subway lines out to Vnukovo Airfield, about 17 miles southwest of the Kremlin, and from there flying to remote facilities. They also have a fleet of aircraft, trains, and other vehicles that provide yet another option for survival; these platforms have extensive communications support, which would permit the surviving leadership to reconstitute Soviet military power for ensuing military operations. While Soviet preparations for leadership protection are most intensive around Moscow because of its critical role in wartime management, there are similar programs in other key cities. Moreover, Soviet planning calls for the leadership's evacuation from several hundred additional cities to rural relocation facilities.

The Soviets also use worked-out mines to increase the number of relocation facilities. These old mines have the added advantage of reducing the cost of the passive defense program since the excavation costs have already been recovered. The mines would also provide concealed storage sites for military stores and equipment, expanded storage capacity for the strategic stocks reserve network, and improved continuity of economic activity in wartime. By using these old mines, the Soviets can expand the already large number of underground facilities available for leadership protection quickly and inexpensively.

The Soviets' experience with civil defense, leadership protection, and massive relocation efforts during World War II has taught them the benefits of a leadership protection program. While continuing improvements indicate the program does not yet fully meet Soviet requirements, the Soviets have made extensive preparations to give the leadership the potential for effective performance in a nuclear war. The enormous and continuing Soviet investments in the leadership protection program indicate that they believe its benefits

The SL-4, operational for 24 years, is still the workhorse of the Soviet space program.

are well worth the large cost. Unceasing efforts in strategic offensive forces and active defensive forces modernization, when coupled with efforts to protect the leadership, clearly indicate that the USSR expects to exercise national command and control through all phases of protracted nuclear war.

SPACE FORCES

The continuing evolution of Soviet military space doctrine, the increasing number of military-related launches, and the high priority given to development of space-related strategic offensive and defensive systems reflect the Soviet determination to use space primarily for military purposes. The long-term Soviet commitment to space was reaffirmed by General Secretary Gorbachev in May 1987 when he declared, "We do not intend to relax our efforts and lose our vanguard position in the conquest of space."

Space Programs and Capabilities

The Soviets currently operate about 50 types of space systems for military and civilian uses, including manned space stations (MIR and the inactive SALYUT 7), and reconnaissance, launch-detection, navigational, meteo-

rological, and communications satellites. Some types of satellites — the Soviet space station, the materials processing satellite, the radar ocean reconnaissance satellite (RORSAT), the electronic intelligence (ELINT) ocean reconnaissance satellite (EORSAT), and the radar-carrying oceanographic satellite — are unique to the Soviets.

The USSR conducts approximately 100 space launches annually from its three "cosmodromes." One of these, Tyuratam, is the world's largest. To maintain their impressive launch rate, the Soviets have about 20 launch pads and use eight operational types of boosters to launch their payloads. A ninth booster, the SL-X-17, is in development and testing. Their high launch rate allows the Soviets to maintain an increasing number of active satellites in orbit — up from about 120 in 1982 to about 150 in 1987. At least 90 percent of the Soviet satellites in orbit have a military purpose and can support offensive or defensive operations.

Although the Soviets steadfastly maintain they have no military space program, about 150 of the approximately 200 operational Soviet satellites projected to be in orbit by the mid-1990s will most likely have purely military missions such as ocean reconnaissance

62

US and Soviet Space
Launches 1957-1987

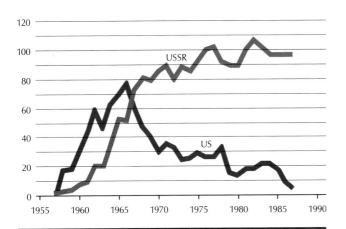

US and Soviet Operational Satellites
in Orbit 1957-1987

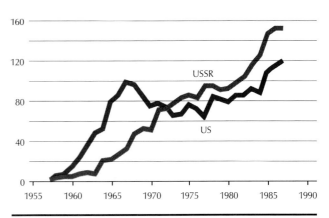

and targeting, electronic intelligence, imagery reconnaissance, and communications. Another 40 will probably support joint military-civilian functions, including communications, navigation, and weather data. The approximately 10 remaining satellites are likely to conduct interplanetary probes and other scientific missions. The lifetimes and survivability of Soviet satellites are expected to increase during the next 10 years because of more sophisticated technology and the placement of satellites at higher altitudes.

Military Support From Space

The Soviets continue developing and deploying space systems designed to support military operations on Earth. They now have a fully operational network dedicated to warning them of an ICBM attack, and they operate several types of space-based reconnaissance systems. Two of these, the RORSAT and EORSAT, can be used to locate naval forces. Moreover, the Soviets practice their detection and targeting techniques, routinely launching these satellites to monitor both their own and NATO naval exercises.

Moscow continues to expand its sophisticated satellite reconnaissance program. Several planned improvements such as a data-relay satellite system could improve the timeliness of Soviet intelligence. Demonstrations of flexibility and versatility in launching and deploying surveillance systems have continued, and the Soviets are capable of redirecting them for worldwide missions as required. Meanwhile, their satellite imagery reconnaissance capability has been refined, and space-based electronic intelligence is being upgraded.

While the Soviets are expected to maintain their cur-

rent launch-detection satellite network, they are probably working on a space-based surveillance system to detect the launch of US SLBMs, as well as European and Chinese missile launches. Although the USSR's land-based ballistic missile defense radar network permits detection of inflight SLBMs, a space-based geosynchronous launch-detection satellite system could increase warning time significantly. The Soviets will probably have the technical capability to deploy such a satellite system within the next several years.

The Soviets continue deploying their space-based global navigation satellite system known as GLONASS. This system will probably provide highly accurate positioning data for military and civilian users by 1992. GLONASS is similar to the US NAVSTAR Global Positioning System (GPS). In fact, the Soviets used digital signal-processing data from GPS documents to develop GLONASS. GLONASS is being placed in a GPS-like orbit. Based on the 9 to 12 satellites announced for the system, GLONASS would have a worldwide, two-dimensional navigation capability. If the Soviets want GLONASS to provide worldwide, three-dimensional navigation upgrades, they would have to orbit 18 to 24 satellites.

The Soviets have continued developing and deploying radar-carrying satellite systems. Designed for mapping ice formations in polar regions, these satellites can greatly enhance the Soviet Navy's ability to operate in icebound areas by facilitating navigation of northern sea routes and assisting in such activities as routing naval ships from construction yards in the western USSR to new ports in the Pacific.

In July 1987, the Soviets orbited a very large, new

type of satellite using their PROTON booster rocket. According to the Soviets, COSMOS-1870 has an Earth-resources, remote-sensing mission, which reportedly includes experiments related to hydrology, cartography, geology, agriculture, and the environment. It uses an onboard radar unit to gather data. Since no scientific data attributed to this spacecraft has even been discussed or publicly acknowledged to date, a strong military affiliation cannot be ruled out.

Manned Operations

The Soviet manned space program occupies a unique position in Moscow's space efforts. It is heavily publicized to promote the perception of the peaceful nature and technological superiority of the USSR's space program. Nonetheless, the Soviets have made a strong commitment to using their manned space program to accelerate their drive to achieve military superiority in space. For the Soviets, having a man in space provides unique observation, experimentation, execution, and command functions — functions which the US frequently uses remote systems to perform.

Soviet literature indicates that the military applications of remote sensing, oceanography, meteorology, and geodesy have been the focus of repeated cosmonaut investigations. Even civil investigations such as astronomical observations, also performed by cosmonauts, have military uses. The USSR may be using such investigations to develop techniques useful for maintaining the orientation of certain equipment to an accuracy of

The Soviet manned presence in space accords the USSR an extremely valuable capability for repair and maintenance (shown here is a cosmonaut welding), military support, and even the potential for interfering with other satellites.

a few arc-seconds, a capability needed to aim directed-energy weapons.

The ability to rendezvous and link up with uncooperative spacecraft, which Soviet cosmonauts demonstrated in 1985 and 1986, also has military applications. Cosmonauts use equipment such as a laser rangefinder, a night-vision device, and an optical sensor while performing this type of operation. The Soviets state that this rendezvous procedure will allow the rescue of cosmonauts stranded in orbit, but it could also be useful both for repairing friendly satellites and for inspecting and disabling enemy satellites.

A crucial cosmonaut activity is Earth observation, which has applications for reconnaissance and targeting. The Soviets report that their cosmonauts have used visual observations, cameras, spectrometers, and multispectral electro-optical sensors in their observations from the SALYUT and MIR space stations. These experiments suggest the Soviets are evaluating their ability to locate, identify, and track targets from outer space. Developing this ability could be the first step toward designing a space weapons platform for use against targets in space and on Earth. Such a platform may eventually be used for ASAT and ballistic missile defense operations, as well as for space station defense.

In 1986, the USSR launched a new-generation space station — MIR — to replace the aging SALYUT-7. MIR is an impressive advancement over SALYUT-7, having enhanced solar energy and electrical power systems, greater computer capabilities, and individual "cabins" for crew members. Most significantly, while SALYUT-7 had only two docking ports, MIR has six.

With the launch of MIR, a space station module, and regular crew rotations with the SOYUZ-TM capsule, the Soviets have probably begun their permanent manned presence in space. The crew launched in February had a partial crew change in July 1987, and the remaining cosmonaut, Colonel Yuri Romanenko, was relieved in December 1987 after setting two space endurance records. In the early-to-mid 1990s, the Soviets should be able to construct a very large modular space station. They have discussed housing up to 100 cosmonauts in such a space complex.

Antisatellite Operations

In addition to space programs which could be construed as having both military and civilian applications, the Soviets have space systems that are purely military in nature. Indicative of the Soviet military program for space is their development and maintenance of the world's only currently operational ASAT system, a ground-based orbital interceptor. Using a radar sensor and a pellet-type warhead, the interceptor can attack all current low-altitude satellites. A target engagement during the first orbit of the intercept leaves little time for a target satellite to take evasive action. The interceptor can reach targets orbiting at an altitude of more than 5,000 kilometers, but it is probably intended for high-priority satellites at lower altitudes.

The ASAT interceptor is launched from Tyuratam on SL-11 launch vehicles. Two launch pads, storage space for many interceptors, and the launch vehicles are available at the Tyuratam facility. Several interceptors could be launched each day from each of the pads.

Given the complexity of launch, target tracking, and radar-guided intercept, the Soviet ASAT system is far from primitive. Soviet ASAT tests have been largely successful, providing them with an operational system fully capable of performing its mission. Although the Soviets have not launched their ASAT system in several years, in an effort to forestall US development of an ASAT weapon, they have maintained their ASAT readiness. Over the past several years, the Soviets have routinely launched the SL-11 ASAT booster with other payloads, thereby ensuring the reliability of this system component. Other components can be tested on the ground without actually having to launch the ASAT system itself. The nuclear-armed GALOSH ABM also has an inherent ASAT capability against low-altitude satellites. The Soviet Union also has ground-based lasers with some capability to irradiate US satellites.

New Space Launch Systems

The Soviet space program's success is due largely to its versatile and reliable inventory of space launch vehicles (SLVs) and its space launch and support facilities. The Soviets send a satellite aloft every three or four days, using one of eight types of operational SLVs. The USSR's impressive ability to launch various spacecraft quickly gives the Soviets a distinct operational military advantage in any crisis. Most malfunctioning satellites could be rapidly replaced, and additional satellites could be launched to cover new or expanding areas in a crisis. In fact, if all deployed Soviet satellites were destroyed, the Soviets have sufficient standby lift capability to replace them within two to three months, provided reserve satellites were available.

Even with their current launch capability, the Soviets are expanding their extensive family of SLVs with

new expendable launch vehicles and reusable manned spacecraft. The deployment of the medium-lift Titan IIIC-Class SL-16 and the heavy-lift Saturn V-Class SL-X-17 will increase the payload weight of satellites the Soviets will be able to orbit.

On 15 May 1987, the Soviets conducted the first flight test of the SL-X-17, which they designated "Energiya" (Energy). They openly announced that "military experts took part in creating and testing" the new launch vehicle. The Soviets reported that "Energiya's" first stage (the strap-on boosters) and the second stage (the core vehicle) operated as planned. They also stated that an attempt was made to orbit a satellite during this test. The satellite mockup engines apparently did not function properly and the satellite splashed down in the Pacific Ocean. The failure of the payload, however, was not due to problems with the booster, which performed as intended.

The SL-X-17 heavy-lift vehicle will be used to launch the Soviet space shuttle orbiter as one of its payloads. Launch-pad compatibility testing of an orbiter attached to the SL-X-17 vehicle may already have taken place, and it appears that a test flight will occur soon. By using US propulsion, computer, materials, and airframe

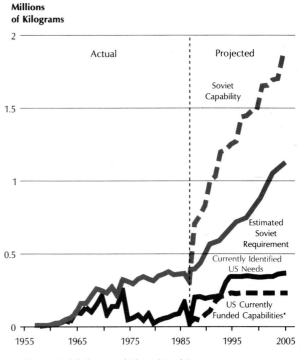

US vs. Soviet Weight to Orbit

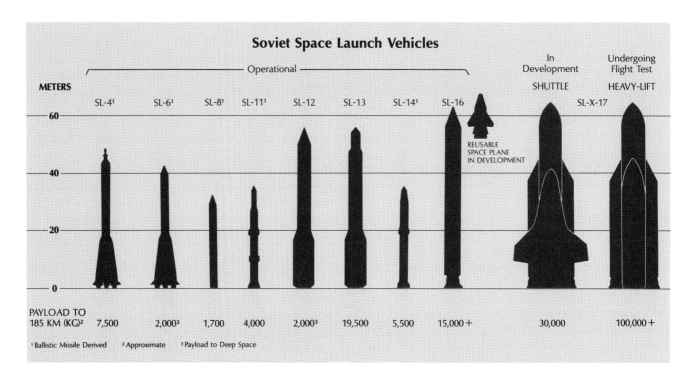

Soviet Space Launch Vehicles

METERS	SL-4[1]	SL-6[1]	SL-8[1]	SL-11[1]	SL-12	SL-13	SL-14[1]	SL-16	SHUTTLE SL-X-17	HEAVY-LIFT
PAYLOAD TO 185 KM (KG)[2]	7,500	2,000[3]	1,700	4,000	2,000[3]	19,500	5,500	15,000+	30,000	100,000+

Operational — In Development — Undergoing Flight Test

REUSABLE SPACE PLANE IN DEVELOPMENT

[1] Ballistic Missile Derived   [2] Approximate   [3] Payload to Deep Space

Estimated Soviet Space Launch Requirements

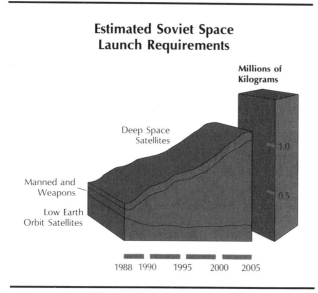

Saturn V rocket. Potential payloads for the SL-X-17 include modules for a large space station, components for manned and unmanned interplanetary missions, and perhaps directed-energy ASAT and ballistic missile defense weapons and other space-based components of the Soviet strategic defense program.

The SL-16 booster is capable of placing a payload of more than 15,000 kilograms into low-Earth orbit. This capability filled a gap in the Soviet SLV inventory by providing an economical means of launching medium-weight payloads. One candidate payload for the SL-16 could be a space plane, a subscale version of which has been flight-tested in orbit; a full-scale test version is possibly in production. A small, manned spacecraft could be used for quick-reaction, real-time reconnaissance missions, satellite repairs and maintenance, crew transport, space station defense, satellite inspection and, if necessary, satellite destruction.

The introduction of the SL-16 and SL-X-17, coupled with an expected greater use of the SL-12 and SL-13 SLVs, will increase substantially the payloads the Soviets will be capable of launching into space. In fact, during the next five years, the Soviets are expected to double the annual payload weight launched into orbit, and quadruple that weight within 15 years.

PROSPECTS

While the INF Treaty marks an important step in reducing the threat of nuclear war, the residual

technology and designs, the Soviets were able to produce an orbiter years earlier, and at far less cost, than if they had depended solely on their own technology and engineering.

Development of a heavy-lift launch system with its main engines on the core vehicle rather than the orbiter gives the system the versatility to launch either an orbiter or other very heavy payloads. The SL-X-17, for example, will be able to place payloads of over 100,000 kilograms into low-Earth orbit, a figure comparable to that carried by the discontinued US

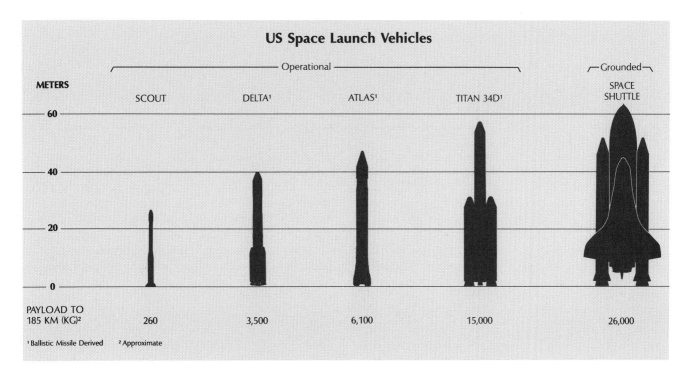

US Space Launch Vehicles

Operational — Grounded

	SCOUT	DELTA¹	ATLAS¹	TITAN 34D¹	SPACE SHUTTLE

METERS

— 60

— 40

— 20

— 0

PAYLOAD TO
185 KM (KG)²

260	3,500	6,100	15,000	26,000

¹ Ballistic Missile Derived   ² Approximate

Soviet nuclear arsenal will still contain some 1,400 ICBMs, nearly 1,000 SLBMs, and a large number of cruise missiles, short-range ballistic missiles, and tactical missile and artillery systems.

Even if a strategic arms reduction treaty is concluded and ratified, the Soviets can be expected to continue to improve their strategic nuclear weapons, especially for accuracy, mobility, and survivability. Their short-range ballistic missile force, which is expected to grow steadily, will remain a potentially devastating strike force. Continued Soviet development of a new class of cruise missiles with greater accuracy than currently deployed ballistic missiles will enhance the deep-strike capability of theater bombers and increase bomber survivability by providing a standoff capability. Furthermore, the Soviets show no sign of abandoning any aspect of their strategic defense program, despite its approximate $20 billion per year cost.

Research and development trends suggest that the Soviets fully intend to use space for both offensive and defensive purposes. If current trends continue, space will become the fastest growing industry in both the military and civil sectors, although all available evidence suggests that military requirements drive the Soviet space program.

Projected Soviet Space Launch Capabilities

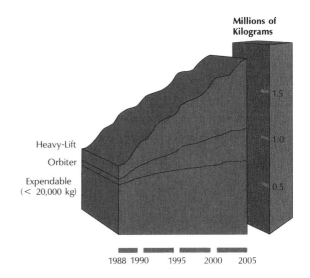

Millions of Kilograms

Heavy-Lift
Orbiter
Expendable
(< 20,000 kg)

1988 1990   1995   2000   2005

CHAPTER V

Soviet Conventional Forces

In this decade, no element of Soviet military power has undergone more profound improvement than Soviet conventional forces. Enhancements in Soviet ground force equipment such as armored vehicles, air defense weapons, and tactical missile systems have been complemented by advances in Soviet tactical aircraft and naval forces. The following upgrades are representative of the overall buildup in Soviet conventional forces:

- The number of T-64 and T-72 main battle tanks has grown at a steady rate while the new T-80 and, within the last several years, a new tank derived from the T-72 tank, also entered the inventory.
- Towed artillery and mortar systems continue to be replaced by self-propelled systems, all of which are capable of firing chemical rounds, with those 152-mm and larger capable of firing nuclear rounds.
- The number of fighters and fighter-bombers, which now include the sophisticated MiG-29/FULCRUM, the MiG-31/FOXHOUND, the Su-27/FLANKER, and Su-24/FENCER, has increased by 38 percent.
- The Il-76/MAINSTAY is operational, significantly improving Soviet early warning and battle management capabilities.
- Several new air defense weapon systems have been deployed, including the all-altitude SA-10 and the SA-12 surface-to-air missile systems. Both are mobile and have a capability to intercept (cruise and some tactical ballistic) missiles.
- More than 20 warships (carriers through destroyers), including two KIEV-Class carriers, have entered the inventory.
- Seven new classes of general purpose submarines have been introduced.

In terms of manpower, the Soviet military's largest component is its general purpose conventional and theater nuclear forces. These forces are equipped to operate in land and oceanic theaters of military operations on or adjacent to the Eurasian landmass. All five branches of the Soviet Armed Forces — the Strategic Rocket Forces, Ground Forces, Naval Forces, Air Defense Forces, and Air Forces — contribute to the USSR's theater forces. In addition, the armed forces of the USSR's Warsaw Pact allies add significantly to the Soviet military capability against NATO.

The profound effects of new nonnuclear technology on modern warfare have triggered sweeping changes in Soviet military strategy and doctrine. Advanced weaponry has increased greatly the threat and likely damage to Soviet forces from potential adversaries, and it has offered prospective new capabilities and opportunities to Soviet forces with weaponry incorporating these new technologies.

Yet underlying Soviet responses to these changes is a basic concern that the United States and its allies are maintaining or acquiring a distinct advantage in critical technologies, while at the same time adopting a more offensive military strategy. Soviet planners believe that the development of US/NATO operational concepts involving deep strikes, such as the Follow-on Forces Attack strategy, stem from NATO's determination to seize the initiative in a war in Europe and conduct operations deep in Warsaw Pact territory.

Soviet strategic planners are highly concerned about the effects that standoff and penetrating weapon systems incorporating newly developing advanced technology will have on their own offensive capability. Such US systems as the Joint Surveillance and Target Attack Radar System (JSTARS), the Army Tactical Missile System (ATACMS), and the Joint Tactical Fusion Program, which the Soviets refer to generically as "Reconnaissance Strike Complexes," are designed to "look" and "shoot" deep into Warsaw Pact territory and substantially increase NATO's combat power. These Western plans and programs would imperil the reinforcing waves, or echelons, of Soviet troops moving toward the battle area and the elements that resupply them. Moreover, the Soviets believe these NATO reconnaissance strike complexes present a fundamental challenge to the Soviet ability to execute their theater strategy of conducting high-speed, deep-offensive operations. In response to these NATO initiatives, the Soviets have expanded and modernized their own forces and formulated new strategies to counter what they perceive as an effective counter to Soviet strategy.

This chapter will highlight significant developments observed in Soviet conventional military forces, which include:

Increasingly quiet, modern general purpose submarines such as the 16,000-metric-ton OSCAR-Class, shown here, can challenge Western navies with highly accurate, lethal antiship cruise missiles and torpedoes. Each OSCAR unit carries 24 SS-N-19 550-kilometer-range missiles.

- Theater strategic operations and the nuclear and non-nuclear forces designed to wage a combined-arms campaign;
- Ground forces, which now include 211 active divisions and thousands of improved weapon systems;
- Conventional air forces, which have been restructured and equipped with several types of sophisticated new aircraft;
- A navy and naval air force which has introduced several new weapon systems and substantially increased the firepower carried on each ship and submarine.
- Force-wide trends, which include a formidable command, control, and communications network; a high readiness posture; a comprehensive manpower and materiel mobilization system; and a logistics and sustainability infrastructure which can support multiple strategic offensives.

THEATER STRATEGIC OPERATIONS

A key part of the Soviets' response to change has been the development of what they term the Theater Strategic Operation. This concept provides a framework for the integration of forces and strategy designed to wage a rapid nonnuclear or, if imposed by the enemy, nuclear, combined-arms campaign in a Theater of Military Operations (TVD). The increasing prominence of the Theater Strategic Operation reflects emphasis on coordination of efforts and resources to achieve success in an intense and costly conflict, in which enemy strategic objectives located up to a 1,500-kilometer depth must be successfully attacked and neutralized.

The Theater Strategic Operation comprises a series of component suboperations designated front, air, antiair,

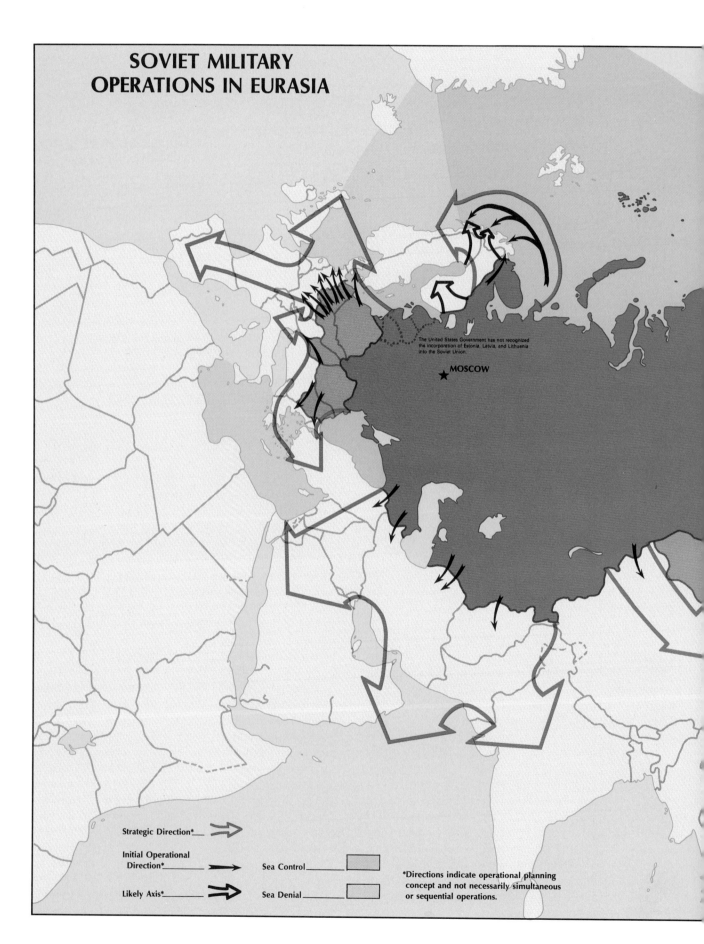

SOVIET MILITARY OPERATIONS IN EURASIA

The United States Government has not recognized the incorporation of Estonia, Latvia, and Lithuania into the Soviet Union.

★ MOSCOW

Strategic Direction*⎯

Initial Operational
Direction*⎯⎯⎯⎯⎯

Likely Axis*⎯⎯⎯⎯⎯

Sea Control⎯⎯⎯⎯

Sea Denial⎯⎯⎯⎯

*Directions indicate operational planning
concept and not necessarily simultaneous
or sequential operations.

70

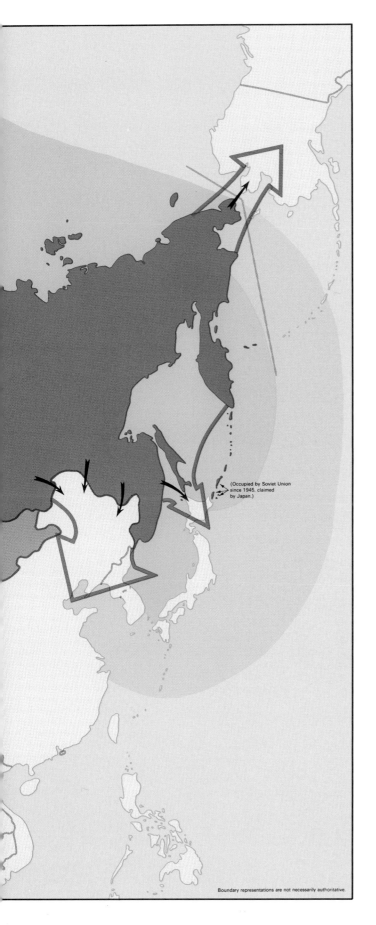

(Occupied by Soviet Union since 1945, claimed by Japan.)

Boundary representations are not necessarily authoritative.

airborne, naval, and nuclear. They are controlled and coordinated by the High Commands of Forces (HCFs) in each continental TVD. In 1984, permanent peacetime High Commands of Forces headquarters in the Western, Southwestern, and Southern TVDs were established. These joined an existing Far Eastern TVD HCF. These peacetime HCFs permit the establishment of a permanent command structure closer to that required in wartime, allowing a more rapid generation of forces and increasing the prospects of the Soviets' success before an opponent's preparations to resist were complete.

The ground maneuver portion of the Theater Strategic Operation is conducted by Soviet fronts. The front operation is executed by three to five combined-arms armies consisting of tank, motorized rifle, and fire support elements, and supplemented by additional front, army aviation, and fire support units. In the Western TVD, for example, the Soviets expect up to five first-echelon fronts to be committed to achieving initial objectives 600 to 800 kilometers into Western Europe. Subsequent front operations would operate against objectives up to 1,500 kilometers deep.

In the past 10 years, the deep operation has emerged as a primary means to neutralize and seize Soviet objectives deep in an opponent's rear area. This operation consists of deep strikes by aviation, rocket, and artillery forces, as well as attacks into the enemy's deep rear areas conducted by Soviet operational maneuver groups, or OMGs. OMGs can be formed at front- or Army-level. Multiple OMGs would be employed to isolate front-line defending forces; disrupt rear area logistics; threaten key command-and-control, economic, and population centers; neutralize nuclear attack systems; and disrupt the mobilization and reinforcement process critical to a successful NATO defense.

The air operation component of the Theater Strategic Operation would include a massive nonnuclear offensive campaign by front and theater air assets designed to gain air superiority and disrupt and destroy NATO's command, control, and nuclear capability. Frontal ground forces would contribute to the air operation by attacking enemy air and air defense facilities with surface-to-surface missiles, artillery, and ground attacks. In turn, the air operation, by degrading and disrupting enemy command, control, and communications systems, as well as aviation and nuclear capabilities, would create favorable conditions for the fronts to accomplish their objectives quickly.

To counter enemy air operations, Pact offensive and defensive forces would conduct a coordinated, theater-wide antiair operation involving both attacks

MITSUO SHIBATA

In addition to having an integrated suite of antisubmarine systems, the KIEV-Class carrier's complement of FORGER VTOL fighters, ASW helicopters, and antiship missiles gives it surface-attack and limited power-projection capabilities as well. It is thus well suited to operate in defense of Soviet SSBNs, to participate in sea-control operations, and to project Soviet military power.

To help ensure the continuous and effective control of forces in wartime, the Soviets would use multiple and well-disguised field command posts, such as this one observed in Eastern Europe.

against NATO aircraft in the air and against their bases. Pact naval forces would operate off coastal flanks to destroy NATO naval forces, secure the theater's coastal flanks, and participate in amphibious operations, while thwarting any NATO attempt to employ amphibious forces.

A naval operation employing surface ships, aircraft, submarines, and naval infantry would be an integral part of the Theater Strategic Operation in a continental TVD. In addition to securing and protecting the theater's coastal flank, amphibious operations would be conducted in support of overall theater objectives. Amphibious assaults would be directed against targets such as major islands or straits and would be closely coordinated with the advance of frontal forces. For example, a joint air-sea assault landing would likely be directed against the Danish straits area, specifically the islands of Zealand and Lolland, and potentially Fyn, during the first weeks of war.

In oceanic TVDs, such as the Arctic or Pacific, Soviet fleets would conduct complex operations hundreds of nautical miles from the Soviet coastline. Major Soviet objectives would include deploying and protecting the strategic ballistic missile submarine force and defending the USSR from seaborne attack.

Although the Soviets would prefer to fight using only conventional forces in a theater conflict, they are prepared to use nuclear and chemical weapons. If nuclear use becomes necessary, the Soviets would hope to preempt an impending enemy escalation to nuclear combat with a massed nuclear strike throughout the TVD against air, nuclear, command-and-control, and ground forces targets, with the Soviet Supreme High Command exercising overall control. Nuclear weapons would be delivered by frontal aviation, artillery, missiles, and some naval systems, as well as the Strategic Rocket Forces and Strategic Aviation. Chemical strikes could also be employed independent of, or in coordination with, nuclear attacks. The Soviets would launch subsequent strikes based on damage assessments.

Theater nuclear capabilities are complemented by extensive measures to ensure the survivability of Soviet forces. Forces are dispersed, key facilities are hardened, and redundant command-and-control systems have been deployed. Soviet radiological and chemical protection capabilities have long been rated as the world's best.

Despite doctrinal, organizational, and equipment enhancements since 1980, recent Soviet writings reflect concern that they may be unable to initiate offensive operations immediately. One factor highlighted is the growing importance of initial defensive operations. The contest for early successes and momentum may require the Soviet Union and its allies to wage defensive operations to defeat the enemy's initial strikes, retain or gain the initiative, and eventually deploy the forces necessary to conduct a war-winning theater offensive.

Another related doctrinal change has been an increasing Soviet concern that they may no longer be able to defeat an opponent totally in a short, rapid, offensive campaign lasting several weeks. Rather, a future war may be a succession of operations and campaigns conducted over an extended period, due, in part, to the enormous resources of present-day coalitions. Recent conflicts in the Middle East and South Atlantic are cited as indicative of the enormous losses in personnel and equipment that can be expected and underline the growing importance of strategic reserves. The increased capability of both sides to attack forces and facilities deep in an opponent's rear is an additional factor likely to extend the scope and lethality of a future conflict.

GROUND FORCES

The Soviet Ground Forces comprise the largest branch of the Soviet Armed Forces. In the 1980s, they have made remarkable strides in maintaining their offensive capability in the face of developments by US/NATO forces and other potential adversaries. The Soviet Ground Forces have expanded in size and structure, readiness, sustainability, survivability, and command-and-control capability. The Soviets now have two Unified Army Corps (UAC), 211 active divisions with five additional inactive wartime mobilization bases, plus numerous independent regiments and brigades.

Since 1980, Soviet divisions have increased their combat potential significantly through extensive restructuring and expansion. Artillery and motorized rifle (MR) assets have been increased in tank divisions. Within MR divisions, the number of BMP infantry fighting vehicles (IFVs) and BTR armored personnel carriers (APCs) has grown significantly, and the improved BMP-2 vehicle has appeared in increasing numbers. In divisional artillery regiments, self-propelled artillery has replaced towed pieces, and the total number of guns has risen. Thus, a typical motorized rifle division is composed of 270 tanks, 680 APC/IFVs, 215 artillery pieces, and 13,500 troops, while a typical tank division is composed of 330 tanks, 255 APC/IFVs, 165 artillery pieces, and 11,100 troops.

Soviet efforts since 1980 to develop forces and capabilities to sustain a high-speed, deep-striking offensive have been highlighted by the establishment of over 20 air assault brigades and battalions within fronts and armies. The necessary helicopter-lift resources to employ them against targets in the enemy rear also have been added.

Organizational and structural changes have been reflected most dramatically by the establishment of two Unified Army Corps (UAC) for an apparent wartime role as front OMGs. While roughly equal in equipment and personnel to a combined tank and MR division, the UACs have received the latest Soviet equipment and are organized into combined-arms tank and mechanized brigades, integrating tank and MR forces down to

Front-line Soviet troops in Eastern Europe are the priority recipients of the newest ground force equipment. This T-80 tank features greater firepower, armor protection and mobility than old model T-62 tanks.

battalion level. This organization has resulted in a formation well suited for relatively independent, fast-moving deep operations.

Equipment Growth

Overall, the Soviet Ground Forces now contain over 53,000 main battle tanks; 60,000 APCs/IFVs; 48,000 artillery pieces, mortars, and multiple rocket launchers (MRLs); 4,600 SAM launchers (excluding the thousands of handheld systems); 7,000 antiaircraft artillery (AAA) pieces; 1,600 surface-to-surface missile (SSM) launchers; 4,500 helicopters; and more than 1,900,000 personnel.

The number of newer T-64, T-72 and T-80 main battle tanks in the Soviet ground forces is steadily increasing, replacing the older T-54/55 and T-62 vehicles in front line units. Additionally, a new Soviet tank derived from the T-72, exhibiting improved protection, better mobility, and enhanced firepower is being fielded. Modern tanks now comprise approximately 40 percent of the force. At the same time, the Soviet Union and its Warsaw Pact allies have programs under way to upgrade many of their older tanks with newer guns, power/transmission plants, and fire control equipment, as well as providing them with improved protection. A high-priority program also has been implemented to add reactive and wrap-around armor and side skirts to some of their tanks, as well as to improve their upper surface protection substantially against new Western precision top-attack weapons.

New IFV and APC vehicles also are replacing older models in Soviet tank and MR divisions. The number of divisions with the BMP-2 IFV is steadily increasing, and BTR-70 and -80 model APCs are supplanting the older BTR-60. Unlike their Western counterparts, all of these vehicles can be made amphibious with little or no preparation, greatly enhancing the ground forces' ability to negotiate water barriers.

Over the past seven years, the Soviets also have replaced towed artillery systems with self-propelled 122-mm 2S1 and 152-mm 2S3 howitzers in tank and MR divisions in the TVDs opposite NATO. Similar changes are now being implemented in the Southern and Far Eastern TVDs. Self-propelled 152-mm 2S5 and 203-mm 2S7 guns, as well as 240-mm 2S4 mortars, are also replacing older towed models in front and army artillery divisions and brigades. In addition, the 120-mm SP 2S9 howitzer, with unique direct and indirect fire capabilities, is replacing towed artillery weapons in airborne divisions and air assault brigades. Besides the increasing availability of enhanced-blast and subprojectile warheads, all of these new gun and howitzer weapons are capable of firing chemical rounds, while 152-mm and larger guns are nuclear capable. The availability of improved conventional and, probably, chemical war-

At the tactical level, camouflage, concealment, and deception, illustrated here by field-deployed 2S1 122-mm howitzers, is an important aspect of *maskirovka,* which the Soviets emphasize throughout their military forces.

Soviet high-powered artillery such as this 203-mm self-propelled 2S7 gun can disrupt an opponent's defensive preparations by firing nuclear, high-explosive, or improved conventional rounds deep behind his lines.

Light, responsive surface-to-air missiles such as this man-portable SA-16 threaten low-flying, fixed- and rotary-wing aircraft.

heads for high-volume-of-fire MRL systems provides front, army, and division commanders with additional fire support resources.

Short-range ballistic missile (SRBM) and tactical rocket assets available to frontal forces have been significantly improved. The older, inaccurate FROG artillery rocket is being replaced with the vastly improved SS-21. Besides improved reliability and accuracy, the SS-21, as do the newer gun and rocket systems, benefits from new families of highly lethal improved conventional munitions. SCUD SRBMs are assigned to front and army SSM brigades.

The new self-propelled antiaircraft gun system (SPAA-Gun M1986) is now appearing in selected first-line divisions in place of the long-proven and still-effective ZSU-23-4. Unlike the ZSU-23-4, which has four 23-mm weapons, the M-1986 is believed to mount twin rapid-firing 30-mm guns, as well as a state-of-the-art radar and fire control system. The newest Soviet man-portable, shoulder-launched surface-to-air missile

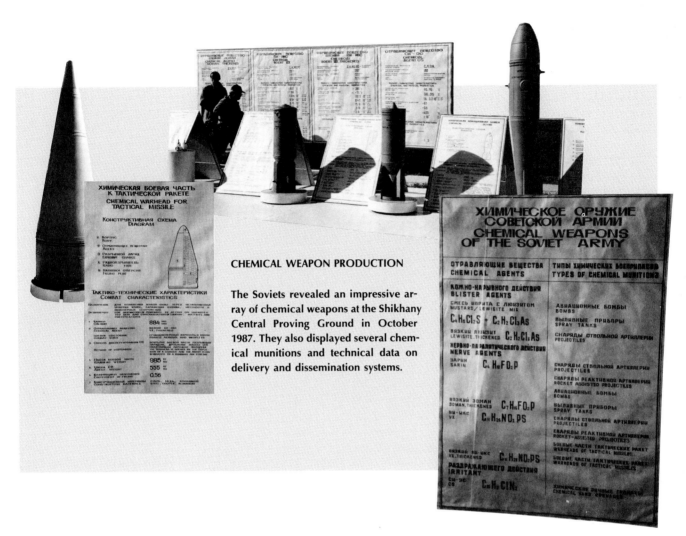

CHEMICAL WEAPON PRODUCTION

The Soviets revealed an impressive array of chemical weapons at the Shikhany Central Proving Ground in October 1987. They also displayed several chemical munitions and technical data on delivery and dissemination systems.

(SAM), the SA-16, also is entering service, supplementing or replacing older SA-7 and SA-14 weapons. At higher command echelons, the SA-11 is replacing the SA-4 in army air defense brigades, while the even newer SA-12A is being deployed. Improved versions of the SA-6 and SA-8 systems also have been deployed in recent years.

The Soviets also have improved the capabilities of their helicopter forces over the past eight years. The introduction of two new attack helicopters, the HAVOC and HOKUM, is expected shortly, while existing HIND and HIP attack helicopters have been upgraded with a variety of new gun, rocket, and aerial mine armament options. In addition, all attack and transport helicopters that would likely operate in the vicinity of the front line have been equipped with active and passive self-protection jammers and flares. Some helicopters have been fitted with add-on armor plates to protect flight crews or vital components and with engine exhaust filters to reduce emissions that could attract heat-seeking SAMs.

Chemical Warfare

The Soviets maintain and continue to upgrade the world's most extensive chemical warfare program. In an April 1987 speech in Prague, General Secretary Gorbachev declared that the Soviet Union had stopped producing chemical weapons and denied that it had deployed such weapons outside its borders. Nevertheless, the Soviet Union and its Warsaw Pact allies are still emphasizing new agent testing, research and development, and training which could lead to employment in a future conflict. In summary, the Soviets continue to consider chemical weapons a useful military option.

About the time the US began to modernize its chemical warfare capabilities, the Soviets began to assert their support in principal for a treaty banning chemical weapons. In October 1987, they invited representatives from 45 nations to view their chemical weapons and witness a demonstration of a mobile chemical weapon destruction facility at Shikhany, their primary research, development, testing, and evaluation site. The Soviets also accepted a longstanding invitation and visited the US CW destruction facility at Tooele, Utah. While the events and statements of the past year portray the Soviets as being willing to relinquish their offensive chemical warfare superiority, neither the Soviet Union nor its Warsaw Pact allies have serious intentions to eliminate unilaterally their formidable chemical warfare capability.

The Soviet Union has acknowledged that it has up to 50,000 tons of poisonous substances, the world's largest known chemical warfare agent stockpile. The USSR's stockpile includes mustard blister agents and a mustard-lewisite mixture, and the nerve agents sarin, thickened sarin, soman, VX, and thickened VX. These agents can be delivered by FROG or SCUD warheads, and by a wide range of chemical bombs, artillery shells, and MRL projectiles. The Soviets did not, however, show the complete range of chemical weapons and agents they possess. They continue to develop new agents and chemical delivery systems.

In a war with NATO, the Soviet Defense Council decision to employ chemical weapons would be weighed against the consequences of US retaliation. If the Soviets calculate that they could achieve significant benefits at what they considered an acceptable risk, they might employ chemical weapons. If such a decision were made, the Supreme High Command would execute the decision and integrate chemical weapons employment into the overall operations. Short-range ballistic missiles, ground-attack aircraft, and artillery would deliver the chemical munitions. Aircraft- and helicopter-mounted spray tanks also would be used to disseminate agents.

The Soviet chemical warfare organization has undergone significant restructuring since 1980. Support units have been reduced from battalions to companies at division level, and from companies to platoons at regiment level. At higher levels, however, the size of chemical units has been expanded. Army-level chemical defense battalions have been reorganized into specialized battalions and companies such as nuclear burst location units, radiological and chemical reconnaissance battalions, analytical computation stations, smoke battalions, flame battalions, and several types of decontamination battalions. At the front level, the chemical defense brigade has been augmented by a variety of independent battalions. Units at all levels are being fully equipped and continue receiving new and more modern equipment.

The reorganization of chemical troops improves the Soviets' ability to conduct operations in a contaminated environment. Increased reconnaissance and detection capabilities at army and front levels allow the Soviets to evaluate quickly the effects of a nuclear or chemical strike. This evaluation allows units to bypass contaminated areas or to conduct partial decontamination, thereby maintaining the tempo of the offensive.

To support the Soviets' chemical warfare effort, there are in the ground forces alone between 45,000 and 60,000 chemical troops and 30,000 special vehicles for reconnaissance and decontamination. Some of these forces assisted in the Chernobyl cleanup efforts, decontaminating personnel, vehicles, structures, and terrain.

The Soviets have improved both their defensive and offensive chemical warfare capabilities in recent years. Every combat vehicle fielded today is equipped with a collective protection system, thereby facilitating the crossing of contaminated areas. Decontamination capabilities have been enhanced by the introduction of the ARS-14 decontamination apparatus, which has a larger chassis and greater tank capacity than its ARS-12U predecessor.

SOVIET CONVENTIONAL AIR FORCES

Three major elements comprise the Soviet Air Forces — the Strategic Air Armies (SAA) of the Supreme High Command (VGK); Air Forces of the Military Districts and Groups of Forces (AF MD/GOF); and Military Transport Aviation (VTA). One SAA, the Moscow Air Army, which has intercontinental bomber assets postured for nuclear war, is discussed in Chapter III. VTA's logistics and power-projection capabilities are covered in the section on readiness and sustainability. The remaining four SAAs — the Smolensk, Irkutsk, Legnica, and Vinnitsa Air Armies — and AF MD/GOF are the subjects of this section.

The Soviets have always respected NATO's air power. In the 1980s, however, the Soviet Air Forces have made great strides to overcome their shortcomings. They developed and deployed new aircraft with improved range, weapons loads, and avionics. They also structured their air forces to provide dedicated air support at all levels of command — from maneuver division to VGK — and modified operational concepts by supplementing the offensive air operation with the antiair operation oriented against NATO's combat aviation.

Strategic Air Armies

Since 1980, the Soviets have steadily modernized the intermediate-range bomber units assigned to the Smolensk and Irkutsk Air Armies, which are arrayed against NATO Europe and China/East Asia, respec-

The MiG-29/FULCRUM, a state-of-the-art air-superiority fighter, can detect and intercept low-flying aircraft.

tively. In 1980, about 50 BACKFIREs were deployed and accounted for only slightly over 10 percent of the Soviet Air Forces theater bomber strike assets. Now more than 160 BACKFIREs are deployed with SAA, accounting for 30 percent of Smolensk and Irkutsk Air Army strike assets. Most, if not all, of the aging BADGER bombers will likely be replaced by BACK-FIRE bombers in the coming decade. The BACKFIRE is superior to the BADGER and the BLINDER in combat radius, survivability, and weapon versatility. It can perform a multitude of missions, including nuclear strike, conventional attack, antisurface warfare, and reconnaissance. Its low-level supersonic dash capabilities make it a highly capable weapon system for theater military operations. In addition, BEAR long-range bombers, including BEAR G AS-4 carriers, have been reassigned to a theater role, and have been observed conducting regular combat training exercises against naval and land targets in the northern Pacific Ocean region.

The Smolensk and Irkutsk Air Armies have 375 BADGER and BLINDER bombers assigned to them. The Irkutsk Air Army also has about 70 BEAR bombers, including 45 BEAR Gs. Almost 180 additional specialized BADGER and BLINDER reconnaissance and electronic countermeasures (ECM) aircraft round out the assets available for conducting theater bombing operations.

The strike component of the Legnica and Vinnitsa Air Armies consists largely of Su-24/FENCER fighter-bombers. Currently, these SAAs have more than 500 FENCERs, 200 other fighters of various types, and 120 reconnaissance/ECM aircraft. Fighter aircraft assigned to these SAAs currently include the MiG-21/FISHBED, MiG-23/FLOGGER, and Su-27/FLANKER. The pri-

mary mission of these fighters is to escort FENCER strike aircraft. The fighter components of both air armies will convert completely to the FLANKER for strike support because of its longer range and advanced avionics.

SAA reconnaissance and ECM assets currently include MiG-25/FOXBAT, Yak-28/BREWER, and FENCER variants, with the FENCER replacing the BREWER. High-altitude, high-speed, pre- and post-strike reconnaissance would be conducted by FOX-BATs, while FENCERs will probably accompany strike aircraft formations for immediate, post-strike bomb damage assessment and follow-on targeting.

Frontal Aviation

The Air Forces of the Military Districts and Groups of Forces (AF MD/GOF) would be assigned to various wartime fronts to support ground troops or to conduct interdiction in support of front objectives. Most air support to ground forces, however, would be provided by combat helicopters.

Deep-interdiction missions would be accomplished by AF MD/GOF FENCER regiments. The majority of AF MD/GOF strike assets, however, are composed of Su-17/FITTER and MiG-27/FLOGGER fighter-bombers. A new aircraft, the FOXBAT F, a variant of the MiG-25/FOXBAT specifically designed for defense suppression, is entering service. Although other Soviet aircraft carry antiradiation missiles (ARMs) to attack air defense radars, the FOXBAT F/AS-11 ARM weapon system appears to be especially designed to attack the NATO air defense missile belts from a long-range standoff posture. The mission of this weapon system in a massive air strike would be to degrade NATO

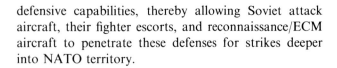

The capabilities of the Su-27/FLANKER give it the versatility to fly both escort and air defense missions.

The MiG-31/FOXHOUND, designed specifically for air defense, is equipped to engage a variety of targets with air-to-air missiles.

defensive capabilities, thereby allowing Soviet attack aircraft, their fighter escorts, and reconnaissance/ECM aircraft to penetrate these defenses for strikes deeper into NATO territory.

Fighters assigned to AF MD/GOF include the aging MiG-21/FISHBED, the MiG-25/FOXBAT, the MiG-29/FULCRUM, and the ubiquitous MiG-23/FLOG-GER. The newest aircraft to enter the inventory is the FULCRUM, which now numbers around 450 and is operationally based entirely west of the Urals, indicating Soviet concern for countering the latest NATO fighters. Fighter aircraft missions include conducting fighter sweeps, escorting fighter-bombers, attacking high-value NATO platforms such as the AWACS, and maintaining fighter combat air patrols.

The decade's most noteworthy trend in both the SAAs and AF MD/GOF has been the remarkable expansion in ground attack capability. For example, the number of fighter-bombers has increased from 2,100 in 1981 to 2,900 today, an increase of 38 percent. This trend forcefully underscores the key role Soviet military planners give to air power to ensure the success of their offensive operations.

Some of this increased ground attack capability has been developed at the expense of counterair fighters. Their number has declined from 2,100 in 1981 to 1,800 today, a decrease of over 14 percent. Nevertheless, the Soviets have gained more in ground attack capability than they have lost in fighter capability. Reconnaissance/ECM assets have stabilized at around 700 — the same level as in 1981. In sum, Soviet Air Forces of today are better postured and more capable of conducting conventional air operations than they have ever been.

Air Defense Forces

The 1980s have been a period of modernization and growth for the Soviet Air Defense Forces. Years of research and development efforts have borne fruit in the deployment of several new air defense weapon systems. Soviet Air Defense Forces structural readjustments and disposition have been consistent with their goal of making an already formidable air defense system even more effective.

Soviet air defense weapon systems are better able today than in 1981 to degrade effectively strikes by US and NATO air forces. Significant progress is being made in countering Allied cruise missiles and cruise missile carriers. In contrast to the air defense weapons of the 1970s, the new Soviet SAMs and supporting radars possess increased mobility, making them more survivable. In addition, a greater number of Soviet interceptors are able to engage low-altitude targets and can fly longer missions, thereby permitting projection of air defenses well beyond the borders of the USSR.

The 1980s have witnessed changes in the air defense forces as Soviet commanders seek to achieve the optimum structure for controlling their SAMs, radars, and aircraft. At the beginning of the decade, both strategic and tactical border air defenses were subordinate to the local MD commanders. Since 1986, however, the trend has been back to centralization under the strategic homeland Air Defense Forces. All strategic SAMs, radars, and air defense aircraft are once again under direct control of air defense headquarters in Moscow. Conversely, tactical SAMs and radars have been resubordinated to the Soviet Ground Forces, whose combined-arms formations they chiefly support.

The MAINSTAY AWACS was developed to enhance the effectiveness of Soviet air defense efforts, for both Soviet homeland defense and probably defense over the battlefield.

Surface-to-Air Missiles

The major strategic SAM development of this decade has been the deployment of the SA-10, which reached initial operational capability in 1980. It has been entering the inventory as a replacement for three older strategic SAM systems — the SA-1, -2, and -3. Its introduction enhances the Soviet SAM forces' capability to track and engage multiple targets simultaneously. It also promises to fill a low-altitude coverage gap that has historically plagued the strategic SAM forces. Supported by new phased-array acquisition and guidance radars, the SA-10 represents the Soviets' first credible capability against targets with a small radar cross section — cruise missiles. Since 1981, about 150 SA-10 launch units have been deployed in defense of major military industrial centers, with one-third of the force around Moscow. The even more capable all-altitude SA-X-12B/GIANT will soon become operational, thus further enhancing Soviet strategic defenses.

Even as they have deployed new SAM systems, the Soviets have continued upgrading existing systems and adjusting their deployment to maintain a multilayered homeland defense. A recent example of this approach has been the deployment of long-range, high-altitude SA-5 systems to Eastern Europe, where they now provide overlapping coverage over the Baltic Sea and inter-German border. By exporting this system to their Warsaw Pact allies, the Soviets have not only enhanced the air defense of those countries but have extended the air defense buffer zone for the defense of the USSR as well. SA-5s in East Germany pose a particular threat to key NATO reconnaissance and air warning aircraft such as AWACs even when they are operating in West German airspace.

The SA-13 on a tracked vehicle, shown here, gives the Soviets yet another layer and option in their tactical air defense network.

Aircraft

While the number of Soviet aircraft committed to strategic air defense has remained at about 2,250 for the last several years, the interceptor force has nonetheless been improved significantly. Over the past eight years, the force has evolved from one consisting almost entirely of 1950s and 1960s vintage aircraft to a rapidly modernizing inventory that includes over 160 MiG-31/FOXHOUND and 100 Su-27/FLANKER aircraft. These new generation fighters have a true look-down/shoot-down capability — the capability to detect and destroy targets flying at low altitudes against ground clutter — using modern air-to-air missiles like the AA-9 and AA-10. The new-generation aircraft entering the force are replacing interceptors like the FIREBAR, FIDDLER, and FLAGON. The net effect is a force better able to threaten both US strategic bombers and US/NATO theater aircraft.

To add to their growing interceptor capability, the Soviets are expected to produce two new fighters in the mid-1990s — an offensive counterair fighter, the air-superiority fighter (ASF); and a defensive counterair fighter (CAF). The maneuvering capabilities of the ASF and CAF will be significantly greater than those of the FLANKER B and FULCRUM A. Initial operational capability for both aircraft is expected in the late 1990s.

Increasing numbers of MAINSTAY AWACS aircraft are being made available to Soviet air defense forces, with more than a dozen having been produced. The MAINSTAY has both an airborne radar platform for detecting low-altitude targets and the capability to direct air defense interceptors to targets beyond the range of ground-based systems. The combination of the MAINSTAY and longer range interceptors like the FOXHOUND gives the Soviets their first capability to project strategic air defenses far beyond the USSR's periphery. The MAINSTAY also provides the Soviets with a better capability to manage the air battle over the TVD.

RADARS AND COMMAND, CONTROL, AND COMMUNICATIONS

The capability to conduct successful air defense operations depends in part on the air defense radar's capability to acquire accurate air surveillance data, as well as on the speed and efficiency of command, control, and communications (C^3) systems. Over the past decade, developments in Soviet air surveillance radars and C^3 have produced significant technological advances in these systems. In addition to the phased-array radars associated with both the latest SAM and AAM systems, major advances include early warning radars with three-dimensional (azimuth, height, and range) capabilities and improved effectiveness against low-altitude targets.

The Soviet Union is expanding its electronic surveillance of the Western Pacific, probably to improve tactical early warning and tracking of US and Allied aircraft and ships. There is evidence of a Soviet over-the-horizon radar east of Vladivostok. The radar could operate continuously to determine the force composition, speed and direction of targets traveling in the area between Japan, the Philippine Islands, Guam, and Wake Island.

MARITIME FORCES

The evolution of the Soviet Union's maritime forces during the 1980s saw the expansion and modernization that began in 1963 continue to transform what was essentially a coastal defense force into an ocean-going fleet capable of executing a full range of naval tasks. The Soviets' concept of seapower envisions the use of all maritime resources, including naval surface combatants and submarines, amphibious forces, naval aviation, maritime border guards, coastal missile and artillery forces, as well as their large merchant, fishing, and research fleets, in support of state policy in both peace and war. Since 1981, Soviet maritime forces have become increasingly capable of conducting wartime operations at greater distances from home waters, in either a conventional or nuclear environment, and better able to support state interests abroad during peacetime. Complex multitheater and combined-arms exercises; the assumption of maritime missions by nonnaval forces; increased logistic sustainability; a permanent presence and growing naval influence in distant ocean areas; and the continued construction of more capable surface combatants, submarines, and aircraft characterize Soviet naval power growth.

Maritime Strategic Defense

The Soviet Navy's primary wartime mission is to protect its ballistic missile submarines (SSBNs). To ensure a naval strategic nuclear strike force, assets must be protected from attack by Western antisubmarine warfare (ASW) forces through effective control of selected sea areas contiguous to the Soviet Union. A second aspect of Soviet maritime strategic defense is the destruction of those enemy sea-based forces that pose a strike threat, especially a nuclear one, to the Soviet Union and its allies, including Western ballistic missile submarines, aircraft carriers, and land-attack cruise missile-equipped units operating in selected areas contiguous to the USSR. Because of the perceived threat, the Soviets consider ASW and antisurface warfare (ASUW) platforms to be the fleet's most significant conventional forces.

The recent introduction of long-range, land-attack cruise missiles onboard US Navy submarines and surface combatants has significantly complicated Soviet ASUW and ASW efforts. The Soviets have reemphasized the development of ASUW and ASW platforms and tactics to counter the increased threat from these units. In the past seven years, the Soviets have developed new antiship missile-equipped surface combatants and submarines and have continued to modernize their naval intermediate-range bomber force. Additionally, new classes of attack submarines and ASW ships and helicopters have been constructed, and the long-range BEAR F force has been modernized in an attempt to counter the Western submarine threat. In spite of this recent emphasis, the Soviet Navy has not abandoned its traditional coastal defense mission, and the Soviets continue to acquire submarines, corvettes, and missile combatants specifically designed to operate in coastal waters peripheral to the Eurasian landmass.

Support of Ground Forces

Although the Soviet Navy has evolved into an ocean-going force with major offensive and defensive strategic tasks, the support of Pact ground forces remains an important mission. This task entails protecting the ground forces' flanks from attack by enemy naval and amphibious forces and providing naval gunfire, amphibious, and logistics support to land operations.

Interdiction of Sea Lines of Communication

The interdiction of Western sea lines of communication has been a longstanding mission of the Soviet Navy. Early in the nonnuclear phase of a NATO-Warsaw Pact war the Soviets are expected to assign relatively few attack submarines to disrupt the flow of reinforcement and resupply to Europe, due to higher priority tasks such as protecting their SSBNs and destroying enemy sea-based nuclear delivery capability. If a NATO-Warsaw Pact war evolved into an extended conventional conflict, additional attack submarines could be assigned for increased interdiction of NATO's strategic shipping. The release of these additional units, however, is considered to be contingent on the successful achievement of those other, more important tasks.

Support of State Policy

The Soviet leadership has continued to use its ocean-going navy and other maritime elements to support its international economic, political, and military policies. Today, Soviet naval and merchant forces are deployed continuously around the globe to perform a variety of political, economic, and military tasks. They provide Soviet presence during port visits, assert Soviet rights in international waters, protect the interests of the Soviet merchant and fishing fleets, demonstrate support for Soviet client states, and counter Western naval presence. Some prime examples include:

- A well-established periodic Soviet naval presence in the Caribbean, including port visits and naval air deployments to Cuba and joint training with Cuban forces;

- A continued Soviet naval or naval air presence in both Syria and Libya, and the possible support of indigenous forces during periods of tension;
- Port visits to, and use of the ship repair facilities in, Yugoslavia and Tunisia;
- A continued Soviet naval and periodic naval air presence in Luanda, Angola;
- Periodic naval and naval infantry presence in Port Victoria, Seychelles;
- A long-term, Soviet naval presence in Aden, South Yemen;
- A permanent stationing of Soviet naval, naval air, and air force elements at Cam Ranh Bay, and a periodic naval presence at Da Nang and Ho Chi Minh City, Vietnam;
- Soviet Navy port visits to Kompong Som, Cambodia, since 1980; and
- Navy visits to Wonson, North Korea, since 1985 and combined North Korean-Soviet exercises in 1986 and 1987.

Soviet Naval Developments

The decade began with the introduction of three surface warship classes, two attack submarine classes, and a new helicopter class. The KIROV, the Soviet Navy's first nuclear-powered surface combatant, entered the fleet with the antisurface ASUW oriented SOVREMENNYY-Class guided-missile destroyer (DDG) and the ASW-oriented UDALOY-Class DDG. Among them, these three classes introduced six new weapon systems: the KIROV's SS-N-19 antiship cruise missile (ASCM) and its SA-N-6 surface-to-air missile (SAM); the SOVREMENNYY's medium-range SS-N-22 ASCM, SA-N-7 SAM, and a new 130-mm dual-purpose, twin-gun mount; and the UDALOY's SA-NX-9 SAM. The Ka-27/HELIX A ASW helicopter, which entered service with Soviet Naval Aviation the same year, can operate from the helicopter decks of these three combatants as well as from the KIEV-Class carrier, the MOSKVA-Class aviation cruiser, and other surface combatants and auxiliaries.

Entering the Soviet fleet during 1980 were two general purpose submarine classes, the OSCAR I and the KILO. The OSCAR I-Class nuclear-powered cruise missile attack submarine (SSGN) has slightly over three times the displacement of its functional predecessor, the CHARLIE II-Class SSGN, and can carry 24 ASCMs. In wartime, its 24 submerged-launch SS-N-19 ASCMs will be targeted primarily against NATO carrier battle groups. In contrast, the KILO-Class diesel-electric attack submarine (SS) is relatively small (about 3,000 metric tons), relies on antisurface or ASW torpedoes, and was designed for operations primarily in sea areas

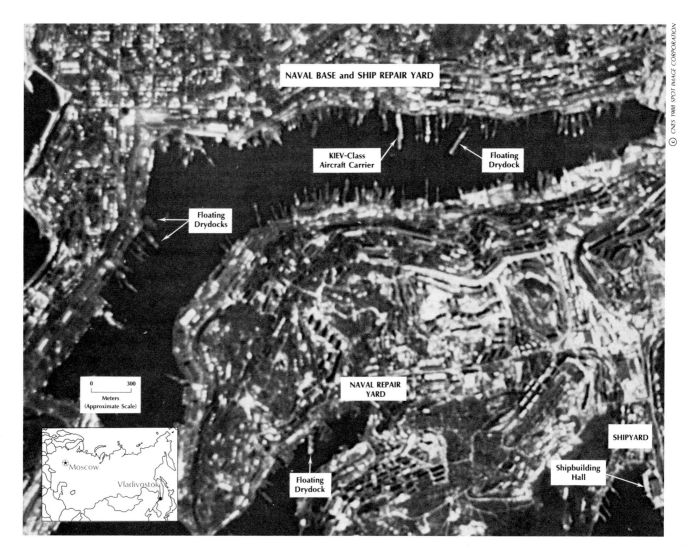

NAVAL BASE and SHIP REPAIR YARD

KIEV-Class
Aircraft Carrier

Floating
Drydock

Floating
Drydocks

0   300
Meters
(Approximate Scale)

Moscow

Vladivostok

NAVAL REPAIR
YARD

SHIPYARD

Shipbuilding
Hall

Floating
Drydock

Vladivostok, headquarters of the Pacific Ocean Fleet, is the Soviet Union's largest naval complex. Located on the Sea of Japan, it is home port to more than 80 principal surface combatants and 95 submarines.

peripheral to the Soviet Union. These two classes of attack submarines are noteworthy in that they typify recent Soviet naval construction trends. Specifically, the Soviets have continued building platforms capable of operating in the open ocean without sacrificing those platforms designed to perform the Soviet Navy's traditional coastal defense mission.

A new SLAVA-Class cruiser and two new aircraft types entered service with the Soviet Navy. Additionally, the Soviets have constructed three new classes of nuclear-powered attack submarines (SSNs) and three unique auxiliary submarines designed for research and development purposes. In addition to new classes of combatants and combat aircraft, the navy has continued to convert and modify platforms for new roles and capabilities. These new, evolutionary, and existing classes of ships, submarines, and aircraft complement the navy's ability to fulfill its assigned missions.

Surface Combatants

The trend in Soviet major surface warship construction has been toward larger units with more firepower and more sophisticated weapon and sensor systems. An ambitious building program has resulted in the construction of over 20 warships of destroyer size or larger since 1980. In 1982, the initial unit of the SLAVA-Class guided-missile cruiser (CG) joined the fleet. Designed for ASUW and fleet air defense, the SLAVA-Class carries 16 SS-N-12 ASCMs and 64 SA-N-6 SAMs. The second unit of this class joined the fleet in 1986, and a third is fitting out. Other surface warships which began sea trials during this period include the second unit of the KIROV-Class CGN in 1983, and the third and fourth units of the KIEV-Class VTOL aircraft carrier in 1981 and 1986, respectively. A new, larger 65,000-metric ton aircraft carrier will probably commence sea trials in 1989. This ship will improve Soviet tactical aviation capability significantly beyond the range of coastal air defenses.

By the end of 1987, eight SOVREMENNYYs and nine UDALOYs were operational or on sea trials, and additional units are under construction. The Soviets have also continued to construct or acquire smaller combatants, amphibious ships, and auxiliaries to conduct operations in sea areas contiguous to the Soviet Union and to support amphibious, logistic, and intelligence collection missions.

Submarines

A major portion of Soviet naval strength lies in its general purpose submarine force, the world's largest. Today, this force numbers some 300 active units, about one-half of which are nuclear-powered. Recent Soviet submarine designs emphasize improved quieting, speed, weapons versatility, and the incorporation of advanced technology. Since 1983, the Soviets have introduced three new classes of SSNs. These include the MIKE-Class, a sole unit which is estimated to be serving as a testbed, as well as the SIERRA-Class, which is a series production SSN and follow-on to the successful VICTOR III-Class. Both were first launched in 1983. In 1984, the lead unit of a second class of VICTOR III follow-on boats, the AKULA-Class SSN, was launched. The AKULA, with significant improvements in quieting technology, is believed to be the most capable attack submarine yet developed for the Soviet Navy. An additional submarine development of the early 1980s was the conversion of dismantled YANKEE SSBNs to other configurations. The first YANKEE conversion is the YANKEE SSGN, the probable testbed for the SS-NX-24 SLCM. In 1983, a conversion resulted in the YANKEE SSN and included the installation of updated fire control and sonar systems and other modifications that will enable the YANKEE SSN to launch a wider variety of weapons. Another conversion of the YANKEE SSBN in 1985 has resulted in a variant designated the YANKEE NOTCH SSN, probably equipped to fire the SS-N-21 SLCM. Since the early 1980s, three unique auxiliary submarines have been constructed. The nuclear-powered XRAY and UNIFORM, and the BELUGA-Class are designed for research and development purposes.

Naval Aviation

In recent years, Soviet Naval Aviation has seen a marked proliferation of operational naval air tasks and related aircraft. The year 1985 was a banner year for Soviet Naval Aviation as two new aircraft and two evolutionary variants entered service with the Soviet

SLAVA-Class guided-missile cruisers, still being produced, are outfitted with surface-to-surface, antisubmarine, and surface-to-air weapon systems.

The MIKE-Class nuclear-powered attack submarine is currently used as a testbed.

The BACKFIRE bomber of Soviet Naval Aviation poses a potent threat to Allied naval forces.

Navy. The Ka-27/HELIX B combat assault helicopter was assigned initially in the Northern and the Pacific Ocean Fleets in 1985. This helicopter enhances Soviet naval aviation airlift and attack support for amphibious assault operations. By 1986, the HELIX B had been deployed to all but the Black Sea Fleet. During the summer of 1985, the Su-24/FENCER E fighter-bomber reconnaissance aircraft arrived in the Baltic Fleet as a replacement for obsolescent BADGER reconnaissance aircraft. With its comparatively enhanced sensor package and penetration capability, FENCER E significantly upgrades the Baltic Fleet's maritime air reconnaissance capability. The BEAR F Mod 4 ASW aircraft entered service with the Northern Fleet, probably before late 1985. The BEAR F Mod 4 has been fitted with self-protection ECM that should enhance warning and survivability in a hostile air defense environment. Also in 1985, the Soviet Black Sea Fleet Air Force, which was the recipient of the first BACKFIRE Bs deployed operationally within Soviet Naval Aviation, also received the first of the BACKFIRE Cs.

Since 1981, Soviet Naval Aviation (SNA) has increased its aircraft order-of-battle by approximately 23 percent. Most of the increase is the product of continued deployments of aircraft initially introduced prior to 1981. BACKFIRE B/C antiship missile-equipped aircraft have supplanted many aging BADGERs as the first-line strike aircraft. The BEAR F Mod 3/4 long-range aircraft and Ka-27/HELIX A helicopter have assumed prominent ASW roles in the modern Soviet

Navy. More than 100 carrier-based FORGER As and land-based FITTER C fighter-bombers and FENCER E fighter-bomber reconnaissance aircraft have been added to SNA over the past seven years. Mine-countermeasures helicopters are now in all fleets, and BEAR J aircraft recently have been introduced into the Northern and Pacific Ocean Fleets.

Naval Warfare Areas

ASUW Forces

The ability to attack and sink any type of surface shipping is a critical requirement of Soviet maritime strategy. The antiship category of ships and submarines has experienced both quantitative and qualitative growth during the 1980s, particularly in antiship missile capabilities. Today, the Soviet Navy includes about 185 surface combatant ships and craft that carry surface-to-surface missiles. In addition, nearly 70 submarines carry subsurface-to-surface missiles. KIROV- and SLAVA-Class guided-missile cruisers and SOVREMENNYY-Class guided-missile destroyers have greatly increased cruise missile firepower and carry antiship missiles with performance characteristics that make them increasingly difficult to defend against. OSCAR series SSGNs carry similar submerged launch antiship missiles. In addition to missiles, today's general purpose platforms carry a vastly more sophisticated array of weapons, radar, sonar, electronic warfare systems, and communications, with further developments constantly in progress.

ASW Forces

As in other warfare areas, a progression of improved platforms with associated sensors and weapons has expanded Soviet capabilities in the area of antisubmarine warfare. Evolutionary improvements of existing ASW aircraft have produced the HELIX A ship-based helicopter and the long-range BEAR F Mod 4. Similar improvements in ships designed primarily for ASW have been observed, with the UDALOY-Class DDG designed specifically for this task. Even the largest modern Soviet combatants, including the KIEV-Class carriers and the KIROV-Class CGNs, carry sensor and weapon suites which include powerful low frequency sonars; ASW rockets, missiles, torpedoes; and ASW helicopters.

The Soviets' design and construction of late-generation attack submarines demonstrate marked improvements in submarine quieting. This feature reduces their acoustic detectability under certain operating conditions, while improving their effectiveness against opposing submarines.

Although the Soviets have expended considerable resources in recent years on developing ASW platforms and systems, particularly nuclear-powered attack submarines, they have not yet resolved the difficult problem of locating Western submarines in the open ocean. The Soviet ASW problem, like that of the West, has been exacerbated by the continued NATO deployment of longer range ballistic missiles and the advent of the submarine-launched and surface ship-launched land-attack cruise missile.

Amphibious Warfare

Although very small in comparison to the US Marine Corps, Soviet Naval Infantry (SNI) is made up of approximately 18,000 troops. Since 1981, a 40-percent increase in personnel, a 70-percent increase in vehicles and equipment, a growth in assault-lift capacity, and an organizational restructuring have combined to improve the SNI's strength, organic firepower, and mobility. Although not capable of conducting independent, large-scale assaults in countries distant from the Soviet Union, SNI can be expected to play an important role in wartime. Potential missions would include spearheading a large ground forces amphibious assault, acting as a mobile coastal defense force, conducting small-scale landings or raids in lightly defended peripheral areas, and providing security to important installations.

In peacetime, the potential power of even a few hundred Soviet marines afloat during a Third World crisis provides the Soviet Union with a valuable political-military instrument. For example, on several occasions when the Rene government of the Seychelles was threatened by internal unrest, the Soviet Union dispatched combatants, including an amphibious ship with SNI embarked, to the capital to provide visible and tangible support to the regime. Such contingency operations are facilitated by the routine deployment of Soviet amphibious ships off Angola and in the Indian Ocean. Soviet amphibious forces maintain a near-continuous presence in the South China Sea, the Indian Ocean, and off the West African coast.

Coastal Missile and Artillery Forces

The Soviet Navy also maintains a little known but significant force of coastal missile and artillery troops. With coastal defense cruise missile and numerous coastal artillery sites in all fleet areas, coastal defense remains an active part of Soviet planning for wartime operations, including those that might take place in a nuclear environment. The Soviet Union has fielded coastal missiles since the late 1950s and currently has launch sites for the 160-nautical-mile-range SEPAL coastal defense cruise missile in all four fleet areas. In 1984, the Soviets began an expansion of their coastal missile force with the initial deployment of the SSC-3/STYX antiship missile to operational sites in the Pacific Fleet area. The STYX, in its coastal defense role, is expected to supplement rather than replace the existing SEPALs.

Sealift

The USSR's military sealift capability results from its large merchant fleet of more than 1,700 ships, which has grown steadily in the past two decades to a cargo carrying capacity of nearly 22 million deadweight tons. Nearly half of Soviet cargo ships are equipped with cranes capable of lifting the heaviest armored vehicles, thereby reducing the Soviets' dependence on prepared port facilities. The inventory includes 100 modern barge carriers, roll-on/roll-off cargo ships, and roll-on/float-off ships. All these ships have direct military applications. In wartime, the merchant fleet would move troops and military equipment, and support the Soviet and Warsaw Pact navies. In peacetime, Soviet foreign policy goals are fulfilled through the use of Soviet merchant ships to deliver arms to client states, while passenger ships transport troops.

The merchant marine's capability to support the military is enhanced by its quick responsiveness to central control. Additionally, most ships are commanded by naval reserve officers. As a result, the fleet is a valuable asset in crisis situations, particularly in circumstances requiring troop movements, amphibious operations, or arms deliveries. The operational readiness of the merchant marine is enhanced through routine participation in major naval exercises.

To facilitate responsiveness to Soviet military needs, merchant ships incorporate features normally seen only on other nations' naval combatants, including increased speed and endurance capabilities; improved cargo handling capabilities; decontamination systems which would permit the ship to operate in a chemical-biological-radiological environment; and advanced communications, navigation, and electronics systems.

Naval Summary

Today's Soviet Navy is larger, better equipped, and far more balanced in structure and capabilities than ever before to meet the requirements of conventional or nuclear war at virtually any level. Future Soviet naval policy and programs will be directed toward broadening the range of military and political options available to the leadership across the entire spectrum of conflict — from peacetime competition to nuclear war. The Soviets can be expected to increase their emphasis on making general purpose naval forces more capable and to continue challenging the West's traditional dominance of the open oceans.

PROSPECTS FOR SOVIET GENERAL PURPOSE FORCES

Soviet conventional forces will continue to grow in size, capability, and mobility. Despite a declared policy of "reasonable sufficiency," the Soviets will develop their conventional and tactical nuclear forces to maintain a rigorous capability to execute Soviet offensive strategies in a global conflict. They perceive that ongoing developments in NATO forces may challenge their ability to conduct an offensive operation. The prolonged, complex, and highly lethal operations of theater warfare, in their eyes, require increased sustainability, large numbers of forces, and a redundant, survivable command-and-control system. The Soviets will make the force structure developments and tactical and operational innovations required to ensure that they can achieve their strategic objectives.

FORCE-WIDE TRENDS

Radioelectronic Combat

The Soviets recognize clearly the systemic dependencies of modern military forces on command, control,

and communications (C^3). As a result, they have developed a formidable capability to degrade the C^3 assets of enemy forces. The Soviet doctrine of radioelectronic combat (REC) includes an integrated program of C^3 countermeasures using a combination of reconnaissance, jamming, firepower, and deception to disrupt effective command and control. REC is integrated into all aspects of the Soviets' combat operations, displaying their intention to control the electromagnetic spectrum and deny it to their enemy.

Deception in REC is part of an overall program called "maskirovka." In the realm of REC, "maskirovka" tactics in the form of deception are used to cause delays and can be divided into disinformation practices and counter-reconnaissance techniques. Disinformation includes the transmission of false information to confuse the enemy. Counter-reconnaissance techniques are used to mask troop movements and deployments. The Soviets use a variety of means for this purpose. Because the enemy is unable to distinguish between real and decoy targets, the resulting confusion leads to uncertainties about enemy intent, deployments, and troop movements. Thus, REC, the electronic portion of "maskirovka," when used with other denial and deception measures, ensures that, at the very least, the Soviets can deny the enemy the use of the electromagnetic spectrum and could exploit or manipulate those emissions that are not jammed or destroyed.

The Soviets are continuing to modernize the equipment needed to support radioelectronic combat at all echelons of their military services. When the Soviets' impressive electronic warfare resources are combined with the use of combat forces, they achieve an unmatched capability to disrupt effectively the command and control of enemy forces.

The Soviets have deployed increasingly modern electronic collection systems. New-generation signal-intercept and direction-finding systems, in variations designed to cover high frequency (HF), very high frequency (VHF), and ultra high frequency (UHF) communications bands, complement the Soviets' fielding of new noncommunications (radar) intercept systems. There is mounting evidence that the Soviets have benefited from Western technology-transfer in modernizing these signals collection systems.

To degrade an opponent's organization, the Soviets have begun deploying a communications jamming variant of their armored personnel carrier, the MTLB. This system is believed to be replacing older truck-mounted jamming systems. It improves operator and system survivability and better supports fast-moving Soviet armored formations. Advances in Soviet ground-based communications jamming systems have been reinforced by the deployment of ECM-modified helicopters. These heliborne systems offer the distinct advantages of greater mission flexibility, mobility, and brute jamming power, factors that hinder the effectiveness of an opponent's conventional forces.

Soviet communications-jamming capability is supplemented by a considerable number of ground-based radar-jamming sets. The Soviets continue to modernize their radar-jamming assets in response to Western advances in radar technology. This effort emphasizes the Soviets' intention to disrupt enemy airborne radars, thereby supporting both their air operations and their air defense of high-value rear area targets. Soviet advances in this area provide them with an ever-increasing advantage over similar Western capabilities.

The Soviet Air Forces have continued to upgrade REC assets. Modern fighter aircraft are equipped with internally mounted self-protection ECM systems that reduce aerodynamic drag over externally mounted systems and provide increased free space on the wings and body to carry additional ordnance. An ECM variant of the Su-24/FENCER is currently undergoing system development that will enable it to assist penetrating ground-attack aircraft by electronically suppressing SAM and early warning/ground-controlled intercept radars. Even Soviet cargo aircraft have been equipped with infrared countermeasure flares for self-protection and could, undoubtedly, be equipped with jamming equipment if the mission dictated.

The Soviet Navy has dedicated substantial resources to conducting electronic reconnaissance and countermeasures with its major combatants. The Soviet auxiliary intelligence collection ship classes BALZAM, PRIMORYE, and VISHNYA are dedicated reconnaissance platforms capable of conducting intelligence operations throughout the world, and they are frequently seen off major military installations and near fleet exercises. Both the BALZAM- and VISHNYA-Classes are equipped with self-defense weapon systems, indicating they are prepared to operate in a hostile environment. Virtually all major combatants possess signals intercept and jamming systems to assist in defense against attacks by aircraft, guided missiles, and submarines.

Readiness

Soviet military doctrine holds that the initial period of war is critical to determining the overall course of a conflict. Thus, the Soviets are continually enhancing the combat readiness of their armed forces to ensure that large, well-equipped forces can be committed rapidly. In support of this doctrine, Soviet Air and Air Defense Forces are at high readiness. The Soviet Navy routinely has less than 10 percent of its major combatants deployed out of area but has the readiness capability to deploy up to 50 percent on short notice. The ground forces have the lowest peacetime manning levels of the major force components. They are dependent to varying degrees on mobilizing manpower and equipment from the civilian economy to reach wartime status. Overall, the Soviets have developed a posture in which the most ready forces are deployed in the area of the greatest perceived threat, backed up by the capability to mobilize and move their entire force structure as required.

The Soviets maintain their ground forces at so-called ready and not-ready levels. Ready divisions are manned with a high percentage of their planned wartime personnel and equipment requirements. These forces are trained extensively during peacetime. Not-ready units are divided into active cadre divisions, with less than 50 percent of required manpower, and inactive mobilization divisions, which are unmanned equipment sets. The ready divisions constitute about 40 percent of Soviet forces, including all the forces stationed in Eastern Europe, and can begin combat operations after a brief period of mobilization and preparation. The not-ready cadre divisions can be assembled in about a week, and the mobilization divisions require even more time. An extensive period of training may be conducted before these units are committed to offensive combat, although Soviet doctrine allows for their commitment to combat almost immediately after mobilization. Although the Soviets emphasize the rapid mobilization of their entire force structure, recent enhancements have stressed the mobilization responsiveness of the not-ready forces.

Since the late 1970s, the Soviets have converted over 30 unmanned mobilization divisions into low-strength cadre-level units with a personnel complement of 10-20 percent of wartime levels. This process has involved the assignment of experienced personnel, some expansion and modernization of equipment holdings, and the construction or expansion of garrison facilities. These enhancements improve the mobilization capability of these divisions and make them available for earlier commitment as more effective formations. As noted above, only five unmanned, inactive, mobilization-base divisions remain in Soviet forces.

Mobilization System

The USSR has developed a comprehensive mobilization support system. Soviet doctrine calls for two

The large 280-mm multiple rocket launcher under development by the Soviets is capable of laying down a broad field of fire, threatening armored vehicles, infantry, airfields, and rear service areas.

levels of mobilization — general and partial. General mobilization involves all the armed forces and pursues a full, rapid transition of political, economic, and manpower resources to a wartime posture. Partial mobilization involves selected military districts using limited numbers of military units and installations.

At the heart of the system is a network of about 4,200 military commissariats ("voyenkomaty") located throughout the USSR. They are subordinate ultimately to the General Staff and are found at local and regional administrative levels. They serve as draft boards, armed forces reserve centers, and the veterans administration.

Currently, the Soviets are emphasizing both speed and flexibility in their mobilization system. A rapid mobilization system allows the Soviets to prepare their forces quickly to take advantage of surprise by initiating combat before the enemy is fully deployed. The regimented nature of Soviet society facilitates rapid mobilization. The Soviet system is also flexible. In addition to its ability to achieve rapid, comprehensive, and relatively hard-to-conceal national mobilization for global war, it can gradually, sequentially, and covertly

raise the readiness of selected elements of the armed forces. The Soviets thus can maintain a large degree of secrecy while preparing their forces for war.

Logistics and Sustainability

Over the past decade, Soviet logisticians have developed a logistics support structure and management system that can effectively support simultaneous strategic offensives by the Warsaw Pact in multiple TVDs. Significant logistics support improvements have been achieved in sustainability, survivability, mobility, efficiency, and standardization. Extensive and ongoing efforts to ensure adequate logistics support have focused on the restructuring of rear service support units, creating a theater-level rear service management agency, and vastly increasing stockpiles of materiel, particularly ammunition.

To improve their logistics support capability of theater strategic operations, the Soviets have activated theater-level rear service control and planning headquarters. In the past, there was no intermediate control structure between Soviet central rear services and individual fronts. The Soviets have realized that a broader, more strategic viewpoint is required in order to coordinate the logistics support of the fronts, fleets, air armies, and other elements assigned to a TVD. Consequently, theater-level logistics chiefs within the High Command of Forces in the various TVDs have been appointed to centralize and implement theater-wide rear service plans.

Connected with the concept of theater-level rear service command and control there is the increased Soviet emphasis on the integration and standardization of Warsaw Pact (NSWP) rear service organizations.

Ground Force Logistics

Since 1980, Soviet Ground Forces' ammunition stocks have increased markedly in all theaters of military operations. Stock increases reflect Soviet military doctrine which stipulates the logistics requirement to pre-stock 60 to 90 days of conventional ammunition for wartime use. These ammunition stock increases also reflect Soviet expectations that theater war will be of a more costly and prolonged character, thereby requiring a more efficient and survivable logistics support structure and greater quantities of supplies.

For example, storage facilities in the Western TVD opposite NATO have undergone some of the most extensive enhancements. Several new depots were built and many of the existing depots were expanded. Since 1977, the ammunition storage capacity there has almost doubled and construction continues. The current total for ammunition stocks in the Western TVD is over three million metric tons, which could support combat operations for some 60 to 90 days.

Traditionally, the Far East TVD (the region opposite China and Japan) has maintained large quantities of supplies because of the long lines of communications to the production facilities in the European Soviet Union. The expansion in ammunition stocks has been extensive. The current ammunition stocks there are estimated at over three million metric tons, which would support combat operations for more than 100 days. To enhance the mobility and flexibility of their logistics formations, the Soviets are making changes in their logistics organizations from front to regiment level. In the past, transport, supply, and service operations were under the control of different commanders. This fragmented organization lacked the responsiveness to provide a timely reaction in unexpected situations. The Soviets have now consolidated these different support functions within materiel support units under a single commander. These new units are being formed at all echelons, from front down to regiment. Motor transport

holdings within the materiel support units have been significantly increased (30 percent at the divisional level since the late 1970s). These changes have not only streamlined logistics support but also greatly increased mobility and survivability.

The Soviets have also undertaken efforts to improve and refine ancillary support measures such as computer management, prepackaging and containerization, mobile repair shops, pipeline-laying vehicles, and materiel handling equipment.

Coupled with these improvements is the continuing upgrading of Warsaw Pact transportation routes and infrastructure to support the movement and supply of theater forces. For example, large increases have occurred in the amounts of pre-positioned bridging, rail, road, and airfield repair construction materiel and equipment.

The transport vehicle inventory within Soviet rear services organizations has been modernized. New, heavier load-carrying trucks such as the KaMAZ series (produced with the help of Western technology) have been introduced at all levels, resulting in an increase in tonnage capacity and the ability to support operations with less augmentation from mobilized civilian vehicles.

Air Force Logistics

Over the last decade there has been a significant increase in stock levels used by Soviet aviation units. The Soviets have established a depot system capable of providing air units with sufficient stocks to commence wartime operations effectively. The Soviets have developed plans for dispersing depot materiel to mobile supply bases and have modernized their supply management concepts to ensure timely resupply. Additionally, they have stockpiled large quantities of fuel, air weapons, and spare parts at main operating bases to facilitate the logistics independence of Soviet combat aviation during the initial period of a conflict. Aircraft shelters, support equipment, storage areas, and fuel and air weapons storage facilities at most operational airfields in Eastern Europe have been hardened, concealed, or dispersed to protect against enemy attack.

Most operational airfields have the trucks and equipment necessary to support and resupply the tenant unit when they deploy from that base. Also, large quantities of tactical pipeline have been stockpiled in many fuel depots and other areas for use in transporting fuel to airfields.

The Soviet aircraft maintenance and repair system

provides effective support for peacetime operations. Soviet fighter/fighter-bomber units generally maintain a readiness standard of 90 to 95 percent of assigned aircraft operationally available at all times. Soviet bomber units usually maintain 75 to 80 percent of their aircraft in an operationally ready state.

The aircraft maintenance system appears to operate well enough to guarantee commanders the level of readiness they desire. Low yearly operating rates for most aircraft (approximately 100 to 150 hours for fighters and 100 to 200 hours for bombers) ensure that a combat-ready fleet of relatively new or recently overhauled aircraft is available.

The current level of combat-ready aircraft and spare parts availability appears adequate for the Soviet aircraft maintenance system to support the initial stages of combat operations. The Soviets have centralized their best maintenance personnel and equipment in regimental-level maintenance units for complicated and time-consuming inspections and repairs. Consequently, squadron and flightline maintenance personnel do not ordinarily participate in complex maintenance tasks. Thus, their ability to do so in wartime is suspect.

Naval Logistics

Sustainability is a weak point of the Soviet Navy. Historic Soviet doctrinal emphasis on a short war has led to a navy ill-suited for a long conflict. Although the Soviets now consider the possibility of a more protracted conventional war, this factor is not evident in the overall design of their fleet. Certain newer units are, however, more capable of sustained engagements, as evidenced by increasing use of nuclear power for propulsion and the incorporation of greater weapon loads on new ships and submarines. Nevertheless, the Soviets have little logistics support afloat. These problems are exacerbated by the limited endurance of most naval forces and by onboard munitions which are generally sufficient for only one intense engagement. These shortfalls are minimized in peacetime by relying on the merchant fleet for a large measure of logistics support.

For a variety of reasons, including the improvement of combatant readiness, Soviet naval out-of-area operations have decreased within recent years. Their concept of combat readiness focuses on the ability to generate forces rapidly for short-notice deployment for combat operations. They are less concerned with maintaining large forces deployed in areas distant from the USSR. The Soviets prefer to keep their ships in anchorages or in port much of the time with brief periods of underway tactical training.

While the Soviet naval operating tempo has decreased, their use of foreign ship repair facilities by auxiliaries over the same time period has increased. This increase is due in part to foreign interest in obtaining repair contracts as well as Soviet interest in gaining access to additional repair facilities. Consequently, the Soviets have been able to enhance their influence in certain countries that depend on ship repair work.

To supplement their limited naval auxiliary underway replenishment force, the Soviets continue relying on merchant replenishment ships to support their naval operations. These merchant vessels make port calls in Mediterranean and other Western countries to obtain supplies for naval combatants. By providing logistics support to the navy with their merchant fleet, the Soviets have maintained their capability to support and sustain out-of-area naval operations.

The capability to conduct underway at-sea replenishment remains a low priority in the Soviet Navy. The Navy has not built any new naval oilers or replenishment ships since 1978, partially due to the support provided by the merchant fleet. These merchant tankers, however, cannot provide high-speed underway replenishment. In contrast to some Western navies, alongside underway replenishment is practiced infrequently by Soviet naval oilers. Instead, they prefer to refuel using slower methods like towing bow-to-stern or tying alongside dead in the water.

It is believed that the Soviets have stockpiled in the USSR ammunition, petroleum, oil, lubricants, and other stores in quantities sufficient to conduct naval operations during a war lasting 60 to 90 days. Within the Northern and Pacific Ocean Fleets, the number of ordnance facilities is increasing. This rise probably is the result of a program to construct safer, more survivable, and more dispersed storage facilities developed in response to the disastrous 1984 explosion in a missile storage depot at Severomorsk.

Mobility

During the past two decades, the Soviets have bolstered their overall military force posture by steadily increasing the projection capabilities of their forces through advancements in airlift, sealift, and command-and-control structures. Today, the Soviets can project powerful armed forces into areas contiguous to the USSR and sustain them. With the enhanced capability to deploy light, well-armed, mobile forces in support of political goals and foreign policy objectives, the Soviets are also expanding their ability to exert influence in the Third World.

Soviet Airlift

During this decade, Soviet Military Transport Aviation ("Voyenno-Transportnaya Aviatsiya," VTA) capabilities have increased to match the gains in other components of the Soviet Air Forces and the combat equipment of the ground forces. In 1980, about 25 percent of VTA's assets consisted of long-range transports such as the Il-76/CANDID and An-22/COCK. Today, about 75 percent of VTA's assets are long-range transports, including the recently introduced An-124/CONDOR.

The An-124/CONDOR, the world's largest military transport aircraft, can carry outsized cargo such as tanks and mobile missiles.

Replacement of the medium-range, four-engine turboprop An-12/CUB by the newer and more capable long-range CANDID jet transport is nearing completion. Only about 150 CUBs remain with VTA forces. Although the number of transports assigned to VTA has stayed about the same (some 600), the cargo and range capabilities of newer airframes now entering Soviet military service have greatly improved VTA's support capacity. A clear example of this advantage is seen in the CANDID, which can carry twice the CUB's maximum payload over roughly three-and-a-half times the CUB's range.

The CONDOR, first exhibited at the 1985 Paris Air Show, became operational in 1987 and small numbers are now deployed with VTA. The CONDOR is the USSR's new long-range, wide-bodied jet transport with almost twice the maximum cargo lift capacity of the COCK heavy-lift turboprop transport now in service. The CONDOR can lift 150 metric tons while the An-22 can lift only 80 metric tons. VTA's heavy-lift capability for wide and bulky, or outsized cargo, will increase substantially as CONDOR joins COCK in the VTA inventory.

Additionally, the Soviets continue publicizing CONDOR's significant achievements. In May 1987, a CONDOR carried out a record-breaking unrefueled flight of 20,150 kilometers 25.5 hours around the periphery of the USSR. The Soviets also claim CONDOR has lifted cargos in excess of 170 metric tons. While these record flights are indicative of maximum performance under special conditions, CONDOR's capabilities are still impressive by any standard of measurement. Although the CONDOR is not capable of aerial refueling, its demonstrated range enables the CONDOR to use alternate flight routes to almost anywhere in the world, avoiding overflight/landing problems with politically sensitive nations.

Clearly, the increased payload and range of VTA's modern transport aircraft significantly improve the USSR's ability to move airborne forces and provide logistics support to all Soviet military forces. The CONDOR can lift virtually all vehicles currently assigned to the ground forces. The new transport's range will enable the Soviets to respond rapidly to any wartime military transport requirements on the Eurasian landmass. Additionally, the USSR can now respond more rapidly to the economic or military needs of its client states in distant regions.

The USSR's civil aviation organization, Aeroflot, is the world's largest airline. On wartime mobilization, Aeroflot would increase the military passenger transport capacity significantly. Aeroflot's organizational structure lends itself to a rapid transition to a wartime mobilization role, and its aircraft could be deployed almost immediately to meet urgent requirements. Its greatest military utility is that it serves as a primary source for troop transport, while the military aircraft provide the bulk of equipment and cargo transport capacity.

Since the beginning of this decade, the number of long- and medium-range aircraft available to Aeroflot has increased from about 1,400 to about 1,600. As with the military airlift forces, the Soviets are developing a new generation of civil airliners for the 1990s which will provide capabilities similar to those of present civil airliners in the West.

PROSPECTS

The across-the-board modernization of Soviet conventional forces in the 1980s, including tanks, artillery, fighter aircraft, and surface and submarine combatants, represents a true revolution in Soviet military capabilities. The scale and momentum of these programs will carry them forward well into the next decade. As the accuracies of delivery means increase, and the explosive power of improved conventional munitions grows, the tactical and strategic missions of conventional assets will grow in importance as well.

2

An Assessment of the Threat

- The Strategic Balance

- Regional and Functional Balances

- Research and Development: The Technological Competition

- Collective Security: Our Risks and Responsibilities

The many dimensions of Soviet military power described in Part I do not exist in isolation. Soviet military capabilities are a threat insofar as they afford the USSR the ability to support its overall policy goals, its military strategy and its ability to achieve peacetime and wartime objectives. Recognizing that many elements of Soviet policies conflict with those of the United States, our allies and friends, we have constructed a system of collective security to counter the most ominous and threatening Soviet aims. Together we and our allies and friends have acquired the military capabilities we believe to be minimally necessary to deter the Soviets from military action or, should deterrence fail, to prevent the Soviets from using military power to achieve political and military objectives. Yet the question persists: How well can we achieve national security goals given the nature of the threat?

In an effort to address this question, the Soviet threat is examined, US capabilities to counter the threat — together with those of our friends and allies — are assessed, and then an evaluation is made of how well US military forces help meet US objectives. A particular military balance can then be judged as favorable or unfavorable in terms of how well US national security objectives can be met in a given area. An especially useful aspect of this process is its focus on identifying long-range trends as they relate to the military balance, as opposed to merely examining the current status. Thus, by assessing the military balance as it has developed over time, the assessment can assist in outlining relevant actions and policies, which would further a positive trend or redress a negative trend.

There has yet to be devised a single measure of merit that would allow an assessment of the global military balance. National security objectives can and do vary from region to region, and the number of other variables, contingencies, and inherent uncertainties increases exponentially as the focus of the assessment is widened. As a result, an effort has been made here to evaluate the overall military balance by assessing the balances in a number of significant regional and functional areas, while keeping in mind the relationships that exist among various balances.

Although disaggregating the overall military balance into discrete area balances simplifies the analytic process somewhat, the assessment of those individual balances is by no means easy. Constructing an appropriate analytic framework, identifying the key factors affecting each balance, and developing rigorous, comprehensive, and accurate ways of measuring those factors all pose difficult problems. Even then, a host of less tangible factors — like the military effects of weather or surprise — may be crucial; these, by and large, are not subject to quantification, but nonetheless may prove to be critical in any military contingency.

Thus, we have not attempted to lay out these assessments in a consistent format. Rather, having compared and contrasted military goals and objectives and then presented the trends in the relevant military forces, we provide the reader an assessment of the key trends and issues in a particular area.

These assessments are by no means comprehensive. Rather, they are intended to serve as a point of departure for more informed debate and decisions regarding the nature of the Soviet threat and what we collectively should do about it.

CHAPTER VI

The Strategic Balance

United States strategic nuclear forces are designed to deter nuclear attack and to help deter conventional attack on the United States and its allies. To execute this policy of deterrence credibly and effectively, US strategic nuclear forces and support elements must generally balance corresponding Soviet forces and be able to inflict unacceptable damage to the USSR under all conditions of retaliation. Force structure alone, however, will not guarantee deterrence. It is also important that the Soviet leadership be convinced of the US willingness to use such forces in response to sufficient provocation, while simultaneously being uncertain as to the exact circumstances, conditions, and targets of the retaliatory response.

A balance of forces, and Soviet perceptions of US capability and resolve, are particularly important in view of the opposing US and Soviet attitudes toward nuclear war. While US leaders have consistently maintained that a nuclear war cannot be won and should never be fought, Soviet civilian and military leaders have historically indicated their belief that such a war may well be fought, and won, under certain circumstances. Although recent Soviet statements appear to reject their previously held positions, these cannot be accepted solely at face value, particularly in light of unabated Soviet efforts to develop and deploy the forces necessary to support a nuclear-war-winning strategy.

There is a tendency among some observers to evaluate the strategic balance only in terms of quantitative measures such as the number, yields, and types of offensive weapons. These static measures certainly have validity and, in fact, often figure prominently in arms control negotiations. They are at best, however, only one factor in a complex strategic balance equation in which qualitative differences in the forces themselves, as well as in supporting elements, operational planning, leadership, training, and morale, factor into the analysis.

A strategic balance acceptable to the United States must be consistent with our national security objectives and supportive of America's basic defense strategy — deterrence of aggression. Above all, it must provide a stable deterrent by ensuring there are no circumstances under which the Soviet leadership might believe it could execute a successful first strike against the United States. Accordingly, the strategic balance should be judged in terms of the ability of each side's forces to survive a first strike and hold the vital assets of the other at risk. Deterrence can only be assured by convincing the Soviet leadership that the probable costs of their aggression will exceed any possible gains. Furthermore, we seek not only to deter actual aggression, but also to prevent coercion of the United States, its allies, and friends through the threat of aggression, since successful coercion could provide the Soviet Union with the fruits of war without actual conflict.

By 1981, the strategic position of the United States relative to that of the Soviet Union had deteriorated substantially from what it had been only a few years earlier. This prompted President Reagan to initiate his Strategic Modernization Program to redress the decline. To comprehend the extent and implications of the deteriorated US position, one must trace the historical evolution of the strategic balance and corresponding US nuclear policy. Only then can one fully appreciate the reasoning behind the President's decision and understand its impact on the strategic balance.

HISTORY

1940s through 1950s

Immediately after World War II, the US demobilized significant percentages of its conventional military power. But during the late 1940s and early 1950s, America's virtual monopoly on intercontinental nuclear systems meant that requirements for conventional forces were relatively small. Moscow understood that under the US strategy of "massive retaliation," Washington might respond to a Soviet conventional attack against the US or its allies with a nuclear attack on the Soviet Union. As the 1950s ended, however, the Soviets began fielding long-range nuclear capabilities. As Soviet nuclear and conventional capabilities grew, the US threat to respond immediately to a conventional attack, or even a limited nuclear attack, with massive nuclear retaliation became increasingly less credible. Accordingly, in the 1960s, the US and the NATO Allies adopted the strategy of "flexible response."

The deployment of the highly accurate PEACEKEEPER ICBM with 10 reentry vehicles represents a significant improvement in the hard-target-kill potential of US strategic forces.

1960s

The alliance strategy of flexible response had two major goals: first, existing US nuclear planning was modified to provide the President with the option of using nuclear forces selectively rather than massively, thereby enhancing the credibility and stability of the nuclear deterrent; and second, the United States and its allies hoped to reduce reliance on nuclear weapons to deter conflict or cope with nonnuclear attack by improving their conventional forces.

Despite increased Soviet nuclear and conventional capabilities, in the early 1960s the United States still enjoyed overwhelming superiority in numbers of strategic nuclear weapons. With over 7,000 strategic warheads, as compared to the Soviet arsenal of fewer than 500, the US nuclear posture presented the Soviet Union with a compelling deterrent. The comparatively small

numbers and ineffectiveness of Soviet nuclear weapons precluded the successful execution of a military attack against US strategic forces. Similarly, an attack against US cities would have invited a much more massive and effective retaliatory attack against Soviet cities. Hence, the Soviets were deterred. Soviet security against a US strategic attack stemmed largely from America's espoused aversion to war in general and nuclear war in particular.

1970s

The Soviets embarked on a massive buildup of their nuclear forces. Beginning in the 1960s and persisting throughout the 1970s, the Soviet arsenal grew both in quantity and in quality (although the US qualitative edge remained). The Soviets expanded their land-based missile forces and hardened their protective silos, and continued improving their defenses against air attack.

The SS-13 is a solid-propellant ICBM that was first deployed in 1969 as part of a major buildup of Soviet strategic offensive forces. While missiles of this class are not capable of destroying hardened targets, they are fully capable of destroying other military or civilian targets. In the ensuing years, the Soviets have enhanced their ICBM force capabilities with several generations of more sophisticated and threatening missile systems.

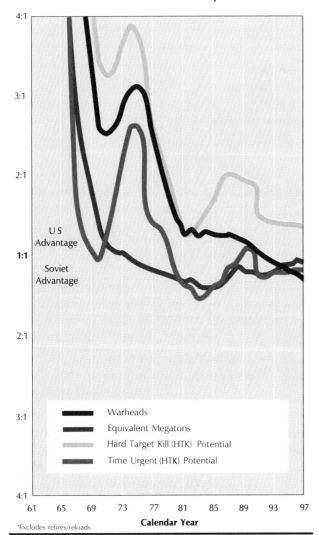

Ratios of Strategic Capabilities
Total Active Inventory*

US Advantage

1:1

Soviet Advantage

— Warheads
— Equivalent Megatons
— Hard Target Kill (HTK) Potential
— Time Urgent (HTK) Potential

4:1 3:1 2:1 1:1 2:1 3:1 4:1

61 65 69 73 77 81 85 89 93 97

Calendar Year

*Excludes refires/reloads

Furthermore, the Soviets continued a vigorous strategic defense program to protect the Soviet leadership and its key warfighting instruments from nuclear attack and enhance the credibility of their strategic offensive forces. During this same period, the United States chose not to invest in strategic defenses and also deliberately restricted yield and accuracy improvements to its own missile forces so as not to threaten the Soviet Union with a sudden, disarming first strike. The disparity between US and Soviet strategic modernization efforts during the decade of the 1970s was substantial.

By purposely restricting improvements to its own strategic ballistic missile systems, the United States acknowledged the potentially destabilizing influence of either side acquiring a credible disarming first-strike capability against the other. Unfortunately, the Soviets did not follow US self-imposed restraint. Instead, they developed a new generation of ICBMs specifically designed to destroy US missile silos — which were hardened far less than Soviet silos — and our strategic bomber bases. By the late 1970s, this combination of vulnerable US missiles and the diminished capability of US ICBMs to maintain a comparable threat against Soviet missiles had caused our deterrent's effectiveness to deteriorate, thereby easing the problems of Soviet war planners. United States defense strategists became increasingly concerned that the Soviets might envision a potential nuclear confrontation in which they could threaten to destroy much of the US deterrent force in a first strike, while retaining in their remaining nuclear arsenal an overwhelming capability to deter Washington from any retaliatory strike contemplated. This scenario raised fears that, by operating increasingly on the margins of deterrence, the United States might tempt the Soviets to use their nuclear forces in a first strike during a crisis.

98

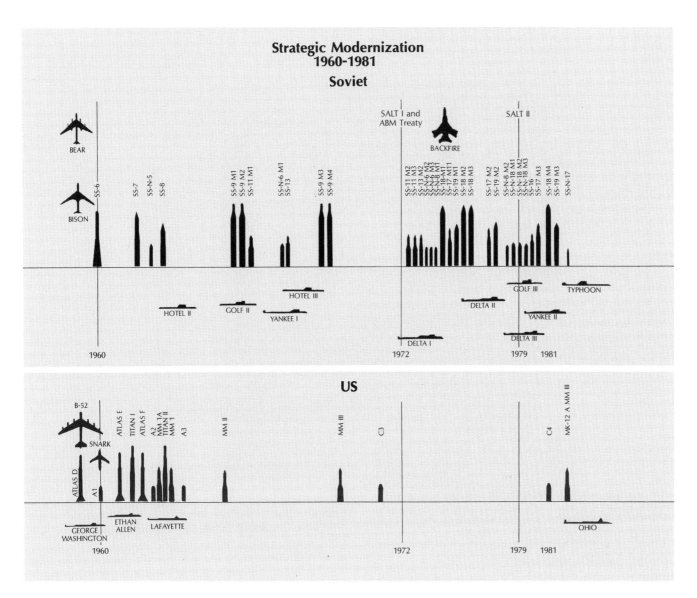

Strategic Modernization 1960-1981

Soviet

US

The asymmetry between the capabilities of US and Soviet forces to hold the other's land-based missiles at risk led to perceptions at home and abroad of US strategic vulnerability. While the effectiveness of its nuclear deterrent (as measured by the balance of strategic forces and capabilities) had eroded to its lowest level ever, the United States was never truly without a credible deterrent to a disabling Soviet first strike, owing to the US reliance on a triad of strategic nuclear weapon systems. In truth, the vulnerability of US silos and the reduced capability of its most accurate ICBMs to hold Soviet silos at risk with confidence may have degraded US flexibility in responding to an attack (particularly by making the timing of certain retaliatory options much more critical). But the hedge provided by US submarine-launched ballistic missiles (SLBM) and strategic bombers ensured that the United States could launch an effective retaliatory response under any conditions of war initiated by the Soviets.

The end of the 1970s left the United States with significant military weaknesses, both actual and perceived, relative to the Soviet Union. The relentless, long-term Soviet arms buildup, which was accompanied in the decade of the 1970s by a 20 percent real reduction in the US defense effort, had taken its toll. By most measures, the strategic balance had clearly shifted in the Soviets' favor. A comparison of selected static capabilities of US and Soviet forces demonstrates just how seriously the US position had deteriorated.

That the US target base (the object of a potential Soviet attack) was considerably smaller and less hardened than the corresponding Soviet target base only exacerbated the problem, especially when the substantial differential between US and Soviet investments in strategic defenses is considered. It was clear that the Soviet strategic nuclear weapons buildup was far more ambitious than was needed simply to deter an attack.

As mentioned previously, these static measures provide only first-order comparisons of strategic capabilities. They do not, in and of themselves, constitute the essence of deterrence. The Soviet Union's modernization of its strategic forces included substantial qualitative improvements in addition to the quantitative increases indicated. Knowing that deterrence depends on the perceptions of Soviet leaders, and given their own values and attitudes regarding US capabilities and will, US leaders were concerned that America's deteriorating position might lead the Soviets to conclude that they had achieved a position of nuclear superiority owing to their massive buildup and the US unwillingness to compete. Furthermore, Soviet intentions to continue the quantitative and qualitative expansion of their strategic arsenal were abundantly clear. Through improved quality and greater numbers, they were threatening US forces directly. As a result of their aggressive program to enhance their offensive forces and their simultaneous pursuit of every avenue to defend themselves from US retaliation, they were attempting to deny the United States the ability to retaliate effectively. In short, Soviet actions threatened the very foundations of US deterrent policy.

US STRATEGIC MODERNIZATION: RESTORING THE BALANCE IN THE 1980s

In response to this significant deterioration of the US strategic position relative to that of the Soviets, President Reagan ordered a thorough review of the status of US strategic forces. The review concluded that each leg of the Triad had deficiencies and was becoming obsolete, and that supporting command, control, and communications systems lacked the survivability and endurance to support fully US deterrent policy and forces. The President responded to the Soviet challenge by initiating the Strategic Modernization Program in October 1981. The program reaffirmed America's reliance on the strategic Triad as an indispensable element of deterrence. Accordingly, it directed the modernization of all three legs along with their associated support systems.

The Strategic Modernization Program recognized that the effectiveness of US forces depended on: (1) the ability to detect an attack confidently and in a timely manner; (2) the ability to communicate with US forces before, during, and after an attack; (3) the survivability of US forces under attack; (4) the ability to locate targets and penetrate defenses; and (5) the accuracy, reliability, and yield of US delivered weapons. It was also recognized from the outset that the program would not be static; rather, it would be responsive to the dynamic nature of the evolving Soviet

The B-1B bomber ensures the US capability to penetrate current and projected enemy air defenses into the next century.

threat. Subsequent directives have kept the program in line with estimates of that threat. Specific provisions of the program have generated a number of near- and long-term modifications to our strategic forces. For example:

- The B-1B bomber is now operational, providing an enhanced capability to penetrate steadily improving Soviet air defenses. Together with air-launched cruise missiles (ALCMs) deployed on selected B-52 bombers, the B-1 provides the United States with an effective and flexible deterrent capability in the air-breathing leg of the Triad. This capability will be further augmented with the introduction of the advanced cruise missile (ACM) and the B-2 advanced technology bomber (ATB).
- The United States continues to build one TRIDENT nuclear-powered ballistic missile submarine (SSBN) each year. Development of the improved TRIDENT II SLBM, the D-5, remains on schedule. The quietness and other advanced features of the TRIDENT subma-

Strategic Modernization
1982-1997
Soviet

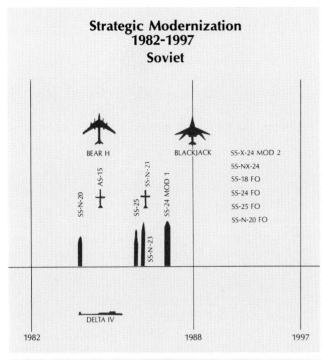

BEAR H   BLACKJACK   SS-X-24 MOD 2

SS-NX-24

SS-18 FO

SS-24 FO

SS-25 FO

SS-N-20 FO

AS-15   SS-N-21   SS-N-20   SS-25   SS-N-23   SS-24 MOD 1

DELTA IV

1982   1988   1997

US

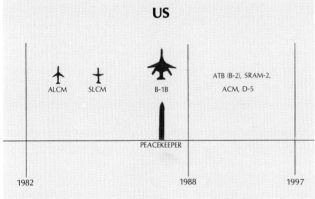

ALCM   SLCM   B-1B   ATB (B-2), SRAM-2, ACM, D-5

PEACEKEEPER

1982   1988   1997

rine increase the very high survivability potential of US SSBN forces. Deployment of the more accurate D-5 will, for the first time, provide US SSBN forces with the capability to hold hardened Soviet installations at risk. This missile will enhance deterrence by denying the Soviet Union the capability to prevent prompt, effective US retaliation, even in the event of a disabling first strike against our land-based strategic forces. The continuing deployment of sea-launched cruise missiles aboard selected surface ships and submarines will make it even more difficult, perhaps impossible, for the Soviets to design an attack that effectively compromises the US retaliatory capability.

- The initial deployment in Minuteman silos, of 50 PEACEKEEPER ICBMs, each with 10 very accurate warheads, will reduce the current disturbing asymmetry in US-Soviet prompt, hard-target-kill capability. The long-term US plan is to deploy 100 PEACE-KEEPERs in the rail-garrison mode, including the

50 missiles initially deployed in silos. These 100 PEACEKEEPERs are not sufficient to threaten the entire Soviet ICBM force but will strengthen the US deterrent capability.

- A less publicized but equally important part of the Strategic Modernization Program concerns improving the survivability of US command, control, communications, and intelligence systems. This improvement helps deter a nuclear attack designed to incapacitate the US National Command Authority (NCA) and its control over US nuclear forces.

A comparison of actual and projected deployments since 1981 indicates a better balance between US and Soviet strategic force modernization programs than had occurred during the 1970s.

The impact of the US modernization effort on the strategic balance, as reflected in static measures of force capability, has been positive. In all cases, the precipitous deterioration of the US position through 1981 will have been arrested, and in some cases, reversed. Recall that the US does not seek superiority in these measures for itself, but rather to avoid perceptions of Soviet superiority and the potential erosion of America's deterrent posture likely to accompany significant Soviet advantages in these measures.

Of the qualitative enhancements to US offensive weapon systems, improvements in accuracy are particularly important. An increased hard-target-kill potential, to be attained primarily through accuracy improvements, is necessary to counter Soviet efforts to undercut the US deterrent by hardening key Soviet military installations, particularly ICBM silos and leadership facilities. Accuracy improvements also contribute to the operational flexibility of strategic weapons systems by increasing their effectiveness against a broader spectrum of targets. Similarly, increased accuracies can limit unwanted collateral damage, helping to convey US intentions more clearly and aiding the US objective to limit escalation should deterrence fail. Given the reliance on the strategic Triad, it is particularly noteworthy that accuracies have improved for all legs, thereby ensuring that the Soviets could never believe that by destroying one leg they would destroy the ability to retaliate effectively. It is also encouraging to note that continued deployment of the highly accurate PEACEKEEPER and D-5 missiles will redress most of the asymmetries in US and Soviet capabilities to hold each other's silo-based nuclear missiles at risk. These asymmetries resulted from Soviet silo hardening and deployments of accurate ICBMs in quantities more than sufficient to threaten the survivability of the US ICBM force.

A clear picture of the strategic balance does not rest on merely counting the number of systems each side has. As the foregoing discussions have shown, a more appropriate way of assessing the strategic balance may be through evaluating compensating responses. Depending on specific circumstances, one side can compensate for an opponent's destabilizing offensive deployments with deployments of its own — offensive, defensive, or some combination of the two. For example, the Soviets gained the initiative in the 1970s with their massive and continuing buildup of nuclear forces, and the US Strategic Modernization Program and Strategic Defense Initiative (SDI) are responses to that challenge. Accordingly, it is most appropriate to address the program's responses to Soviet initiatives designed to erode the US nuclear deterrent. This approach provides a more realistic assessment of the contributions of strategic modernization toward restoring and maintaining a strategic balance. Examples of current and projected US responses include the following:

- The improved time-urgent, hard-target-kill potential of US missile forces in response to Soviet advantages discussed earlier is being complemented by the increased accuracy and penetrating ability of US air-breathing systems, specifically the B-1B, ALCMs, and ACMs. These improvements provide redundant backup capabilities that will ensure an effective retaliation against Soviet silos under any conditions of war initiation or technological breakthrough. The Soviet leadership places significant emphasis on ICBMs for achieving their strategic nuclear objectives. Failure to maintain a credible retaliatory threat against those systems could undermine the US deterrent and increase the Soviet leadership's confidence in being able to achieve its objectives.
- The Soviets are attempting to assure an ICBM survivability by deploying the road-mobile SS-25 and the rail-based, multiple-warhead SS-24. US plans for compensating responses include improved sensors and retargeting capabilities to locate and attack mobile Soviet targets. The B-2 ATB and other systems under development are expected to play a prominent role in this mission.
- The Soviet SSBN fleet is being enhanced by deployment of the long-range, more accurate SS-N-20 and SS-N-23 SLBMs, as well as the more advanced, quieter DELTA IV- and TYPHOON-Class submarines. An improved version of the SS-N-20 is estimated to be under development. The long-range SS-N-21 SLCM has also become operational and the Soviets are testing another new long-range cruise missile, the SS-NX-24. Compensating US responses include not only a vigorous antisubmarine warfare program designed to improve detection and neutralization of Soviet submarines, as well as improved sensors to detect SLBM launches, but also planned enhancements to US air defenses.

- The Soviets continue deploying the new BEAR H bomber, armed with modern ALCMs, and are developing another intercontinental bomber, the BLACK-JACK. The US is responding by upgrading its air defenses through deployment of over-the-horizon backscatter (OTH-B) radars and upgrades to the Distant Early Warning Line radars through the North Warning System (NWS). The combination of the OTH-B and NWS will assure detection of Soviet ALCMs and their carrier aircraft at ranges sufficient to provide the NCA with decision time, and US offensive forces time for survival actions. The Air Defense Initiative technology program is the key to developing the technologies to counter future generations of Soviet air threats.
- Countering the Soviet Union's superiority in air defenses is particularly challenging. US responses to date include the increased penetration capability afforded by ALCM and the B-1B, together with planned deployments of the Short-Range Attack Missile (SRAM) II, the ACM, and the B-2.

For the immediate future, planned US offensive force modernization and surveillance system upgrades appear sufficient to maintain a strong deterrent to a Soviet nuclear attack on the United States and its allies. The Soviets seek a capability to combine offensive strikes and defensive preparations to limit greatly the damage US retaliation could inflict. To ensure that the Soviets do not achieve this aim in the foreseeable future, it is imperative that the Strategic Modernization Program be continued to its logical conclusion. It is important to remember that the elements of that program are designed not only to redress past and current deficiencies but also to counter projected Soviet plans to undermine the strategic balance.

The trends of the past two decades in the balance of strategic defensive forces also require a vigorous US response. While the United States greatly deemphasized strategic defenses beginning in the late 1960s, the Soviet Union continued to spend as much in this area as on its strategic offensive forces. Soviet passive defenses of both civil and military targets and strategic air defenses dwarf those of the United States, and the USSR maintains the world's only operational antiballistic missile (ABM) capability. Soviet missile silos, other military installations, essential industry, government, and military relocation facilities have all been hardened extensively. The Soviets have about 2,000 dedicated strategic defense interceptor aircraft (the United States has 300), 7,000 strategic air defense radars (the United States has 118),

The imminent introduction of the BLACKJACK intercontinental bomber will make the third leg of the Soviet triad far more robust.

and more than 9,000 strategic air defense surface-to-air missile launchers (the United States has none). In the mid-1970s, the United States deactivated the one ABM site allowed under the ABM Treaty; the Soviet Union maintained its site and has almost completed expanding and upgrading it. The US SDI is an essential response to those active Soviet efforts in strategic defense; even more important, it offers the promise of a more stable, secure basis of deterrence for the longer term.

The SDI is making substantial progress in developing technologies to make defense against ballistic missiles feasible. When these efforts come to fruition, the United States can move away from its almost exclusive reliance on offensive strategic forces. To the extent that defenses render ballistic missile forces militarily

ineffective, any temptation Soviet leaders might have to use their offensive forces would be overcome, not simply by their calculations about the prospect and effects of US retaliation, but by an assessment that their attack would fail to achieve their military objectives.

As described in Chapter IV, the Soviets are pursuing advanced defenses, including research on many of the technologies being examined in the US SDI program. Their ballistic missile defense program enjoys certain advantages over the SDI. First, the Soviet leadership has long believed in the importance of defensive forces to a balanced military posture, and Soviet military doctrine prescribes a key role for strategic defenses. Over the years, Moscow has consistently provided strong financial support for defensive programs. Over the last

Because it operates in the vast expanses of the world's oceans, the TRIDENT nuclear-powered ballistic missile submarine is the most survivable of US strategic forces. These submarines enhance deterrence by ensuring effective retaliation, even in the unlikely event of a disabling Soviet first strike against US land-based forces.

two decades, fully half of the Soviet strategic forces budget has been devoted to defenses. Thus, over the past ten years, the Soviet Union has spent significantly more than the United States on strategic defense activities.

Second, the modernization of the Moscow ABM system has given the Soviets a formidable ballistic missile defense infrastructure. This infrastructure provides the Soviet Union with active missile interceptors and radar production lines, operational experience with ABM systems and how they interact with strategic offensive forces, and a cadre of ABM personnel.

Third, the large-scale Soviet defensive effort permits broad and intensive programs involving a wide range of competing technologies. This substantial effort will provide the Soviets with significant advantages in exploiting future defensive options. Those advantages and the programs behind them antedate the US SDI program by many years.

While the Soviets enjoy significant advantages in the development of effective ballistic missile defenses, they generally lag behind the United States in some related technologies such as reliable, high-speed data processing. In the past, the Soviets have compensated quite successfully for this disadvantage through the legal and illegal acquisition of Western technology, by fielding weapon systems quickly with advanced technology acquired from the West (frequently more quickly than in the West), and by relying on greater quantities of weapons however, inferior they may be individually. As the Soviet Union continues to reduce the advanced military technology gap with the West and expands its range of compensating techniques, technology may be less of a limiting factor on development of Soviet advanced ballistic missile defense capabilities.

By contrast, although the United States strategic defense program does not share the Soviet program's strengths, it does enjoy significant benefits from the West's broad and deep technical superiority. Ballistic

The B-52 has served as the backbone of the US strategic bomber force for some three decades. The majority of the B-52 force is now ALCM capable. Eventually the B-52 will be replaced by the B-1B and B-2.

Both the United States and the Soviet Union have operational and developmental air- and sea-launched cruise missiles. These classes of weapons have the potential for a significant impact on the strategic balance.

missile technology is relatively mature, being understood well and applied by both the Soviet Union and the United States. Conversely, advanced technologies for ballistic missile defense are relatively immature; conse-

quently, significant efforts by the United States in this field have the potential to pay major national security dividends in the years to come.

In summary, the US Strategic Modernization Program, in combination with the SDI, will enhance the ability to deter aggression, strengthen crisis stability, and provide the Soviets with incentives for suitable arms reductions, thereby increasing the security of the United States and its allies. The force-wide improvements in the US nuclear deterrent have helped increase the chances for equitable and verifiable arms reductions by signaling American resolve and allowing the United States to bargain from a position of strength. The dynamic nature of the Soviet threat, however, and the consequences Soviet actions have on the strategic balance, demand vigilance to preserve the capability and credibility of the US strategic deterrent.

CHAPTER VII

Regional and Functional Balances

A comprehensive balance assessment requires a comparative analysis of US and Soviet military capabilities across the spectrum of conflict. In doing so, similar forces, like armor, and opposing forces, like aircraft and antiaircraft air defense systems, are compared to identify relative strengths and weaknesses. The strategies, operational concepts, readiness and a host of nonquantifiable factors comprise further components of each balance. In this chapter, US and Soviet military capabilities and those of relevant allies and friends are compared within certain geographical areas and along functional lines.

THE MILITARY BALANCE IN EUROPE

One way to evaluate the NATO-Warsaw Pact military balance is to measure each side's relative military capabilities against NATO's objectives. NATO's primary objectives have long been to deter aggression against any Alliance member and to defend successfully against aggression should deterrence fail.

To achieve these objectives, NATO since 1967 has followed a strategy of flexible response. Flexible response entails maintaining a combination of nuclear and conventional forces, including US strategic nuclear forces, permitting NATO to respond effectively across the spectrum of conflict. This force posture is designed to deter aggression by ensuring that NATO's commitment to respond remains credible while posing for an aggressor uncertainty and the possibility of unacceptable consequences. Should war occur, the flexible response strategy calls for a direct response in order to defend NATO territory as far forward as possible and, as necessary and appropriate, for deliberate escalation.

As a defensive Alliance, NATO does not maintain a capability to initiate aggressive war or conduct extensive offensive operations. NATO would seek to hold the line by containing any Warsaw Pact attack across the border while attacking Pact reinforcements before they arrive at the front and, as necessary, consider escalation to use of nuclear weapons. NATO has historically relied on the quality of its conventional and nuclear forces to offset the Warsaw Pact's large numerical advantages. While both alliances are modernizing, the USSR continues to narrow NATO's technological lead.

The policy deliberations of the Soviet Defense Council and the Warsaw Pact are, of course, shrouded in secrecy. It does, however, seem clear from Soviet actions and public statements that one of their primary peacetime objectives is to fracture the Alliance, especially to split the United States from Europe. Failing that, they appear determined to degrade NATO's cohesion in order to constrain the Alliance's deployment of adequate defense capabilities.

In the event of a war with NATO, it is likely the Soviets would seek to achieve a quick victory, perhaps with limited objectives. Soviet military leaders maintain that they intend to fight future battles on the territory of the enemy. In Europe, this would entail an invasion of western Europe advancing deep, perhaps driving to the English Channel with a *blitzkrieg* attack similar to the German attack on France in World War II.

As Soviet Defense Minister Dmitri Yazov recently wrote, Soviet doctrine must be designed to secure the destruction of the invading forces. Yazov went on to say that it is impossible to destroy the aggressor only through effective defense; forces must be capable of conducting *decisive offensive* operations.

By winning quickly, the Soviets would seek to foreclose NATO's option to use nuclear weapons. Additionally, a long war would provide an opportunity for NATO to reinforce with American and British forces and to bring to bear the Alliance's economic might. Furthermore, a long war could present the non-Soviet Warsaw Pact countries with the time and incentive to withdraw from the conflict.

The Soviets divide the European theater into what they call TVDs, which translates as theaters of military operations. Their Northwestern, Western, and Southwestern TVDs correspond roughly to NATO's Northern, Central, and Southern Regions. The Soviets view their Western TVD as being strategically decisive in the event of a war with NATO and, therefore, their military operations will be weighted opposite NATO's Central Region. Consequently, although the Pact has sizable force advantages in both the Northwestern and Southwestern TVDs, and would conduct offensive oper-

For more than 40 years, the peace, security, and economic prosperity of Western Europe have been fundamental elements of US and Allied collective security. The starkness of the inner-German border, dividing east from west, demonstrates the basic differences in political and economic philosophies, attitudes toward elemental human rights, and requirements for military power. Thus, a stable military balance in Europe — in the Northern, Center, and Southern Regions as well at sea — remains essential for Alliance security.

ations in those regions, those operations on the flanks, at least initially, would be expected to have more limited objectives.

NATO's flanks — the Northern and Southern Regions — are viewed by the Soviets as theaters of military operations with strategic importance. In the Southwestern TVD, for example, they have even established in peacetime a High Command of Forces headquarters as they have in the Western TVD. The military geography of these regions also features strategically significant bodies of water. Thus, the Soviets probably view them as requiring extensive maritime and air operations. Thus, a key difference between the flanks and the Central Region is the greater saliency of maritime and air operations on the flanks.

In the Northwestern TVD, Soviet operations are likely to include a combined-arms front operation against northern Norway in which ground forces, supported by land-based air and naval amphibious forces, would seek to seize critical airfields and destroy early warning installations. It is in this region that the Soviets perceive a significant strategic air defense requirement against Western air-breathing threats, notably air- and sea-launched cruise missiles and penetrating bombers. Modern air defense aircraft, mainly FOXHOUND and FLANKER supported by MAINSTAY AWACS and MIDAS tankers and by naval forces with modern air search/early warning radars and surface-to-air missiles, will form an extended line of defense into the Arctic. The ground balance significantly favors the Soviets in the Northwestern TVD. The air balance in the

Northwestern TVD may be to the Pact's advantage. NATO has certain advantages in surface, subsurface, and naval air warfare capabilities.

In the Southwestern TVD, Soviet strategy is expected to consist of operations to secure the southern flank of the Western TVD. This would include ground and air operations against Italy and Austria; a combined-arms front operation of ground, air force, and air-sea landing operations against Greece and Turkey to secure the Turkish Straits as well as a naval-air operation to gain sea control on and over the Black Sea. Soviet maritime operations would consist of amphibious operations to seize the Turkish Straits and naval operations in the form of surface and submarine forces as well as Soviet Naval Aviation to attempt to deny NATO naval forces access to the Black Sea, and eventually to the eastern Mediterranean Sea. In recent years, the Soviets have put increasing emphasis on the speed with which they can move amphibious forces to their objectives, as evidenced by the introduction of air cushion vehicles (ACVs) and wing-in-ground effect craft (WIGs) which give the Soviets the ability to move forces more rapidly across the Black Sea to the Straits. Soviet air operations are designed to establish an air defense sector over their maritime and ground force operations, and to deny NATO's carrier-based air access to the Soviet homeland. Because there is a lack of territorial contiguity between the three major Allied nations, the Pact could conceivably achieve major territorial gains in one part of the region despite Alliance success in defending the other parts. The ground balance in the Southern Region, depending on the amount of warning and Pact objectives, initially favors the Soviets, although not so much as in the Northwestern TVD. NATO has certain maritime advantages in the Mediterranean, but the Soviets have advantages in the Black Sea. The air balance in the Southwestern TVD favors the Pact initially, although modernization of the Greek and Turkish Air Forces will improve NATO's position.

In analyzing NATO's capabilities to meet its objectives in the Central Region of Europe, one might first examine the trends since 1981 in several major areas of the European military balance. Since the Soviets regard the Western TVD as the most important theater of military operations, the trends are evaluated primarily as they relate to that theater. Following a discussion of those trends, their impact on deterrence and defense is evaluated.

Trends Since 1981

Nonstrategic Nuclear Forces

Nuclear forces with ranges of less than 5,500 kilometers are often referred to as Nonstrategic Nuclear Forces (NSNF). They are normally deployed in or around the theater to which they are assigned. In NATO, NSNF provide a link between NATO's conventional forces and the Alliance's strategic nuclear deterrent.

There have been five significant changes in the NSNF category since 1981. First, to counter the Soviet deployment of SS-20 intermediate-range missiles, NATO, in accordance with its 1979 decision, began in 1983 deploying Pershing II and ground-launched cruise missiles (GLCMs), while at the same time continuing to negotiate for the reduction of these and other intermediate-range nuclear forces (INF).

The Soviet Union is significantly upgrading its ground attack air capabilities with the continuing introduction of the Su-24/FENCER into its Air Armies opposite NATO. The FENCER has greatly increased range, payload and combat capabilities.

Second, the Soviets began modernizing other missile systems, such as replacing the SCUD with the SS-23, a more modern, longer range and more accurate system. The vast majority of short-range NSNF missiles in Europe are deployed with Warsaw Pact forces. Compared to NATO's 88 operationally deployed LANCE missile launchers, the Warsaw Pact deploys about 1,400 FROG, SCUD, and SS-21 missile launchers west of the Urals. About 1,000 of these short-range launchers are assigned to Soviet units.

Third, NATO ministers decided at Montebello in 1983 to reduce the NATO nuclear stockpile by 1,400 warheads, while taking the steps to modernize and improve the survivability of the delivery systems that remain. Together with earlier NATO reductions, the Montebello reductions have brought NATO's nuclear stockpile to its lowest level in 20 years. Carrying out the Montebello modernization commitment must remain a top Alliance priority.

The fourth major change is the increased number of refire missiles deployed by the Soviets for their short-range (less than 500 kilometers) missile launchers in the forward areas. These missiles are not constrained by the INF Treaty. The refires for these launchers are estimated to have been increased by between 50 and 100 percent over the past several years. Consequently, the Pact has been able to plan on using these missiles, armed with non-nuclear warheads, to strike NATO air defenses, airfields, and command-and-control nodes without sacrificing their ability to plan on using the same missiles, if needed, in theater nuclear strikes.

The fifth major change in the NSNF category has been the nuclear capability of Soviet artillery. The Pact's increased deployment of nuclear-capable artillery has significantly enhanced the flexibility of Warsaw Pact battlefield nuclear forces.

The overall trend in NSNF has been the increase in Warsaw Pact theater nuclear capability to the point where today they have a substantially greater capability than the NATO Alliance in this category, notwithstanding the asymmetrical reductions that will result from the elimination of the INF category of weapons.

NATO-Warsaw Pact
Nuclear-Capable Aircraft*
Land-Based in Europe

Nuclear-Capable Aircraft

NATO ▬▬▬▬▬

Warsaw Pact ▬▬▬▬▬

As of 30 September 1987

*These estimates include systems that could be capable of performing a nuclear mission regardless of assigned mission.

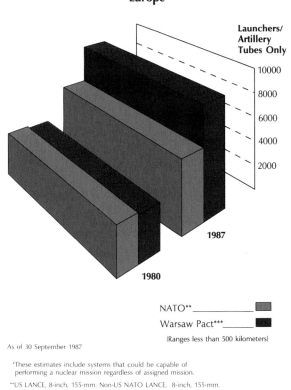

NATO-Warsaw Pact
Short-Range Nuclear-Capable Forces*
Europe

Launchers/ Artillery Tubes Only

NATO** ▬▬▬▬▬

Warsaw Pact*** ▬▬▬▬▬

(Ranges less than 500 kilometers)

As of 30 September 1987

*These estimates include systems that could be capable of performing a nuclear mission regardless of assigned mission.

**US LANCE, 8-inch, 155-mm. Non-US NATO LANCE, 8-inch, 155-mm.

***Soviet SCUD, SS-21, FROG, 203-mm, 240-mm, 152-mm systems. Non-Soviet Warsaw Pact SCUD, SS-21, FROG, 152-mm.

Air Forces

The conduct and outcome of a Pact air campaign would have serious implications not only for the success of ground operations but for NATO's overall defense as well.

By one measure that accounts for both quantity and quality of weapon systems, NATO has done much better in improving the air balance than it has the land balance. In fact, the early 1980s saw the Warsaw Pact's air advantage reduced as a result of NATO air force modernization. In the last few years, however, the Soviets have offset much of NATO's efforts by modernizing their air forces with bombers, ground-attack aircraft, fighters, and interceptors that are as capable as NATO's front-line air forces. An illustration of the current balance, based on an assessment of assigned missions, is shown on page 115.

In addition, projections of Soviet Air Forces modernization indicate that the Soviets will continue well into the 1990s to deploy aircraft such as the MiG-29 and Su-27 that are as capable as NATO's front-line fighters. They are projected to continue improving their air control intercept capability by deploying more of

their version of the airborne warning and control system (AWACS), the MAINSTAY. Moreover, Moscow is showing increasing interest in air-to-air refueling capabilities, including development of the new MIDAS tanker aircraft, that offer the potential to increase the combat radius of their air forces.

In summary, while the trends in the air balance are not as unfavorable as those in the ground balance, they still display a Warsaw Pact capability that poses a serious threat to NATO, the dimensions of which may grow.

Ground Forces

Ground forces are the only type of forces that can seize and hold territory. The Soviets are well aware of this fact, and their history and geography have led them to emphasize the development and deployment of ground forces. The Soviets believe that the ability to project land power is a prime ingredient in the ability to influence directly the political and military decision of an adversary and, as a result, their actions.

NATO remains at a severe disadvantage on the ground. The Alliance's modernization efforts over the

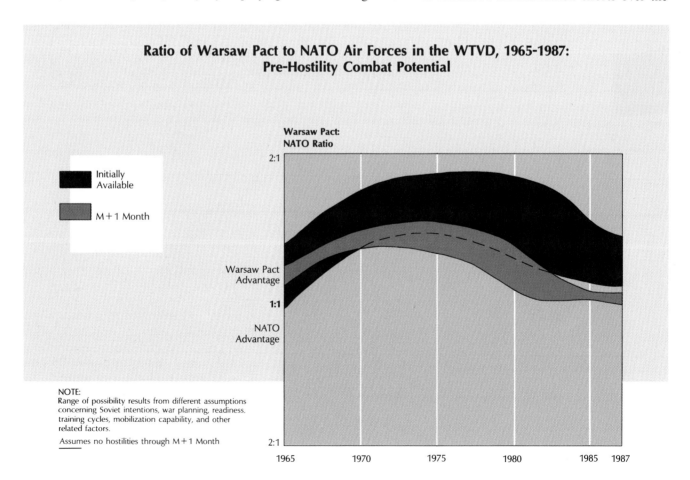

Ratio of Warsaw Pact to NATO Air Forces in the WTVD, 1965-1987: Pre-Hostility Combat Potential

Warsaw Pact:
NATO Ratio

2:1

Initially Available

M + 1 Month

Warsaw Pact Advantage

1:1

NATO Advantage

NOTE:
Range of possibility results from different assumptions concerning Soviet intentions, war planning, readiness, training cycles, mobilization capability, and other related factors.

Assumes no hostilities through M + 1 Month

2:1

1965   1970   1975   1980   1985 1987

110

past seven years, however, especially in tanks, infantry fighting vehicles, and artillery, have prevented the Pact from increasing significantly its force potential advantage in initially available in-place and mobilization forces. However, the situation of near parity in other categories such as theater nuclear and air forces, makes NATO's substantial ground force disadvantage much more significant and a priority concern for the West.

Sustainability

The ability to sustain forces in combat is as vitally important to the military balance as their structure, training, and deployment. Failure to acquire such an ability can result in what some military officers have referred to as a "hollow" force.

Within the complex category of sustainability, two areas stand out: ammunition stockpiles and support infrastructure. In terms of ammunition stockpiles, NATO has made some progress since the 1970s. The Warsaw Pact has also made progress in sustainability, as evidenced by increased ammunition storage capacity, not only in Eastern Europe, but also farther to the rear in the Western military districts of the Soviet Union. As a result, Pact forces in the Western TVD currently may have sufficient munitions to support 60 to 90 days of offensive operations.

NATO Main Battle Tanks*

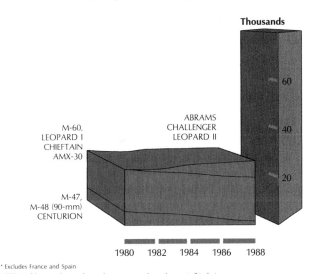

* Excludes France and Spain
NOTE: Model nomenclatures shown above are examples and are not all-inclusive.

Warsaw Pact Main Battle Tanks

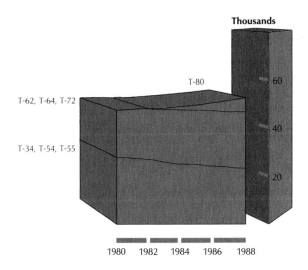

NOTE: Model nomenclatures shown above are examples and are not all-inclusive.

NATO APCs and IFVs*

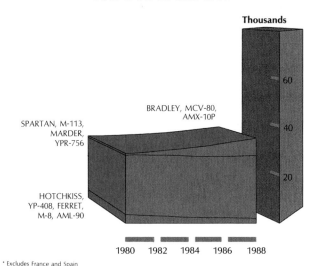

* Excludes France and Spain
NOTE: Model nomenclatures shown above are examples and are not all-inclusive.

Warsaw Pact APCs and IFVs

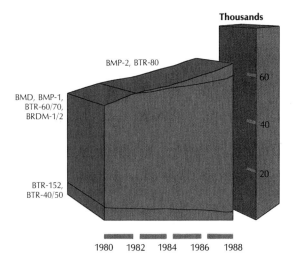

NOTE: Model nomenclatures shown above are examples and are not all-inclusive.

NATO Artillery/MRLs/Mortars*

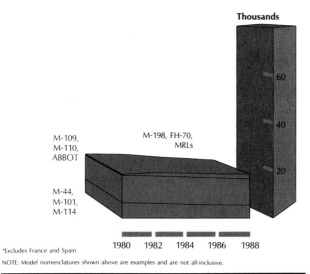

Thousands

M-109,
M-110,
ABBOT

M-198, FH-70,
MRLs

M-44,
M-101,
M-114

60

40

20

1980 1982 1984 1986 1988

*Excludes France and Spain

NOTE: Model nomenclatures shown above are examples and are not all-inclusive.

Warsaw Pact Artillery/MRLs/Mortars

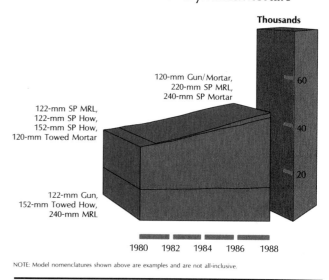

Thousands

120-mm Gun/Mortar,
220-mm SP MRL,
240-mm SP Mortar

122-mm SP MRL,
122-mm SP How,
152-mm SP How,
120-mm Towed Mortar

122-mm Gun,
152-mm Towed How,
240-mm MRL

60

40

20

1980 1982 1984 1986 1988

NOTE: Model nomenclatures shown above are examples and are not all-inclusive.

Ratio of Warsaw Pact to NATO Ground Forces in the WTVD, 1965-1987:
Pre-Hostility Combat Potential

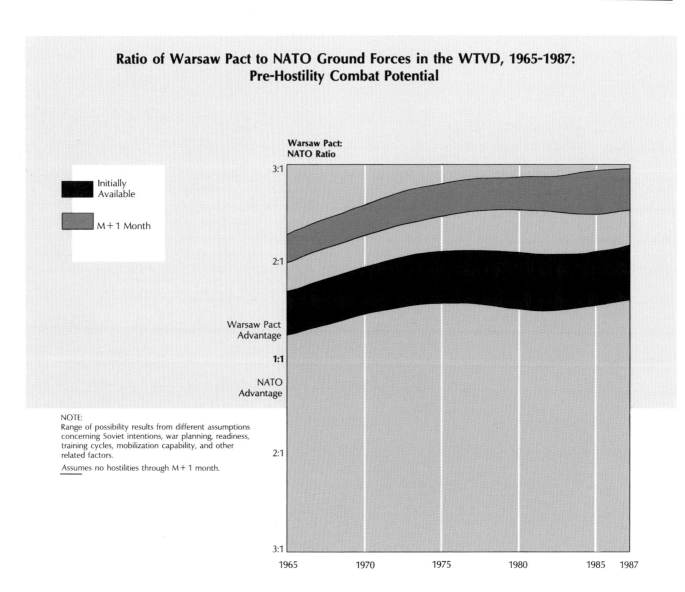

Initially
Available

M+1 Month

**Warsaw Pact:
NATO Ratio**

3:1

2:1

Warsaw Pact
Advantage

1:1

NATO
Advantage

2:1

3:1

NOTE:
Range of possibility results from different assumptions
concerning Soviet intentions, war planning, readiness,
training cycles, mobilization capability, and other
related factors.

Assumes no hostilities through M+1 month.

1965   1970   1975   1980   1985 1987

Furthermore, while NATO has been relying increasingly on reserve forces for its support infrastructure (and host nation support for the US portion), the Pact has been increasing its active force support elements by fielding materiel support brigades and battalions. Consequently, under some scenarios, the Pact would have an advantage in sustaining combat operations since NATO may not have time to activate and put in place an adequate support infrastructure. The net effect of these sustainability trends in NATO and the Warsaw Pact has been a relative increase in the Pact's ability to sustain its forces in the event of a war in Europe.

Operational Concepts

The numbers and types of forces, and how those forces are sustained, provide only a partial picture of the two sides' combat capabilities. Equally important are the operational concepts for employing those forces, which dictate the numbers and types of forces required.

The 1980s have witnessed a period of doctrinal and operational reevaluation for both NATO and the Warsaw Pact. NATO has adopted the concept of Follow on Forces Attack (FOFA) as part of an overall defensive strategy which recognizes the importance of second echelon forces to the Warsaw Pact's attack plan. FOFA is designed to counterattack with air systems Pact forces before they reach the battlefield and to delay, disrupt and to some extent destroy these forces. The actual capabilities needed to implement FOFA are dependent on NATO's willingness to implement necessary force improvement programs.

The Warsaw Pact seems to have taken this new NATO concept seriously and appears to be changing its forces and training to address the role of defensive operations. Rather than emphasizing only offensive operations as they have in the past, they now seem to give greater attention to simultaneous defensive operations than they had previously. Nonetheless, as noted earlier, they continue to believe that defensive operations alone are not sufficient.

Soviet military planning appears increasingly to focus on prosecuting a conventional-only war instead of initiating hostilities with a nuclear strike as appeared to be their approach in the early 1970s. This shift does not mean, however, that they intend to forego the use of nuclear weapons should they prove necessary during the course of a conflict.

Command and Control

The command and control arrangements and the supporting communications for the two sides' forces can have an effect on the efficiency and effectiveness with which those forces can be employed.

In the early 1980s, a new command and control arrangement was instituted that would allow the Soviets to call up non-Soviet Warsaw Pact forces without first obtaining the approval of the various national governments. Such an arrangement is likely to enhance the Pact's capability to transition to war as well as to reduce Soviet uncertainties concerning the participation of non-Soviet Warsaw Pact nations in the event of war.

The majority of NATO forces, of course, remain under national control in peacetime, and the commitment of those forces to NATO command and control requires political decisions by each of the Alliance's sovereign members.

Another major change since 1981 has been the establishment by the Pact of a peacetime headquarters (High Command of Forces) for the Western TVD. This headquarters is provided with the requisite staff, support, and communications for controlling air, ground, and naval operations against NATO's Central Region. As with all major Pact command and control nodes, the headquarters is bunkered and hardened and the supporting communications network is extremely varied, redundant, and, where possible, hardened.

In contrast, many of NATO's key command and control nodes are not hardened and the supporting communications are not as standardized, integrated, redundant, or survivable as those of the Pact.

The Warsaw Pact has an advantage in its ability to mobilize rapidly and move forces to deployment locations. NATO, on the other hand, requires a number of discrete political decisions and the will to take what some will view as escalatory actions. As a consequence, the Pact can transition more quickly from a peacetime to a wartime posture and control sustained combat operations more effectively than NATO.

Deterrence

Attempting to understand the Soviet assessment of the military balance is critical to an accurate evaluation of the deterrent quality of NATO forces. Efforts to evaluate deterrence using Western analyses would be misleading or incorrect if the Soviets do not hold similar assumptions about measures of the balance. Indeed, there are indications that the Soviet assessment of the balance in Europe may be different from NATO's. For example, the Pact appears to calculate weapons

NATO-Warsaw Pact Ground Forces Comparisons[1]

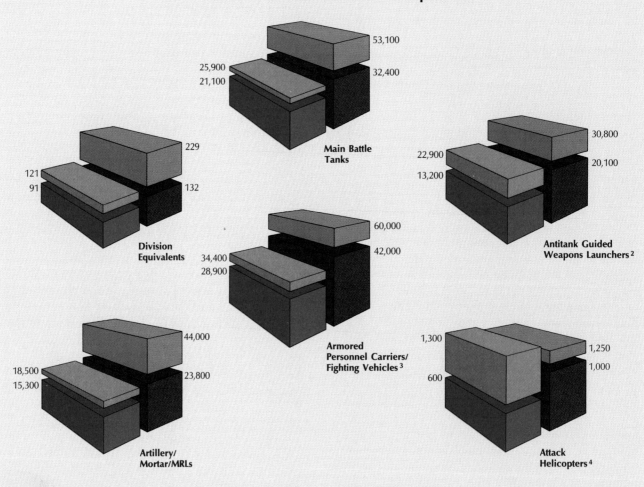

Main Battle Tanks — 53,100; 32,400; 25,900; 21,100

Division Equivalents — 229; 132; 121; 91

Antitank Guided Weapons Launchers[2] — 30,800; 20,100; 22,900; 13,200

Armored Personnel Carriers/Fighting Vehicles[3] — 60,000; 42,000; 34,400; 28,900

Artillery/Mortar/MRLs — 44,000; 23,800; 18,500; 15,300

Attack Helicopters[4] — 1,300; 1,250; 1,000; 600

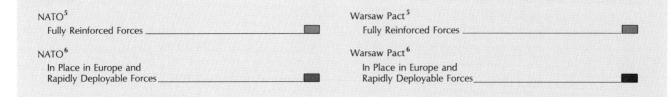

NATO[5]
Fully Reinforced Forces _____

NATO[6]
In Place in Europe and
Rapidly Deployable Forces_____

Warsaw Pact[5]
Fully Reinforced Forces _____

Warsaw Pact[6]
In Place in Europe and
Rapidly Deployable Forces_____

Excludes the following French and Spanish forces: 13 division equivalents, 2,300 MBTs, 3,700 artillery, mortars, MRLs, 5,400 APC/IFVs, 1,700 ATGWs, and 180 attack helicopters.

Warsaw Pact divisions normally consist of fewer personnel than many NATO divisions but contain more tanks and artillery, thereby obtaining similar combat power.

▬▬▬▬

[1] US Estimate of 1987 NATO data.

[2] Excludes shoulder-launched ATGMs, T-64Bs, T-80s and helicopters.

[3] Includes only APCs and IFVs. Excludes armored command vehicles and military support carriers.

[4] Excludes transport helicopters that can be configured for attack roles.

[5] Fully reinforced forces — include North American reinforcements and all Warsaw Pact forces located west of the Ural Mountains.

[6] Rapidly deployable and POMCUS forces include those US forces whose equipment is stored in Europe and high-readiness Soviet forces located in the Baltic, Belorussian, Carpathian, Odessa, Kiev, and North Caucasus military districts. Also includes separate Soviet airborne divisions. All Soviet forces in the Leningrad and Transcaucasus military districts and NSWP mobilization bases are considered in place. Excludes Soviet Artillery Divisions. Increases in many categories due to broader definition of geographic area.

114

NATO-Warsaw Pact Combat Air Forces Comparisons*

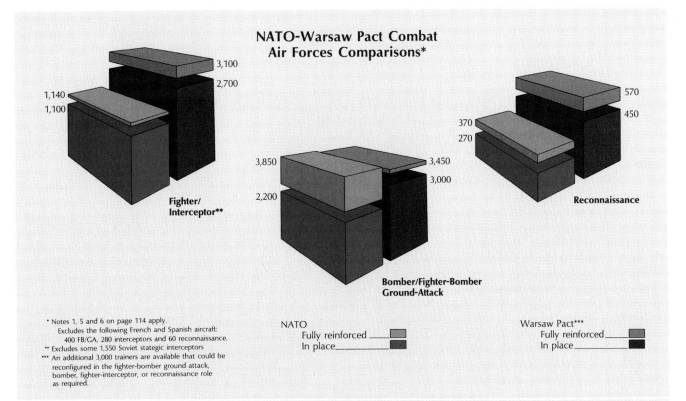

Fighter/Interceptor**

- 3,100
- 2,700
- 1,140
- 1,100

Bomber/Fighter-Bomber Ground-Attack

- 3,850
- 3,450
- 3,000
- 2,200

Reconnaissance

- 570
- 450
- 370
- 270

* Notes 1, 5 and 6 on page 114 apply.
  Excludes the following French and Spanish aircraft:
  400 FB/GA, 280 interceptors and 60 reconnaissance.
** Excludes some 1,550 Soviet stategic interceptors
*** An additional 3,000 trainers are available that could be
  reconfigured in the fighter-bomber ground attack,
  bomber, fighter-interceptor, or reconnaissance role
  as required.

NATO
Fully reinforced ____
In place ____

Warsaw Pact***
Fully reinforced ____
In place ____

NATO and Warsaw Pact Maritime Forces in the North Atlantic and Seas Bordering Europe

Category	NATO*	Warsaw Pact
Aircraft Carriers VSTOL Carriers	11	–
KIEV-Class Carriers	–	2
Helicopter Carriers	6	2
Cruisers	16	22
Destroyers, Frigates, Corvettes	310	201
Coastal Escorts and Fast Patrol Boats	267	586
Amphibious Ships (Ocean-going)	57	25
Mine Warfare Ships/Craft	270	330**
Total Submarines (All Types)	206	258
Ballistic Missile Submarines	35	44
Long-Range Attack Submarines	68	145
Other Types	103	69
% Submarines Nuclear Powered	50%	51%
Sea-Based Tactical, ASW, and Support Aircraft Including Helicopters	832	210
Land-Based Tactical and Support Aircraft Including Helicopters	389	530
Land-Based Antisubmarine Warfare Fixed-Wing Aircraft and Helicopters	462	210

* US Estimate of 1987 NATO data. Excludes approximately 100 French and Spanish warships.
** Excludes minesweeping boats and drones.

effects and military force potentials differently than NATO does. Soviet military planners also appear to use different, relatively more pessimistic (from their perspective) assumptions about relative mobilization capabilities. These differences and other factors may cause the Soviets to believe their advantages to be less than NATO perceives them to be.

The Soviets appear to be strongly deterred by NATO's nuclear forces due, in part, to the escalatory linkages between nuclear and conventional weapons inherent in the flexible response strategy, as well as an apparent lack of Soviet confidence in their ability to keep any conflict conventional and to control escalation should nuclear weapons be used.

However, NATO cannot depend solely on Soviet perceptions of the balance, and their effects on deterrence. Accordingly, NATO remains committed fully to its doctrine of flexible response, which includes the option of making a deliberate political decision to raise the conflict to the nuclear level if necessary.

The Warsaw Pact enjoys a significant advantage in armor which NATO is attempting to offset with a variety of anti-armor systems like the A-10.

At the conventional level, the Soviets may conclude that, despite their advantages, they may not have sufficient forces to assure them a high probability of success in the event of war in Europe. Increasingly in the future, such a Soviet assessment will be influenced by the extent to which NATO is willing to develop and deploy the necessary weapons systems. They will find the prospect unattractive of forward deploying their reserve forces in the face of NATO's FOFA. Furthermore, it is likely that the Soviets remain concerned about the military capabilities and reliability of their allies' forces. In the final analysis, it is the Soviet assessment of the relative state of NATO/Pact force preparations, together with a judgment of the likelihood of NATO's use of nuclear weapons, that will be a critical factor in any Soviet decision to initiate conventional conflict.

While the Soviets desire a capability to prevent NATO from employing nuclear weapons, they probably are not confident of their ability to do so at the present time. Consequently, they are likely to remain concerned about the impact of nuclear use on their combat operations as well as the severe risks and consequences of nuclear escalation. Despite the adverse conditions in conventional ground and air power facing NATO, as well as improvements in Soviet tactical nuclear weapons, it is unlikely that the Soviets would have a high degree of confidence that their current force advantage is sufficient to achieve their political-military objectives in the time they require.

Defense Strategy

Although, as noted above, NATO's nuclear force posture is vital to deterrence, the Warsaw Pact has, and it will continue to have, advantages in the quantity, survivability, and flexibility of its nuclear forces. This situation reduces the effective contribution that nuclear weapons could make to NATO's ability to defend itself successfully should deterrence fail.

Furthermore, the Warsaw Pact currently holds a very large advantage over NATO in chemical offensive and defensive capabilities, although the Soviets may be disinclined to initiate chemical warfare, in part because NATO could retaliate. The Soviets might calculate that their advantages in chemical warfare capabilities would outweigh the risks and could provide them with some distinct military opportunities in the event of war, particularly if NATO did not maintain a capability to respond in kind.

As noted above, NATO remains concerned about the Warsaw Pact's superiority over NATO in conventional forces. While Pact leaders may not feel this superiority

is sufficient to give them a high degree of confidence of victory, given their doctrine of preemption under crisis conditions, their advantages may prove to be sufficient in the event of a war. The situation of near parity in the air balance could make it extremely difficult for NATO to defend successfully against the Pact's intensive air campaign. Not only is the Pact's advantage in ground forces worrisome, but its possible advantage in certain situations in air forces poses additional concerns since NATO's air forces may find it difficult to provide timely air support to its ground forces.

NATO's forward-defense strategy requires sufficient time for its ground forces to move forward and prepare defensive positions prior to a Pact attack. Depending on how a war began, there may not be time to capitalize on the inherent military advantages of defensive operations. NATO's FOFA concept is highly dependent on fielding enough survivable, long-range systems to engage the Pact's follow-on forces, as well as maintaining the command, control, communications, and intelligence (C^3I) fusion to engage them in a timely way. To date, NATO's inventory of those types of systems is uncomfortably low. NATO's defense is also highly dependent on timely reinforcement of in-Theater US forces with ground and air forces from the Continental United States. Should arrival of these forces not be timely, or should the Soviets successfully interfere with air and sea LOCs and in-theater reception facilities (and POMCUS), NATO would be at a serious disadvantage.

The Pact's theater-strategic operational concept, while increasingly incorporating defensive operations into an overall offensive strategy, still seeks a quick, conventional victory over NATO. They intend to execute an initial theater-wide air operation with the aim of destroying NATO's nuclear forces and gaining air superiority. Simultaneously, or shortly thereafter, they would initiate ground operations massing large, combined arms, armored forces to strike against NATO's weakest sectors to affect quick penetrations for subsequent exploitation. The likely overall objectives of this operational concept are to destroy NATO's surviving nuclear capabilities, destroy large groupings of NATO ground forces, and quickly reach the English Channel ports to prevent reinforcement and resupply.

It appears that the Pact has structured its command and control and sustainability elements to support these operations, although they are probably continuing to refine and develop them further. NATO's sustainability posture, as noted earlier, may not be sufficient to support NATO forces adequately in such an intensive, fast-moving campaign.

The above factors, among others, lead to the conclusion that in the event of war in Europe, NATO could be forced within days or weeks to escalate to the use of nuclear weapons in defending against a conventional attack, especially in the Central Region.

Deterrence After An INF Treaty

The conclusion of the INF Treaty has heightened public awareness in the West of continuing imbalances and persisting deficiencies in certain critical categories of NATO's conventional forces. The Treaty also highlights dangerous trends in Soviet force posture and the relative advantages they have in lines of communications and the ability to reinforce and resupply over them. These factors reinforce the importance of maintaining the momentum behind NATO's force improvement efforts.

NATO must continue to maintain a spectrum of conventional and nuclear capabilities to provide the flexibility needed to deter aggression. By following through on NATO's 1983 Montebello decision the Alliance will improve the effectiveness and survivability of its remaining nuclear systems.

The Alliance also must move forward in parallel with these actions by vigorously improving its conventional forces. By following through on the Conventional Defense Improvement Initiative, and obtaining greater defense cooperation among NATO nations, NATO can achieve significant conventional force improvements.

An INF agreement will not change the requirement for deterrence, including nuclear elements of the overall deterrent equation, that has kept the NATO allies free these past four decades. The US commitment to a free Europe remains strong, and should not be misperceived by the Soviet Union. While strategic nuclear forces continue to provide the bedrock of deterrence, the deployment of US theater nuclear and conventional forces in Europe and forward deployed dual capable naval forces also contribute to deterrence and provide the means for executing our flexible response strategy should deterrence fail. To continue to deter Soviet aggression, thereby maintaining the peace in Europe, Alliance plans for nuclear and conventional force modernization must be fulfilled in order to continue to deter Soviet aggression and maintain the peace in Europe.

THE MILITARY BALANCE IN THE MIDDLE EAST/SOUTHWEST ASIA

The geographical area considered here includes most of the countries within the US Central Command's (CENTCOM) area of responsibility, plus Israel, Leb-anon, and Syria. The Soviets refer to a similar area as the Southern Theater of Military Operations. This assessment focuses primarily on USSR and US regional capabilities. Forces of indigenous countries, or forces deployed within the region by outside states, although potentially important in some scenarios, are not addressed in detail. The Soviets' post-World War II occupation of Northern Iran (lasting until 1946) and their 1979 invasion of Afghanistan have demonstrated Moscow's willingness to use force in pursuit of their objectives in this region. In light of this and other regional threats, US policy objectives are to promote the stability and security of friendly states; assure free world access to the region's energy resources; maintain freedom of navigation in international waters; and prevent the domination of the region and its critical resources by any hostile power. This section will provide a summary assessment of the US-Soviet Middle East/Southwest Asia (ME/SWA) military balance within the context of a global war, a major theater war, and a local conflict not involving direct US or Soviet troop commitment.

Strategic Importance of the Middle East/Southwest Asia

The strategic importance of the ME/SWA region is highlighted by its principal resource — oil. Fifty-five percent of the world's proven oil reserves are located in the Gulf region. As world demand for oil continues to grow and reserves elsewhere dwindle, Gulf oil is likely to become increasingly important. The region also includes several of the world's most strategically important international waterways: the Suez Canal and the Bab el Mandeb strait, located at opposite ends of the Red Sea; and the Strait of Hormuz, located at the mouth of the Persian Gulf. Roughly 10 percent of the world's seaborne commerce passes through the Suez Canal — between 50 to 60 ships a day, over 21,000 a year — carrying over 370 million tons of goods.

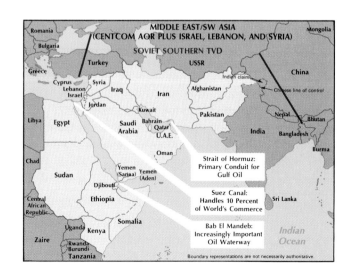

Soviet Forces

The Soviet invasion of Afghanistan in 1979 marked a dramatic shift in Moscow's military focus on Southwest Asia. Since that time, the Soviets have completely reorganized their forces, creating a new Southern Theater of Military Operations (STVD) High Command of Forces similar to TVD command and control structures opposite NATO and the Far East. Roughly 25 active ground and one airborne division are stationed in the Soviet Union's North Caucasus, Transcaucasus, and Turkestan Military Districts (MDs). An additional three motorized rifle and one airborne division, plus one air assault and two motorized rifle brigades, are located in Afghanistan. This organization represents an increase within the region of five divisions over the past decade. Eighteen fighter and fighter-bomber regiments, with over 700 tactical aircraft are available to support ground operations. Although still lagging behind the other TVD's in force modernization, STVD units have been both expanded and modernized with advanced weapons systems such as the BMP and BTR 70 armored vehicles, SA-8 and SA-13 air defense missile systems, and extended range self-propelled artillery tubes, to include the nuclear-capable 2S5 152mm gun. Some of the modern systems, however have been seen only in Afghanistan and are probably deployed there for tests under combat conditions. Tactical air assets have also been expanded and modernized and, more significantly, their composition has shifted to reflect a change in emphasis from an air defense mission to offensive tactical air support to ground commanders.

From staging bases in the Southern-Central Soviet Union, BACKFIRE bombers pose a serious threat to US carrier battle groups and sea lines of communication in the North Arabian Sea. Soviet Caspian Flotilla forces include five frigates/corvettes and 15 amphibious ships. The Indian Ocean squadron could play an important role in some scenarios. Supported by access to base facilities available to them in Ethiopia and South Yemen, the squadron generally includes four to six principal surface combatants, and at times, a submarine. This force, however, could be significantly augmented in a relatively short period. Soviet and Cuban military advisers in the region (including over 7,000 Soviet and Cuban personnel in Ethiopia and South Yemen) also constitute a significant military presence.

US Forces

Although the United States has no forward-deployed land forces in the region, its ability to provide direct military assistance, if necessary, has been significantly enhanced since 1981. In January 1983, a perma-nent, geographically oriented unified command, Central Command (CENTCOM), was established. CENTCOM forces on station in the Middle East routinely include a command ship and four combatants, plus other limited contingents. This force has been substantially expanded, for an unspecified time, with the deployment of the Joint Task Force Middle East (JTFME). The JTFME comprises additional surface combatants, mine countermeasure ships, helicopters, and an aircraft carrier battle group. Total forces available to CENTCOM on a priority basis include five Army divisions and two independent brigades; one Marine Expeditionary Force (a ground division and an air wing); one Marine Expeditionary Brigade; 21 Air Force tactical fighter squadrons; strategic projection forces including B-52s; three carrier battle groups; one battleship battle group; and five maritime patrol aircraft squadrons. CENTCOM's force posture is also enhanced by regular bi-lateral exercises in the region that include the exercise and evaluation of capabilities to deploy military forces from the United States.

Geography and Lines of Communication

Any deployment of US ground forces into the region would require transporting those forces 6,500 to 8,000 nautical miles (NM) by air (almost twice the distance from the US east coast to Europe), or nearly 12,000 NM by sea (more than three times the distance to Europe). Upon arrival, US forces would be operating from ports and airfields that have little of the modern cargo handling equipment found at most European debarking sites. Thus it will be difficult to move US forces rapidly while sustaining those forces already in the theater across extended and potentially vulnerable air and sea lines of communication.

The Soviet Union, on the other hand, enjoys the military advantages of immediate territorial proximity to the region and has a well-developed military infrastructure in its adjacent military districts. Nevertheless, Moscow would also face difficulties in moving ground forces into the region and maintaining a logistics support line. During offensive operations, Soviet forces would be supported by direct overland resupply lines from the Soviet Union, with air resupply available. However, the harsh terrain and limited road network would impede a rapid Soviet advance and create lucrative interdiction targets.

The Middle East/Southwest Asia in A Global War

Soviet forces in the Transcaucasus, North Caucasus, and Turkestan MDs (or Afghanistan) are at a low level of preparation for an immediate major strike in the

ME/SWA region. A month or more would probably be required to prepare for major offensive operations; however, some preparation might be accomplished covertly.

In a global war originating in Europe, the United States would have very limited resources to spare for the ME/SWA. Deployment of US ground forces to the area would reduce the combat capability available for the critical Central European theater. Furthermore, US capabilities may not be adequate to allow a major simultaneous deployment to both Europe and the ME/SWA. On the other hand, Central Europe would also be the main Soviet focus in a global war. Thus, Soviet efforts in the ME/SWA, at least initially, probably would be similarly limited. The oil supplies of this region would become a much more important strategic objective should the Soviets fail to achieve their war aims quickly. In this instance, a Soviet effort in ME/SWA would become more likely.

Although initial Soviet operations in the region would probably focus on limited objectives in eastern Turkey and northern Iran, mobilization and preparation of area forces for offensive operations with strategic objectives would continue. Should Soviet offensive operations in Central Europe drag on with no clear prospects for near-term success, Soviet attention might shift to ME/SWA. They might consider major offensive operations either in Turkey or Iran, or both, although simultaneous major operations in separate directions would severely strain in-place combat and combat support capabilities. Objectives in Turkey would include a link-up with Soviet forces invading western Turkey in support of a broader effort to gain control of the eastern Mediterranean. Objectives in Iran would include seizure of oil fields and key cities along the Persian Gulf in support of a broader effort to deny oil to NATO and Japan and to control important sea lines of communication. As an alternative to a major ground invasion of Iran, the Soviets might attempt to deny oil to the West by conducting air strikes or by mining operations against oil production sources, pipelines, handling facilities, and shipping channels.

Soviet offensive operations in eastern Turkey would be inhibited by rough terrain, the absence of a developed road or rail system, and a highly motivated, but poorly equipped, Turkish defense. Nonetheless, Turkey could probably not successfully resist a full-scale Soviet offensive in the east without significant NATO reinforcement.

Soviet military operations in Iran would also be difficult. If Iran were to make a timely decision to redeploy forces to defend its border with the Soviet Union, then a Soviet invasion could be complicated. Iranian forces have been fighting for seven years and, presumably,

would be highly motivated to defend their country. The rugged terrain in northern Iran is well-suited to defense. Nevertheless, the Soviets have the capability to punch through to central southern Iran. At this point, they would be dependent on extended land lines of communications (LLOCs) crossing very difficult terrain. If the Iranians permitted, US air support could play a major role at this point, particularly in interdicting Soviet LLOCs, and in reducing the impact of Soviet close air support. Without outside support for Iran, the Soviets could probably reach coastal areas without the need to reinforce their own in-place ground forces significantly.

A Middle East/Southwest Asia Theater War

It is also possible that the Soviets might execute an independent campaign to seize Gulf oil reserves without starting a war with NATO. With their 1979 invasion of Afghanistan, the Soviets clearly demonstrated their willingness to employ military force in support of regional objectives. Moscow's assessment of both the capability and determination of the Afghans to resist, however, proved badly flawed. Despite the highly publicized, but largely cosmetic withdrawal of more than 2,000 nonessential personnel in October and November 1986, the Soviets still maintain more than 115,000 troops in Afghanistan. Even this level has proven inadequate to produce a settlement imposed by Soviet use of military power.

The Afghan resistance's military capability and competence steadily improved, taking a major leap forward with the introduction of antiaircraft missiles. Resistance access to military supplies of all types increased significantly over the past year, and resistance military operations were correspondingly more effective. Soviet prospects for a successful military solution to the situation in Afghanistan never appeared more unlikely. In fact, the Soviets and their Afghan clients recently agreed to a nine-month timetable for the withdrawal of Soviet troops from Afghanistan.

Since the Afghanistan invasion, there has been speculation in the West about a possible Soviet invasion of Iran. Much of the discussion of a Soviet invasion of Iran within the context of a global war (see Middle East/Southwest Asia in a Global War) would also apply in a theater war context. Iran could slow a Soviet advance, but would require substantial outside support to successfully resist. There are other non-quantifiable factors, however, which enhance deterrence in the region. On the basis of their experience in Afghanistan, the Soviets will not take lightly a decision to invade Iran, a country with twice the area, and three times the population of Afghanistan, and having equally difficult terrain. Another disincentive would include damage to Soviet political objectives in Western Europe, Japan, and the ME/SWA region as a result of strong political opposition to an invasion. Clearly, the Soviets would prefer to attain their goals through the kind of political maneuvering described in Chapter II. Nevertheless, despite all of the disincentives, a possible disintegration of central Iranian authority following the death of Khomeini, and a request for Soviet assistance from one of the factions struggling for control, might create a tempting opportunity for Soviet intervention.

Local Conflict

Conflicting Arab-Israeli goals in the Middle East remain a source of major tension within the region. The Iran-Iraq war, however, has tended to refocus Arab concerns. In addition to this war, political instability in Lebanon and the disruptive influence of unresolved Palestinian aspirations make continuation of low-level armed conflict in other parts of the region almost a certainty. In this environment, a renewal of the Israeli-Syrian conflict remains a possibility.

In the 1973 Arab-Israeli war, US ability to resupply Israel by air played an important role in that country's victory. The capability of US naval forces to control the air and sea in the Eastern Mediterranean created the benign environment in which this resupply could

occur. Although more than 62,000 tons were eventually delivered by sea to replace Israeli losses, most of the sealifted supplies arrived after the war had ended. Airlifted supplies began arriving in Israel within 48 hours of the political decision to initiate a major resupply effort. Over a 30-day period, the United States airlifted more than 22,000 tons to Israel. In roughly the same period, the Soviet Union is estimated to have delivered to Syria and Egypt some 15,000 tons by air and perhaps as much as 200,000 tons by sea. Far shorter distances made Soviet air and sea resupply operations considerably less demanding (1,700 NM versus 6,500 NM by air). In addition, Soviet resupply by sea was already operating at the beginning of the war with no waiting period for the first ship to arrive.

Should a new crisis develop in the Middle East, the dramatically expanded US in-flight refueling and airlift capabilities would allow the United States to exceed its 1973 effort substantially. On the other hand, the Soviets have also significantly improved their airlift capability since 1973 with the introduction of larger capacity aircraft like the An-124/CONDOR. Short of providing combat troops, however, Soviet support would not alter the outcome of a war between Israel and Syria. Even the introduction of Soviet airborne divisions into Syria would probably be insufficient to affect the outcome, except to the extent that their presence deterred the Israelis from pursuing objectives that would inevitably involve them in combat with Soviet forces. Further-

MILITARY HERALD

The Soviets made a major miscalculation in their invasion of Afghanistan in 1979. As a "guarantor" of the Geneva Accords, they are obliged to remove all Soviet forces from Afghanistan by February 15, 1989.

more, Israeli air defense capabilities make any Soviet attempt to deploy airborne troops directly into Israel unlikely.

Future Trends in the Middle East

Although the ongoing Iran-Iraq War and current Iranian attacks on nonbelligerent Gulf shipping represent a serious threat to regional stability, other elements of Iranian policy may constitute a more serious long-term threat. For example, Iran's expansionist ambitions in the region are closely tied to fundamentalist Islamic religious beliefs. Fundamentalist factions, some with close ties to Iran, exist in almost every state in the region. When radical Iranian leaders speak about the submission of Arab countries to the teachings of the Koran, they have in mind submission to Iranian leadership.

Given the precedent for ethnic unrest in the Soviet Union, the Soviet leadership must also be concerned about the prospects of an Iranian victory over Iraq and the potential subsequent expansion of Islamic fundamentalist influence, perhaps even among the Muslim inhabitants of the south central Soviet Union. Although the Soviets have tried to expand their diplomatic ties and influence in Iran, the Iranians remain suspicious, especially while the Soviets remain Iraq's principal source for arms.

In summary, notwithstanding the limited convergence of US and Soviet goals with regard to Iran, their long-term interests remain opposed. US capabilities to deploy limited forces or to provide military equipment and supplies to indigenous forces within the ME/SWA region have expanded significantly since 1981. Soviet capabilities to intervene with military force into neighboring states in the region have also been augmented significantly. US and Soviet regional capabilities are asymmetric, providing each side with advantages and disadvantages. In many scenarios, local military capabilities will be as important as US or Soviet capabilities in determining the outcome of any potential conflict.

THE MILITARY BALANCE IN EAST ASIA/PACIFIC

The East Asia/Pacific balance is viewed from two different perspectives. First, the overall balance is examined from the perspective of a Soviet/US global war. Second, trends in the regional subbalances that are of importance to the United States or to the Soviets are discussed. Regional subbalances are addressed separately because of their local impact in addition to

their impact on the global balance. These regional subbalances include: the Sino/Soviet; North/South Korea; and Southeast Asia.

Key geopolitical, economic, and military factors which underpin the East Asia/Pacific balance include:

- The immense geographic dimension of the region (including the largest ocean area in the world) is characterized by vast distances between the United States, forward-operating bases, and expected wartime operating areas.
- As history demonstrates, the regional geography and US strategic goals dictate that this is primarily a naval and air theater (from the US perspective) in the context of global war.
- East Asia has emerged as the world's leading economic development region and largest US trading partner.

The military balance in East Asia and the Pacific must be assessed in relation to the primary United States and Soviet objectives in the region. The United States' objective is to support the independence of our allies and other nations against aggression or coercion by the Soviet Union or its allies (North Korea and Vietnam). To provide such support, we maintain military forces and facilities in the region as a deterrent and to provide forward strategic defense for the United States and regional defense for our allies. United States military assets in the Pacific are configured to counter Soviet strike capabilities and place Soviet Far East military forces at risk during global war. Soviet objectives include providing support to socialist governments and revolutionary movements in the region, expanding Soviet diplomatic and commercial presence, and eventually supplanting the United States as the dominant power in the region.

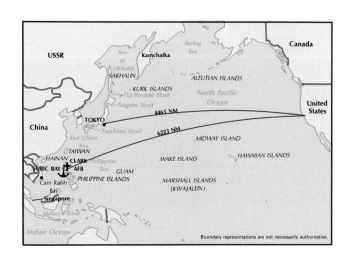

The Global War Perspective

The geography, force dispositions, and strategic objectives of the opponents dictate that the East Asia/Pacific theater will be primarily a naval and air theater in the event of a global war. US objectives in the event of global war are: to conduct an active forward defense of the United States by defending LOCs in and to the region; to counter attacks in-theater against our allies and other friendly nations; to support our deployed military forces in the region; and to conduct offensive actions against Soviet forces in order to neutralize Soviet military capability and inhibit Soviet transfer of Far Eastern forces to the European theater. The US will also take actions necessary to control escalation. Two key missions will be countering Soviet submarines, and dealing successfully with the land- and sea-based threat to our carrier battle groups operating near the Soviet periphery. Soviet wartime goals are to defend strategic strike assets until their use, defend the homeland, and deter opening of a second front by the People's Republic of China (PRC) military forces.

The United States has improved its ability to wage an antisubmarine warfare (ASW) campaign in this theater by increasing the number and quality of its attack submarines in the Pacific. The Soviets, however, have improved the size and quality of their submarine force as well. US superiority in ASW, which is derived from technological advantages — particularly in the area of submarine quieting and underwater acoustics — and from much better ASW training, is expected to persist, but to a diminishing degree. Soviet progress in submarine quieting and weapon capabilities will generate increasing threats to US and allied shipping. To maintain its relative advantage, the United States will have to continue its ASW modernization efforts. These include building attack submarines of even greater quality, increasing ASW surveillance, improving aircraft and surface combatant capabilities for both active and passive ASW operations, and developing better undersea weapons.

Soviet Pacific Ocean Fleet Air Force strike assets (over 90 BACKFIRE and BADGER aircraft armed with cruise missiles), as well as Soviet Air Force strike platforms (BACKFIRE and BEAR G, with AS-4 and AS-6 cruise missiles) and tactical aircraft like the FENCER (about 250 in the theater), are serious medium- and long-range threats to US forces and bases in the region and to US and allied ships in the waters around Japan, the Kuriles, and the Kamchatka peninsula. Improved US fleet capabilities centered on AEGIS-Class antiair warfare cruisers, F-14 aircraft with improved PHOENIX missiles, and F/A-18 fighter/attack aircraft provide a credible defense against long-range bomber strikes. US and allied aircraft operating from land bases in Japan, the Philippines, Korea, and Guam also can play a role in attriting the large force of Soviet bombers.

By virtue of its strong economy, key location, improving defense capabilities, and its assumption of meaningful self-defense responsibilities, Japan provides forces for its own defense and offers essential infrastructure support to US forward-deployed forces.

The Soviet deployment of SSBNs in bastions close to the Soviet Union magnifies the strategic importance of the Soviet and Japanese islands that dominate the entrances to the Sea of Japan and the Sea of Okhotsk. The inclusion of Japan in the Soviet "sea-control" zone underscores Japan's strategic importance and the inherent Soviet threat to Japan. Limitations on Soviet power-projection capabilities constrain Soviet options for addressing such problems, particularly in the face of capable Japanese defense forces and US power-projection capabilities.

The assistance of the Japanese Self-Defense Forces and US aircraft and naval support facilities located in Japan is crucial to defending against the Soviet air threat and in blocking the movement of Soviet naval forces out of the Sea of Japan. The Soviet Union will attempt to coerce Japan into neutrality in a global conflict and into denying the United States the use of Japanese bases and support from the Japanese Self-Defense Forces. Alternatively, the Soviets could attempt to conduct limited amphibious operations against Japan to secure exits from the Sea of Japan. A coordinated allied effort would be required to defend against a determined Soviet amphibious assault.

The primary Soviet goal vis-a-vis China in a global war is to deter attack and thereby avert the opening of a second front. Some 50 Soviet ground divisions deployed near the Sino-Soviet border provide this deterrent. Modernizing these divisions has been the centerpiece of Moscow's ground force activity during the 1980s. Soviet ground forces in East Asia are organized, equipped, and supplied to wage intense warfare for up to several months without reinforcement. It is believed that during a global confrontation these forces would remain "fixed." Indeed ground force operations by the Soviet Union and/or the United States in the region will likely be limited to amphibious operations to secure critical straits or islands guarding Soviet peripheral seas. By posing a threat to Soviet territory, US forces could inhibit redeployment of Soviet Far Eastern forces to other TVDs.

Bases

Access to base facilities in the East Asia/Pacific region provides the United States with the underpinning of its deterrent and forward-defense strategies and is crucial to its warfighting ability. In addition to bases in Japan noted above, South Korea and the Philippines provide forward staging, repair, and resupply facilities 5,000 miles (Korea and Japan) and 6,000 miles (Philippines) from the US west coast. The Republic of the Philippines, located at the juncture of Southeast Asia and Western Pacific sea lanes, is strategically important both geographically and as the host of two large US facilities, Clark Air Base and Subic Bay Naval Base. These bases play a critical role in the maintenance of US forward-deployed forces in the region and in supporting US forces assigned to protect vital interests in the Indian Ocean and Persian Gulf. Recent internal challenges, communist and secessionist insurgencies, and continuing economic problems threaten the stability of democratic institutions in the Philippines. Continued US access to these strategic bases contributes to the economic well-being of the Philippine people and the stability of their government. US forces in South Korea have been a principal factor in the maintenance of peace, stability and unprecedented economic development on the Korean peninsula for more than 30 years. The role of these forces in a global war remains to deter aggression by North Korea and to help defend South Korea if it is attacked.

Soviet naval and air presence in the South China Sea at Cam Ranh Bay has grown during the 1980s and now comprises about 25 ships, two to four submarines, and nearly 40 reconnaissance, ASW, strike, and fighter aircraft. The Cam Ranh Bay facility is the largest Soviet naval base outside the Soviet Union. Soviet forces there pose a limited direct threat to lines of communication to and from the Indian Ocean, and to US bases and forces operating out of the Philippines. While these Soviet forces can be neutralized in a global war with relative ease, this action would divert forces from other missions until this threat had been eliminated.

Global Perspective — Summary

The United States' ASW campaign in the Pacific will become more difficult by the mid-1990s as Soviet submarine quieting and other submarine warfare capabilities improve. In order to counter these Soviet advances, the US must continue the broad-based efforts it is making in ASW.

Soviet strike aircraft en route to targets in the Pacific Ocean would be vulnerable to US Navy air defenses and,

in some cases, to US and allied interceptors operating from land bases. Coordinated land- and sea-based air defense is the method used to destroy strike aircraft en route to a target; however, the best way to attack these aircraft is at their bases. In the Pacific theater, geography and range limitations of US strike aircraft combine to restrict US deep-strike capability. This situation would limit US ability to attack Soviet air power on the ground early in the war and place a premium on attrition of such aircraft by land- and sea-based antiair warfare forces while the aircraft are en route to their targets. US conventional warhead cruise missiles can successfully attack some targets, including support facilities essential for successful Soviet bomber operations; but aircraft on the ground, which may be moved between various dispersal fields, are better attacked by manned aircraft.

The US does not enjoy, nor does its national military strategy demand, predominance in ground forces in the region, and this will remain the case. But the structure, readiness, and deployment capabilities of PACOM forces in the region should permit adequate response to global and regional conflict.

The Soviets would face several uncertainties and constraints in East Asia in a global war. Considering their relative vulnerabilities in the region, the principal uncertainty would likely be the Soviet unwillingness to engage in a two front war. Large Soviet ground and air forces opposite China in peacetime and their "fixed" position in global war are costly to the Soviets in men and materiel, whether or not China becomes involved in a global confrontation. Although geography assists the Soviets in the protection of its SSBN fleet within the waters of the Sea of Japan and the Sea of Okhotsk, Soviet naval forces that venture out of the Sea of Japan for other missions must pass through narrow straits that are controlled by the United States and its allies. The Soviet Union has only limited capability to capture and secure areas bordering the straits, although allied capability to defend some of these areas is also limited. Offensive and defensive mining and mine clearing will play a key role for both sides in controlling the straits; overall the two sides are equal in their mine warfare capability (the Soviets have the larger mine inventory but mine warfare technology and mine delivery capability is viewed as equal). The distances from mainland Soviet air and naval bases to key Pacific LOCs and the requirement to cross over or near US allies to attack the LOCs are additional obstacles to any Soviet effort to interdict the LOCs. Distance and time factors would combine to provide the allies warning and the opportunity to maneuver.

Sino/Soviet Military Balance

The People's Republic of China (PRC) status today is that of a regional military power. It is important to acknowledge, however, that China's large resource base, both material and human, and efforts now underway to improve all aspects of Chinese life mean that the PRC could become a major power early in the 21st century.

In responding to the array of Soviet military power on its northern border, the PRC has embarked on a broad program to upgrade its military forces. This effort, however, is currently viewed as secondary to China's domestic economic development, which the Chinese leadership believes is the key to China evolving as a major power. Beijing is currently addressing technological development and infrastructure shortcomings (distribution systems, rail and road transportation systems, and communications) that are hindering advancements in industry, business, agriculture, and consumer goods production.

Chinese military forces today lack many of the high-technology weapons systems found in the Soviet and US forces. Beijing's defense resources are directed currently toward low-cost military programs designed to lay the groundwork for significant improvement in combat capabilities over the next decade. Improvements in education, training, organization, tactics, and research and development (R&D) will pave the way for the integration of new technologies and upgraded weapons systems during the 1990s. Despite continuing Chinese improvements, the Soviets will remain predominant in all areas of the military balance while the Chinese rely on their large population and geographical size as the bulwark of their conventional deterrent.

The slow growth of China's nuclear forces into the 1990s will likely include the introduction of a small number of operational SSBNs. The Soviets, however, will continue to maintain strategic nuclear superiority over the Chinese for the foreseeable future. Any enhancements to China's strategic forces over the next five years will likely be counterbalanced by Soviet improvements in their missile defense systems.

North/South Korean Military Balance

The regional balance between North and South Korea is of concern to the United States because of the aggressive nature of the North Korean regime and its large and capable military force. The North Korean government has manifested its belligerence by terror and assassination. The military threat that North Korea poses to South Korea is significant, and will continue to be for the foreseeable future. Thus, events on the Korean peninsula and the military balance there are key factors in US military planning for the East Asia/Pacific region.

North Korea's perception of America's resolve to defend South Korea's freedom has contributed to maintaining the peace on this strategic peninsula for nearly 35 years. Yet North Korea continues to modernize its already large armed forces, despite the devastating effects on its weak economy. North Korean advances include upgrading of ground force equipment, continuing reorganization, and forward deployment of its army; increasing naval and air exercises with the Soviets; and fielding of the second largest special operations forces in the world. North Korean forces are postured to attack in ways that would minimize warning and maximize surprise.

Rapid economic growth and political changes occurring currently in South Korea may presage a new era of political maturity and adherence to democratic principles which can only foster even greater growth and prosperity. The Republic of Korea boasts a strong economy roughly four times the size of North Korea's, and growing at a rate two to three times that of the North. South Korea also has been modernizing its forces with US assistance and continues qualitative improvements which will narrow the gap of the North's military superiority in the near term. South Korean military modernization programs however, are generally reactive to capabilities already existing or improvements underway in the North.

Were North Korea to attack, it is estimated that US and South Korean forces, aided by favorable geography and prepared defenses, would hold until a decisive number of US troops could reinforce the South Korean Army and the US 2d Infantry Division. The US and South Korean Air Force and Navy would from the start dominate their spheres of operation. If Pyongyang, aided by the Soviet Union, continues quantitative and qualitative improvements to its forces and does not alter the aggressive nature of its policies, the North can be expected to maintain its military lead over South Korea, and the peninsula will remain one of the world's trouble spots.

Southeast Asia

Southeast Asia is yet another important regional balance of which Vietnam is the centerpiece. Vietnam continues to occupy Cambodia and dominate Laos, and has engaged in a series of border skirmishes with

China. In exchange for base rights, the Soviets provide military equipment and continue to support the failed Vietnamese economy.

Because it fields the world's fourth largest army, Vietnam is in a position to threaten adjacent countries in the region, notably Thailand. Economic realities and lack of progress in resolving the occupation of Cambodia may presage slow movement toward improved relations between the United States and Hanoi.

Future Trends in the Far East

Although some aspects of the East Asia/Pacific balance favor the Soviets and some regional subbalances are currently unfavorable, there are many important theater-wide considerations that favor the United States. The most important of these are staunch allies in key geopolitical locations who provide bases to support our forward-deployed forces. Japan, South Korea, and the Philippines play significant roles in bolstering democratic defenses in the region. The economic dynamism of American allies in East Asia, a dynamism that is particularly striking when compared with the economic stagnation of the Soviet Union's principal client states, Vietnam and North Korea, should in the future create improved possibilities for development. The continued economic well-being of Japan, growth of the newly industrialized countries of the East Asia rim, and anticipated growth of the Chinese economy will serve to broaden the basis for developing the self-defense capabilities of friendly regional countries. Out of these developments will likely emerge new subregional balances derived from economic competition and military developments. The United States is pursuing economic and security policies that tie our nation and those of the Asia/Pacific region more closely together while seeking to maintain peace and stability in the region. The long-term regional trends appear favorable from the perspective of the US and its regional allies.

THE MARITIME BALANCE

The United States depends on a favorable maritime balance to meet its strategic objectives in the regional balances discussed above. The assessment of the maritime balance that follows is based on such important determinants as fleet size, technology, geography, allies, and comparative maritime strategies.

Comparative Maritime Missions

United States national security strategy is founded on deterrence, forward defense, and collective security. The capability to deter aggression is fundamental to our defense plans and policy. Deterrence, in part, relies on forward-deployed combat-ready naval forces that operate in cooperation with allied and friendly navies and air forces. The presence of US naval forces in support of bilateral and multilateral security commitments around the world serves four objectives: first, defending the continental United States far from its shores; second, assuring US control of the sea lines of communication essential to support, reinforce and resupply US forces deployed overseas; third, promoting regional stability by acting as an element of regional power balances to deter Soviet coercion and adventurism; and fourth, functioning as a visible sign of America's capability to deal with crises and low-intensity conflicts on short notice nearly any place in the world.

The US Navy is structured, organized, manned, and equipped to deter and, when necessary, defeat aggression in concert with our allies and on favorable terms. If deterrence should fail, US strategy calls for an early ASW campaign against Soviet submarines and other supporting naval forces. US Navy strike capabilities would be available when needed.

Additionally, to help defend independent nations on the Soviet periphery, we must protect sea lines of communications (SLOCs) from America to Europe and Asia. The United States is a maritime nation, highly dependent on sea-borne trade and linked to Europe and Asia by tradition, commerce, and treaty. The US role in reinforcing our NATO allies makes the Atlantic SLOCs vital to the defense of Europe and the United States. The vastness of the Pacific and Indian Oceans makes the Asian rim countries almost entirely dependent upon sealift for commerce and naval and air forces for protection.

The Soviet Navy's chief wartime mission is to provide "combat stability" (i.e., protection) to Soviet strategic missile submarines so they can be used in attacks on US and theater targets; and to defend the Soviet homeland from enemy sea-based strike forces. The Soviet Navy would also support ground force operations in the land theaters of military operations. This includes conducting amphibious operations on the flanks of the land army, seizing key straits and choke points, and defending against amphibious assaults that threaten land operations. The interdiction of enemy SLOCs is a mission that has received attention in the Soviet Navy over the past two decades.

Operations and Force Structure

The missions of the Soviet and US navies are asymmetrical. This asymmetry has resulted in differences in

Many of the Soviet Northern and Pacific Ocean Fleets' homeports are icebound and some of their suspected wartime operating areas may be in or near Arctic waters. Thus, gaining a better appreciation for the Arctic environment is fundamental for effective allied naval operations, as above, and planning.

force structure, peacetime operations and training, and projected wartime operations of the superpowers and their allies.

During wartime, the Soviet Navy would seek to deny Western navies access to maritime regions from which nuclear or conventional strikes could be launched against either the Soviet homeland or Soviet strategic strike assets operating in protected "bastions." The Soviets intend to establish a "sea-denial" zone about 2,000 kilometers distant from the Soviet periphery in which they would conduct reconnaissance and surveillance operations and attack allied naval forces. Closer to the Soviet periphery, Soviet naval and air forces would conduct joint operations to deny access totally to allied naval forces, thereby creating the Soviet "sea-control" zone.

In conducting peacetime operations preparing for war, Soviet naval forces emphasize pier-side upkeep, and training and exercises in areas within "sea-denial" and "sea-control" zones. This training emphasis assures them an inherent capability to surge-deploy the majority of their naval forces in time of crisis to combat deployment stations close to the Soviet homeland. Because Soviet wartime operating areas are close to their main naval operating bases, the Soviets have not had the requirement to emulate the US Navy's at-sea replenishment capability. Even with the addition of larger and more capable "blue water" surface combatants, an expanded peacetime global presence mission, and expanded "sea-denial" defense zones, the Soviets' capability to conduct underway at-sea replenishment remains a low priority and is regarded as a weak point in the Soviet Navy.

One aspect of deterrence is to render the result of war so uncertain to the enemy that the risk of initiating war and the losses that would result from it become too great. In executing its maritime strategy, the United States Navy plans to conduct offensive operations in Soviet "sea-denial" and "sea-control" zones to impose high attrition on Soviet naval forces early in a conflict, thereby neutralizing their military capabilities, and assuring freedom of the seas to support US and allied military operations and control the critical SLOCs that link America to its allies and deployed forces.

During peacetime, the US Navy trains to maintain the capability to execute the maritime components of the national strategy. The Navy also enhances deterrence by forward-deploying and exercising naval forces in the missions and in the regions where they would be expected to fight. The great distances to many of these operating areas and forward bases dictate that US naval forces remain at sea for longer periods of time than Soviet naval forces. The US Navy's mobile logistics support capability and access to overseas bases permit US naval forces to operate independently over great distances for extended periods of time. Given their strategy, the Soviets do not require a comparable at-sea mobile logistics force. The US also relies on support from the formidable maritime forces of its allies, particularly the Western Europeans and the Japanese, to share certain mission responsibilities. These cooperative efforts enhance greatly its ability to execute naval operations both in peace and in war.

The Maritime Balance — Trends and Asymmetries

The submarine is the Soviet Navy's principal platform. The SSBN is the strategic offensive arm of the Soviet Navy, while attack (SS and SSN) and cruise missile (SSGN) submarines are its principal instruments to counter the allied submarine and surface threat in the Soviets' "sea-denial" and "sea-control" zones. The Soviet submarine force is supported by a modern surface fleet, long-range land-based Soviet Naval Aviation (SNA) bombers and strike aircraft, and Soviet Air Force (SAF) early warning, fighter/interceptor, and bomber aircraft.

The Soviet general purpose submarine force (torpedo attack, cruise missile, and auxiliary) is the world's largest, totaling some 300 active units. The Soviets continue modernizing their SSBN force and upgrading the quality of their new torpedo attack (both conventional diesel and nuclear) and cruise missile submarines. Soviet submarines are becoming quieter and thus slowly closing the acoustic edge maintained by the nearly 100 US attack submarines. The illegal transfer of advanced propeller construction technology from the West facilitates this process. Despite measurable improvements in the Soviet submarine force, however, the United States currently maintains an edge in ASW as well as superiority in open ocean acoustic surveillance and detection capability. A combination of seabed acoustic devices; surface ship towed arrays; a large force of US P-3 ORION ASW aircraft and supporting worldwide base structure; and carrier-based S-3 ASW aircraft, SH-2

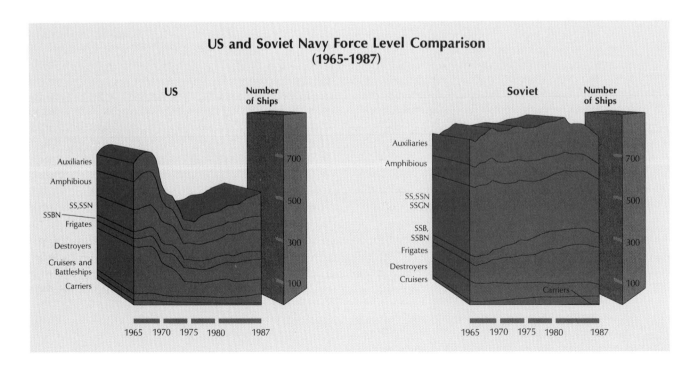

**US and Soviet Navy Force Level Comparison
(1965-1987)**

SEASPRITE, SH-3, and SH-60 SEAHAWK helicopters make potential adversaries' submarines vulnerable to US ASW forces. The Soviets cannot provide similar worldwide coverage.

Soviet surface ships and their supporting naval air arm are being modernized as well. While the Soviets continue to outnumber the United States in the total number of ships (including submarines), the United States has closed the gap during the 1980s due both to our naval ship building program and retirement of a significant number of Soviet diesel submarines and surface auxiliaries. Furthermore, the combined fleets of the United States and its NATO allies far exceed the Soviet and non-Soviet Warsaw Pact fleets in both the number and quality of major surface combatants.

Comparing the size of naval combatants, on the other hand, gives a qualitative comparison of relative warfare capability. These comparisons address displacement in terms of "Full Load Displacement" for surface ships and "Submerged Displacement" for submarines.

Because the US Navy has historically had global missions and presence, while the Soviets heretofore had not, the United States has traditionally built much bigger ships than the Soviets. Now, as the Soviet Navy has assumed a more global character, and especially as the new Soviet aircraft carriers enter service in the 1990s, it can be expected that, eventually, the disparity in the total Full Load Displacement of the Soviet and US navies will be narrowed. The qualitative improvements

found in the new and larger Soviet ships are their new and more sophisticated sensors and weapons, greater range and sea-keeping ability of the ships, greater ordnance load-outs, longer-range weapons, and image of superpower status in operations and port visits.

While the Soviet Navy lacks an at-sea replenishment capability comparable to the US Navy's, this deficiency should not be viewed as a significant impediment to Soviet naval operations since they have different objectives and a different strategy to achieve those objectives. Soviet wartime strategy has substantial elements of its navy positioned to defend SSBNs operating near homewaters, and thus near homeports. During both peacetime operations and in war, the Soviet Navy's limited replenishment capability is augmented by Soviet merchant vessels which are designed and configured to function as naval auxiliaries when needed. This type of support effort has proved capable of sustaining limited routine operations on a worldwide scale. The asymmetry in US and Soviet at-sea mobile logistics support, however, is particularly graphic during crises and in low-intensity conflicts distant from both the United States and the USSR. In such circumstances, the organic replenishment capabilities of the US Navy far outstrip those of the Soviet Navy.

Soviet naval power-projection capability is centered in the Soviet Naval Infantry (SNI). Organized to conduct amphibious landings to support the flanks of the land forces and to seize key objectives and strategic straits near the periphery of the Soviet landmass, this

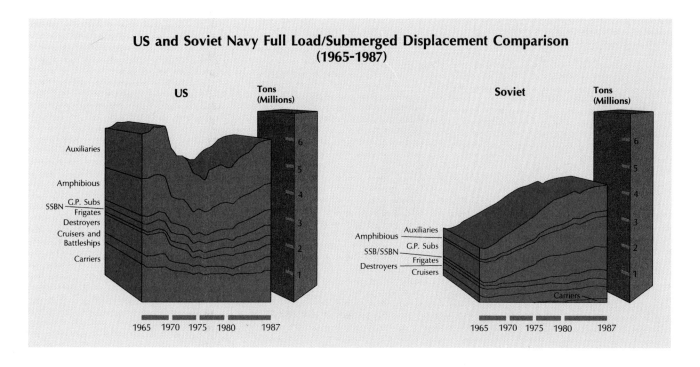

US and Soviet Navy Full Load/Submerged Displacement Comparison (1965-1987)

force is structured appropriately for its mission. Thus, the SNI lacks the US Marines' capability to seize territory at great distances from their homeland and to conduct sustained combat operations as an independent force. Amphibious ships of the two navies differ in number and size but are adequate for the assigned missions of the respective amphibious forces: the Soviets have a larger number of amphibious ships but smaller lift-capacity and overall less capability; the United States has fewer amphibious ships with far greater amphibious capability, greater lift-capacity, longer range, and far superior "blue water" sea-keeping ability. The Soviets, however, can call upon a large merchant fleet, many of whose ships are built to military specifications, to lift both men and heavy equipment.

The US fleet is built around the aircraft carrier and operates primarily in carrier battle groups (CVBG). The aircraft carrier, with its supporting cruisers, destroyers, frigates, submarines, and logistic support ships, is the US Navy's principal conventional deterrent, presence, and power-projection instrument. Carrier battle groups offer a diverse strike capability while providing antiair, antisubmarine, and antisurface ship defense-in-depth. The primary threats to the CVBG are antiship air-to-surface missiles fired from Soviet naval and air force bombers (BADGERS, BEARS, and BACKFIRES) and torpedoes and cruise missiles fired from submarines. The addition of AEGIS-Class antiair warfare cruisers, F/A-18 aircraft, and large numbers of conventional warhead TOMAHAWK and HARPOON antiship cruise

missiles on some submarines and aircraft and nearly all types of surface ships has augmented the capabilities of the US CVBG to counter these threats and compound the Soviets' targeting problem. The Soviet Navy today has no counterpart to the US carrier and its integrated fighting component, the CVBG. Large-deck Soviet carriers now under construction or fitting out may be integrated into the Soviet "sea-control" defense of the homeland strategy, probably to provide improved sea-based long-range tactical antiair capability for the protection of Soviet naval forces operating at sea.

Future Trends in the Maritime Balance

The United States and its allies currently enjoy an advantage over the Soviet Union in nearly all important areas comprising the maritime balance. These advantages however, may be reduced over time as the Soviets continue augmenting and improving their naval forces. By the mid-1990s, improved Soviet submarines and the more capable surface combatants now entering the Soviet fleet will comprise a significant percentage of the Soviet Navy as older units are retired. The US advantage in submarine quieting is being severely challenged by the Soviets and the allied margin of superiority is being narrowed. The US Navy's antiair capability will be increasingly challenged by improved antiship cruise missiles entering the Soviet inventory. The addition of AEGIS to the fleet, innovative antiair tactics and the proliferation of TOMAHAWK and HARPOON missiles will maintain a credible capability

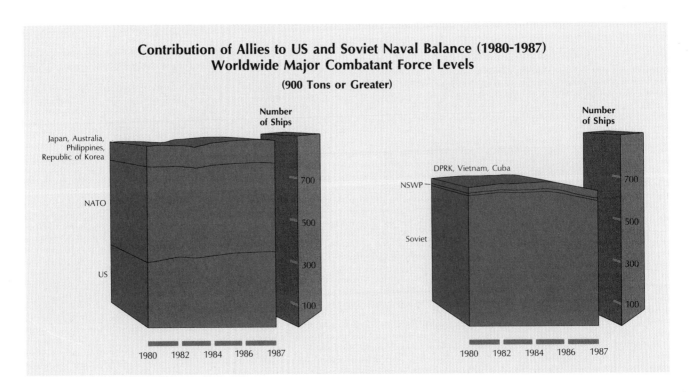

Contribution of Allies to US and Soviet Naval Balance (1980-1987)
Worldwide Major Combatant Force Levels
(900 Tons or Greater)

to counter Soviet cruise missile firing platforms and missiles targeted on US Navy ships. The extent of the Soviet "sea-denial" zones will test US strategy but will also complicate Soviet reconnaissance and surveillance capabilities. The United States will retain significant advantages over the Soviets in tactical sea-based air power, long-range power projection, sustainability at sea, surveillance and reconnaissance, and in its ability to operate and maintain the new and more sophisticated ships entering the inventory.

THE POWER PROJECTION BALANCE

Historically, the Soviet Union's primary power projection mission has been to project military forces to contiguous areas on the Eurasian landmass. To counter the Soviet capability to threaten the independent nations of Eurasia, the United States must move its forces great distances, and so has developed superior long-range power projection capabilities. Thus, one aspect of the power projection balance juxtaposes Soviet short-range power projection against US distant power projection capabilities. For contingencies on the Soviet Union's immediate periphery, the power projection balance has grown increasingly favorable to the Soviet Union.

As Soviet ambitions have expanded beyond Eurasia, and as Moscow has sought to expand its influence and access worldwide, it has become necessary to compare US and Soviet capabilities to project power over long distances. Because long-distance power projection has been a more fundamental and enduring mission for the United States, it is generally better postured than the Soviet Union for any conflict far from both countries. The Soviets, however, have made some progress in overcoming those disadvantages, and have found ways to minimize their disadvantages by using indirect instruments like arms transfers, military advisors, and proxy forces to project power.

Power Projection Near the Soviet Union

US airlift and sealift capabilities for major contingencies on the Soviet Union's periphery have grown less rapidly than the Soviet forces that could invade neighboring states. The United States' ability to deploy men and equipment to those areas has been enhanced by the addition of the KC-10 aerial refueling tanker fleet, increased prepositioning of assets, and a change in operational style of warfare. The acquisition of the KC-10 airlift/tanker aircraft and modifications to the KC-135 fleet provided significant boosts to the US ability to project tactical air power. Since 1980, the introduction of the C-5B, modification of the C-141A to make it refuelable in flight, stretching of the

C-141B, enhancements to the Civil Reserve Air Fleet (CRAF), and improved spare parts availability have raised our airlift capability over 50 percent. The nine maritime prepositioning ships now enable LANTCOM, PACOM, and CENTCOM to support more effectively deployments in the Atlantic, Pacific, and Indian Oceans respectively. Furthermore, the Army's light divisions have improved ability to deploy rapidly, although these divisions have relatively little organic firepower when compared to other US ground forces.

For contingencies requiring projection of military power adjacent to the Soviet Union, the Soviets can deploy more powerful forces and equipment by land much more rapidly and in greater numbers than the United States can deploy with airlift, sealift, and prepositioning forces. Nevertheless, the Soviets have, since 1980, improved their airlift and amphibious lift capabilities. For example, the introduction of the An-124/CONDOR and the Il-76/CANDID transport aircraft has improved significantly the Soviets' ability to move troops and equipment rapidly, not only to contiguous areas, but over extended distances as well. Since 1980, Moscow has increased its amphibious lift, mainly through a 50 percent increase of its air cushion vehicle force and through the addition of more capable amphibious ships. The concurrent growth in Soviet Naval Infantry, however, has resulted in an amphibious lift capability of about 65 percent of overall requirements. Furthermore, while the Soviets lead the world in air cushion vehicle (ACV) technology and their military ACV fleet is the world's largest, they are continuing to pursue new technologies. As an example, they are expected to deploy operationally the first of a new class of "wing-in-ground-effect" (WIG) craft for which there is no US counterpart. If Soviet WIG craft are being built as amphibious transports, the speed and range of these units could provide the means for a relatively small (regimental perhaps), but rapid deployment of forces and their organic air defense — for example, across the Black Sea into Turkey — circumventing local NATO air defense forces. In conclusion, these airlift and amphibious assets are not as effective as their US counterparts at long distance power projection. Nevertheless, they present a formidable increase in capability for the Soviets over short distances and thereby increase the threat to the nations on the Soviet periphery.

Long-Range Power Projection: US and Soviet Forces

For contingencies at great distances from both countries, US power projection forces remain generally superior to those of the Soviet Union. Soviet capabilities for projecting influence at greater distances from the Soviet

SOVIET GLOBAL POWER PROJECTION

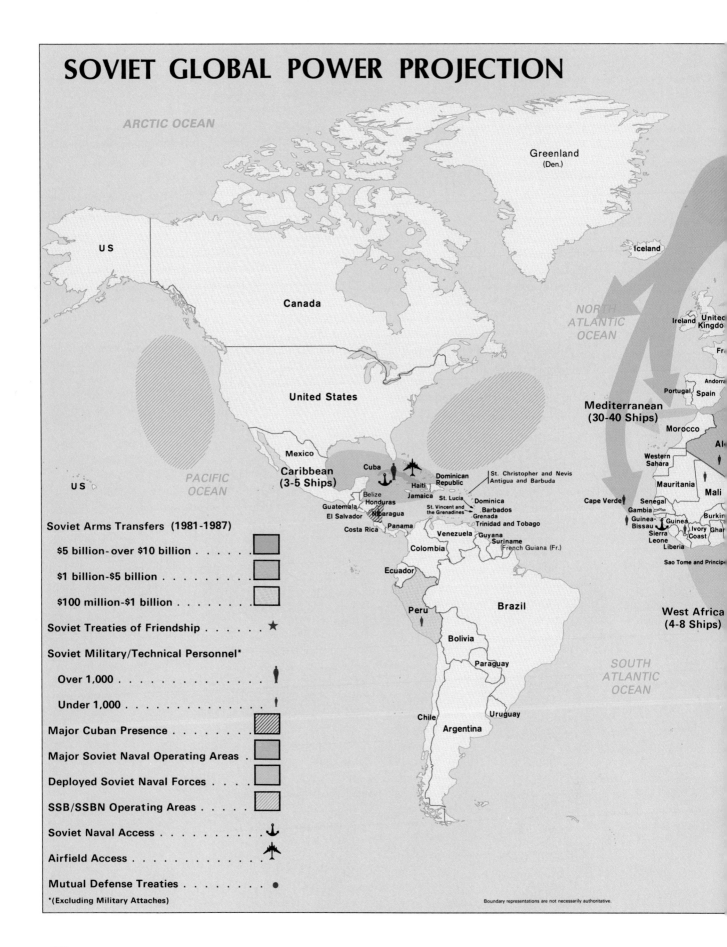

Soviet Arms Transfers (1981-1987)

$5 billion- over $10 billion . . . . . .

$1 billion-$5 billion . . . .

$100 million-$1 billion . . . .

Soviet Treaties of Friendship . . . . . . ★

Soviet Military/Technical Personnel*

Over 1,000 . . . .

Under 1,000 . . . .

Major Cuban Presence . . . .

Major Soviet Naval Operating Areas .

Deployed Soviet Naval Forces . . . .

SSB/SSBN Operating Areas . . . . .

Soviet Naval Access . . . . ⚓

Airfield Access . . . . ✈

Mutual Defense Treaties . . . . ●

*(Excluding Military Attaches)

Boundary representations are not necessarily authoritative.

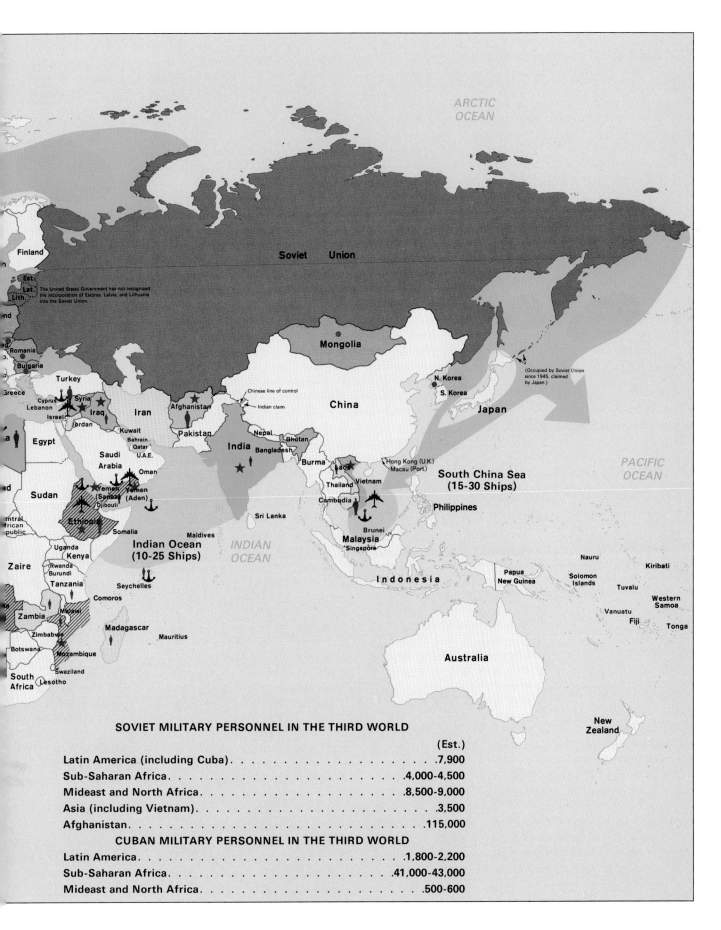

ARCTIC OCEAN

Finland

Est.
Lat.
Lith.

The United States Government has not recognized
the incorporation of Estonia, Latvia, and Lithuania
into the Soviet Union.

Soviet Union

Romania

Bulgaria

Turkey

Greece

Cyprus
Lebanon
Israel
Jordan

Syria

Iraq

Iran

Kuwait

Bahrain
Qatar
U.A.E.

Egypt

Saudi
Arabia

Oman

Sudan

Yemen
(Sanaa)
Djibouti

Yemen
(Aden)

Ethiopia

Somalia

Afghanistan

Pakistan

Nepal

India

Bangladesh

Bhutan

Burma

Mongolia

Chinese line of control

Indian claim

China

N. Korea

S. Korea

Japan

(Occupied by Soviet Union
since 1945, claimed
by Japan.)

PACIFIC
OCEAN

Laos

Hong Kong (U.K.)
Macau (Port.)

South China Sea
(15-30 Ships)

Thailand

Vietnam

Cambodia

Philippines

Sri Lanka

Maldives

Brunei

Malaysia

Singapore

Indonesia

Nauru

Papua
New Guinea

Solomon
Islands

Kiribati

Tuvalu

Western
Samoa

Vanuatu

Fiji

Tonga

Central
African
Republic

Zaire

Uganda
Kenya

Rwanda
Burundi

Tanzania

Indian Ocean
(10-25 Ships)

INDIAN
OCEAN

Seychelles

Comoros

Zambia

Malawi

Madagascar

Mauritius

Zimbabwe

Botswana

Mozambique

Swaziland

South
Africa

Lesotho

Australia

New
Zealand

SOVIET MILITARY PERSONNEL IN THE THIRD WORLD

	(Est.)
Latin America (including Cuba)	7,900
Sub-Saharan Africa	4,000-4,500
Mideast and North Africa	8,500-9,000
Asia (including Vietnam)	3,500
Afghanistan	115,000

CUBAN MILITARY PERSONNEL IN THE THIRD WORLD

Latin America	1,800-2,200
Sub-Saharan Africa	41,000-43,000
Mideast and North Africa	500-600

The Soviets have been investigating Wing-in-Ground effect vehicles for more than two decades. This UTKA-Class vehicle, now under development, carries surface-to-surface missiles. When operational it will significantly enhance Soviet coastal defense and sea control capabilities in the seas near the Soviet Union.

Union, however, have been improving over time with the development of their airlift capacity, amphibious shipping assets, and basing infrastructure. Nevertheless, without vast improvements in ASW and deployed air defense capabilities, a realistic force projection capability at great distance from the USSR is unlikely.

US aircraft carrier battle groups and Marine Corps units are capable of fighting intense battles independently, out of range of support forces based in the United States. While the Soviet Navy would have limited ability to counter US carrier battle groups without the support of their land-based aircraft assets, their capabilities in this area, especially ship- and submarine-launched antiship missiles, are increasing. Indeed, Soviet deployable naval tactical aircraft have increased by 50 percent in the last 10 years. Furthermore, the eventual deployment of the Soviet Union's first large aircraft carrier, which may carry either conventional or vertical takeoff aircraft, will further enhance the Soviet Navy's capabilities. While the aircraft carrier's primary role may be one of bastion defense and sea control, it could have the flexibility to provide, for the first time, sea-based tactical air support for Soviet power projection against limited opposition.

Soviet amphibious forces have also grown somewhat, but remain far smaller than the US Marine Corps

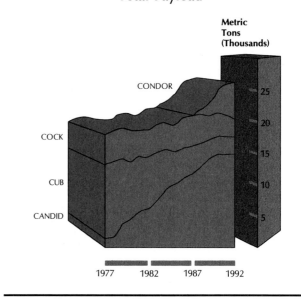

**Military Transport Aircraft
Total Payload**

134

IVAN ROGOV is the first Soviet amphibious assault ship class with a helicopter deck. Its introduction in 1978 fueled speculation that the Soviet Navy was about to expand substantially its amphibious warfare capabilities. A decade later only two ships of this class have been built.

INZHENER YERMOSHKIN is one of four units of the Soviet-built KAPITAN SMIRNOV-Class roll-on/roll-off ships. These 20,000 deadweight ton ships are the fastest ships in the Soviet Merchant fleet. Powered by two gas turbines, they have a crusing speed of 25 knots.

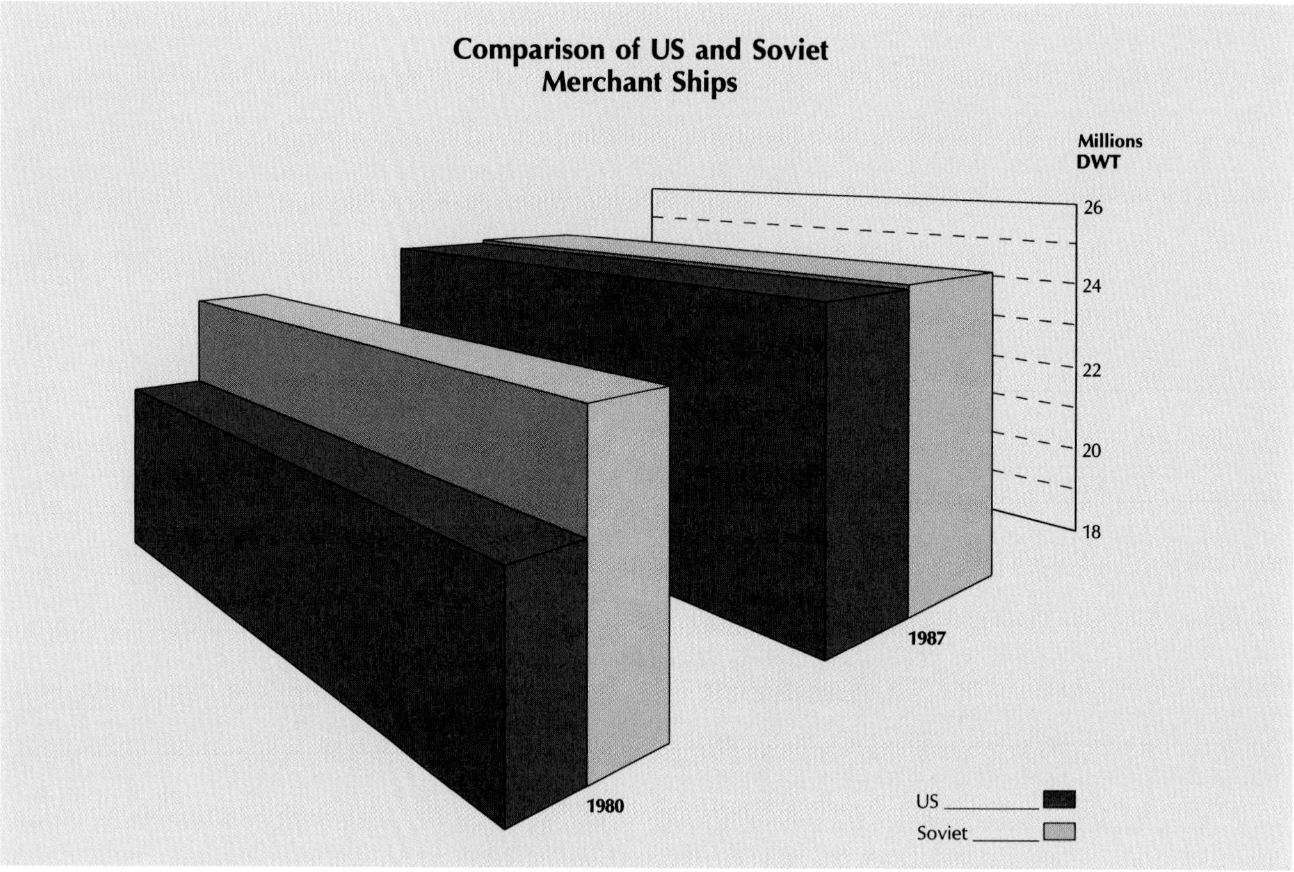
Comparison of US and Soviet Merchant Ships
Millions DWT
26
24
22
20
18
1987
1980
US
Soviet

(approximately 18,000 vs. 198,000 personnel). Soviet amphibious capabilities have increased with the introduction of ships of greater size and endurance; there has also been an increase in the number of air cushion landing craft. The Soviet ROPUCHA-Class LST is configured as a roll-on/roll-off (RO/RO) ship, facilitating rapid on-loading and off-loading. The IVAN ROGOV LPD, launched in the late 1970s, is capable of sustained long-distance operations and is equipped with a command and communications suite that enhances its capabilities as a command vessel. The advent of these two ship classes (ROPUCHA and ROGOV) provides the Soviet Navy with an increased, although still limited, long range amphibious assault capability.

The United States' amphibious assault capability, however, remains superior to the Soviets in quality and endurance. Only two of the IVAN ROGOV-Class, the largest Soviet amphibious ship, are currently operational and they are smaller than most US amphibious ships. Thus, the United States maintains a significant advantage in total lift and assault troop capacity. US amphibious assault capability has been further improved with the recent addition of six air cushion vehicles (LCAC). Combined with the added lift of US new LSD-41-Class ships, LCACs greatly enhance the speed, mobility, and diversity of amphibious assault forces. Until their introduction, only about 17 percent of the world's beaches could be assaulted with conventional craft. That area is now increased to an estimated 70 percent.

Another means of power projection is by air. The USSR has seven active airborne divisions whereas the United States has one. While the Soviets have made improvements in their longer range (over 18,000 nm) airlift capabilities, they are currently limited in the ability to project power to great distances. Since 1981, the Soviets have augmented their lift capability by 72 percent. This trend is a result of the new Soviet An-124/CONDOR heavy transport coming into service, and the replacement of the An-12/CUB by the Il-76/CANDID long-range transport. Furthermore, the Soviets maintain a close integration between civil and military air transport. Virtually all of their civil air transport can be diverted to military use while only a small part of US civil air transport can be so diverted. One impending improvement on the US side will be the introduction of the new long-range C-17, which will be able to deliver forces over intercontinental distances directly to austere forward locations, mitigating the need for additional intratheater lift.

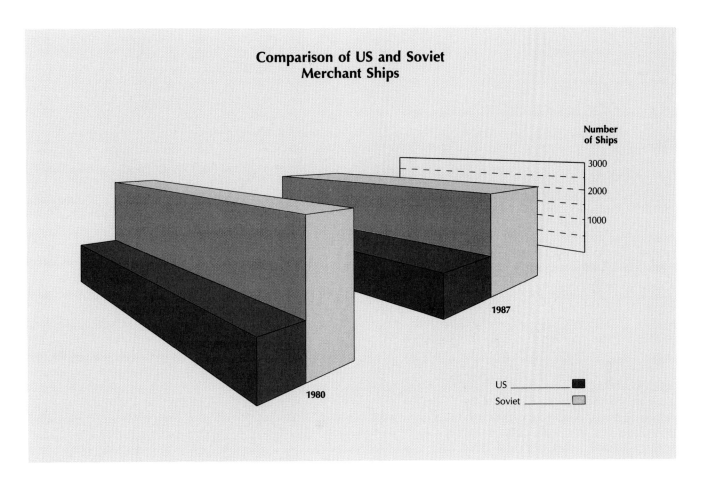

Comparison of US and Soviet Merchant Ships

Number of Ships

3000

2000

1000

1987

1980

US

Soviet

While the Soviets are capable of inserting forces and providing them with airlift support, their in-flight refueling tanker aircraft are few in number and their airlift forces are, for the most part, incapable of refueling in flight and lack overwater and night flying experience. Moreover, crew and maintenance manning of Soviet long-range transport aviation is insufficient to support continued operations at high levels of activity. Consequently, Soviet strategic airlift forces are, to a large extent, still dependent on assistance originating from bases in the Soviet Union or from bases provided by client states. On the other hand, the superior ability of the United States to refuel aircraft in flight greatly enhances the capability to transport troops and equipment to any contingency.

The Soviet merchant marine fleet has grown steadily during the past seven years. The US merchant fleet has declined in numbers and has focused on container ship capacity — which cannot easily be used to transport combat equipment — and on large crude carriers — which cannot easily transport refined petroleum products. While dead weight tonnage is essentially equal, the Soviets retain an advantage in numbers and militarily useful types of merchant ships. This numerical disparity exemplifies the important differences

between the respective commercial fleets. Unlike its US counterpart, the Soviet merchant fleet is built primarily with military uses in mind and performs various military missions, including support for sealift, at-sea refueling of combatants, and transporting arms to Third World countries. Where the US merchant marine emphasis has been to build large ships capable of carrying containers, the Soviets have emphasized smaller merchant ships that can dock at small Third World ports and be loaded and unloaded quickly. Indeed, the Soviet Merchant Marine now has the capability to lift five motorized rifle divisions at one time. The Soviets also appear to be experimenting with vertical take-off and landing (VTOL) aircraft (FORGERS) from specially configured RO/RO ships, an approach used by the British in the Falklands.

Indirect Means of Power Projection

In any direct confrontation, US power projection forces maintain a significant advantage over Soviet power-projection forces operating out of range of forces based in the Soviet Union. Soviet strategy for the Third World has managed to compensate for this imbalance by avoiding direct confrontations with US forces, relying instead on Cuban and non-Soviet Warsaw Pact (NSWP)

The Soviets used the passenger ship *ADMIRAL NAKIMOV* to shuttle Cuban troops from Cuba to Angola and between Angola and Ethiopia. In October 1986, the 51-year old ship sank after a collision in the Black Sea while on a domestic run. Nearly 500 lives were lost.

proxies, arms sales, direct and indirect aid to insurgents, and covert action.

Moscow is systematically developing Cuban and Nicaraguan military capabilities. For example, Cuba, supplied with Soviet arms and trained by Soviet advisors, has more than 41,000 troops in Africa. Cuba today has active duty armed forces numbering more than 162,000 men, with more than 1,000 tanks, 130 modern combat aircraft, including MiG-21s and MiG-23s, and large inventories of other modern combat equipment. Nicaragua has active-duty armed forces numbering 80,000 men, 150 tanks, 56 helicopters, including 12 Mi-24/HIND D helicopters, and 250 armored vehicles. The Sandinistas plan in the next decade to expand their armed forces to 600,000 men, introduce new systems such as the MiG-21, and add significantly to inventories of current weapons systems.

Thus far, Soviet forces have been directly involved only where US action was not anticipated, and only in large numbers on the immediate Soviet periphery. By using an indirect approach in other cases, the Soviets have supported communist or other friendly governments against internal resistance, maintained their own influence with these governments, and supported insurgents against pro-Western governments with little risk of confrontation or strong resistance from the West that the direct employment of troops might provoke. These policies can also result in arrangements that enhance the Soviets' own military power. For example, in the Western Hemisphere, the Soviets already have access to Cuban military facilities. Soviet surface combatants call at Cuban ports; Soviet long-range reconnaissance and ASW aircraft use Cuban airfields; and the Soviets operate communications intercept facilities in Cuba. Nicaraguan facilities are being upgraded, although the

Soviets at present do not have access to them. The Nicaraguan port at Corinto can handle KIEV-Class aircraft carriers and nuclear submarines, while the airfield at Punta Huete can accommodate any aircraft in the Soviet inventory. Because large amounts of US military equipment would move from Gulf Coast ports, use of Cuban and Nicaraguan facilities by forward-deployed Soviet forces to threaten US sea lines of communication in the Gulf of Mexico, Caribbean Sea, and Panama Canal would complicate US defense planning for contingencies or conflicts in Europe and the Persian Gulf, and force the United States to divert resources from other areas.

United States' policies to counter Soviet indirect power projection efforts include providing economic and security assistance to threatened countries, and supporting selected anticommunist resistance movements in countries where Soviet-backed dictatorships have been installed but have not yet gained complete control. In recent years, the success of these efforts to resist Soviet imperialism has been mixed. For example, US support has been quite successful in defending democracy in El Salvador against an insurgency supported by Cuba and Nicaragua. Limited assistance for anticommunist forces in Angola and Afghanistan has helped local forces prevent the consolidation of, but has not yet dislodged, communist power in those countries.

Many clients or proxies of the Soviet Union are highly militarized states — i.e., North Korea, Vietnam, Cuba, Syria, Ethiopia, and Nicaragua. Arms deliveries to these countries and others make the Soviet Union the principal arms exporter to the Third World. In 1987 alone Moscow delivered $21 billion of military materiel to over 30 nations. One expression of the influence gained by arms shipments is the number of military advisors the Soviet Union stations in these countries. Today, there are more Soviet military advisors in Latin America (including Cuba) and Africa than the United States has throughout the world.

Soviet indirect power projection has had a number of successes, but also incurs fairly high costs (although hard currency earnings from arms sales offset some of these costs). The Soviets also face difficulties in some areas where local resistance is strong. For example, Cuban troops in Africa defending Angola's pro-Soviet regimes against insurgents constitute a financial drain on Moscow. Furthermore, the Soviet requirement for Angola to offset partially Cuban and Soviet expenses in Angola has devastated the Angolan economy. Nevertheless, despite their long-term presence, Cubans and Soviets in Angola have not succeeded in cementing the authority of their local client.

Aeroflot, the Soviet national airline, affords Moscow a legitimate means to project Soviet influence in distant areas. The airline's assets, like the Il-76/CANDID shown, are also immediately available to support Soviet power projection or actual combat operations.

The Role of Overseas Bases

The United States relies on a network of overseas bases to project power and support its forward-deployed forces. This base structure has tended to shrink over time, partly from considerations of efficiency, but also due to political changes that have deprived the US access to South Yemen, Libya, Ethiopia, Iran, and Vietnam. In addition to the base negotiations recently concluded in Spain, over the next decade the US will renegotiate its basing agreements in Greece, Portugal, and the Philippines. These bases, due to their location, will remain vital to US national interests.

Although the Soviets may consider bases contiguous or linked by land lines to the Soviet Union extremely important, operating bases outside their immediate periphery historically probably have not seen as essential. The Soviets have tended to employ mostly movable or "removable" assets (e.g., floating piers, tenders, and repair ships; and floating dry-docks) to support an overseas military presence. Generally, the Soviets have been reluctant to invest large sums of money, only to be asked to leave, as has happened in Somalia and Egypt. However, the construction of permanent facilities under way at Cam Ranh Bay, Vietnam, may signal a change in Soviet basing policy.

Future Trends in Power Projection

The relative power of the Soviet Union in areas adjacent to its own borders is expected to grow. For the near future, Soviet distant power-projection capabilities will consist mostly of those merchant and airlift forces capable of operating in a relatively benign environment. Consequently, the Soviets may well continue relying heavily on client states and arms transfers to achieve their objectives.

CHAPTER VIII

Research and Development: The Technological Competition

The application of technology to weaponry is a critical element affecting the specific capabilities of military forces, as well as the larger balance of power between nations. A specific example is the development of the atomic bomb, first by the United States in 1945 and subsequently by the Soviet Union in 1949. Since then, technological advances applied to armaments have had varying, but often significant, effects that threatened the equilibrium of the military balance.

As part of the United States' deterrent strategy, it relies heavily on technological rather than numerical superiority. Its strong technological position has always balanced sheer Soviet numerical advantages and thereby added to deterrence. It has enjoyed technological superiority not only because investments were made directly in research and development (R&D) for national security purposes but also because major technological advances have resulted from government and industry investments in R&D for other purposes as well. If the United States is to take full advantage of its technological strengths as well as exploit Soviet vulnerabilities, it must strengthen cooperation between the private sector, its great centers of learning, and its defense establishment, so that the West's broader technological and industrial base is more thoroughly incorporated into the military sector.

The Soviets are clearly committed to dedicating the R&D resources necessary to improve their weaponry. Indeed, the technological advantages in military capabilities now enjoyed by the West have been threatened, if not eroded. To protect this lead, the West must exploit its technological advantages. Yet these advantages are themselves temporary and can be quickly offset or negated. If the Soviets sustain their concerted efforts, they will eventually have high-technology weapons in areas where they currently lack them. If they seize the initiative and continue to reduce the West's technological advantages, the United States and its allies will be forced to expend even greater resources, or accept greater risks to collective security.

Because of the Reagan Administration's commitment to rebuild US military capability, US procurement expenditures for 1987 are now about 32 percent greater than comparably defined Soviet procurement. However, the Soviets' cumulative defense R&D expenditures have exceeded those of the United States, and as a result of US budgetary constraints, future Soviet R&D investment is expected to grow at rates exceeding US R&D defense investment.

It is imperative, therefore, that the United States invest wisely to maintain its technological advantages. As part of this effort, it seeks to adopt competitive strategies in collaboration with its allies, which will help overcome Soviet numerical advantages, and make Soviet initiatives in technological competition more costly to them. For example, US advantages in low-observable aircraft technology being applied to the US B-2 bomber can cause the Soviets to divert resources from offensive weaponry to defensive systems to counter the problems posed by US "stealth" capabilities. Thus, in the continuing competition for technological supremacy, it is necessary that the United States create strategies that align enduring American strengths against enduring Soviet weaknesses.

Identification of those areas where potential US advantages can be brought to bear with the greatest effect is possible through systematic evaluation of American strengths and Soviet vulnerabilities while appropriately considering the potential impact of trends in technology. In so doing, US competitive strategies seek to enhance deterrence by highlighting new technology efforts that could render obsolete significant components of Soviet warfighting doctrine, equipment, or force structure.

But competition between the Soviet Union and the United States is not purely technological. Technology is but one factor, albeit a major one, that comprises the long-term competition and must be considered in conjunction with the fiscal, quantitative, and qualitative aspects of other factors such as affordability, strategy, doctrine, training, manning, size, and organization of forces. New technologies must be applied to military systems in a cost-effective manner. Sufficient numbers of these new systems must be fielded to make a difference, and they must be sustainable in the rigors of combat. Most importantly, the operating forces of the military must integrate new, advanced systems into

The new SL-X-17 ENERGIYA rocket enables the Soviets to launch their space shuttle or other heavy payloads. This system, which has a payload far larger than any equivalent US space system, also gives the Soviets the capability to orbit large space-based battle stations, directed-energy antisatellite (ASAT) systems or the space-based components of their strategic defense system.

their force structure and devise new tactics and new concepts of operation for the most militarily effective means of employing those systems — all in the face of the interactive challenge of an adversary fielding analogous systems and countermeasures. Thus, pure technology does not, in and of itself, revise any of the military balances previously described. Rather, it is how well technology is applied, and how thoroughly its contributions to military operations are absorbed by those who use that technology, that have the greatest impact upon the military balance.

THE SOVIET CHALLENGE

As part of his plan to restructure the Soviet economy, General Secretary Gorbachev has required that the Soviet industrial base be revitalized. A modernized, vital Soviet industrial base could, in addition to providing high-quality consumer goods, enable Soviet industry to develop the new technologies required for future military competition against the West. In speeches and policy statements, the General Secretary is exhorting the highest levels of the government to accelerate Soviet science and technology initiatives, and to challenge world technological standards.

Although Soviet defense R&D investments exceed those of the US, they have not drawn ahead of the US due to their problems with productivity. A serious concern for future US security is the intensive Soviet effort to improve the quality and productivity of their already extensive science and technology base. Although the current Soviet technology base (with some noteworthy exceptions) is not as advanced as that of the West, their exceptional engineering of inferior or state-of-the-art technology into well-designed weapon systems, with capabilities matching or even exceeding Western counterparts, is impressive indeed. As a result, the United States and its allies face an adversary that is systematically investing substantially more of its gross national product in the development, production, and fielding of large numbers of highly capable weapon systems — in a bid to overtake the West and set the course of the military competition.

Historically, the Soviets have looked to adapt or exploit Western technologies for their own purposes. While the Soviets are not exclusively dependent on Western technology to upgrade their military systems, they are deriving major benefits from applications of Western technology. Although the Soviets have, in the past, relied more on quantitative production to achieve military superiority, they are now emphasizing the acquisition of advanced technology to produce and deploy high-quality weapon systems and narrow the West's lead.

Indeed, numerous Soviet military projects are being improved with advanced technology that has been acquired from the West. Innovation, higher levels of research, accelerated development of sophisticated weapons, avoidance of errors, and reduced costs are among the benefits that the Soviets are realizing. Although much of the technology acquired from the West has been gained through entirely legal means, the Soviets are gathering significant amounts of information through surreptitious and illegal means. As a result of aggressive exploitation and pursuit of technology wherever available, the Soviets are rapidly achieving higher levels of capability within their military forces with a consequent impact upon the military balance.

Continued erosion of the West's lead in technology underscores the importance of preventing additional illegal Soviet technology acquisitions. By illegally acquiring technology, the Soviets are able to forgo the substantial investment costs in basic and applied research and development. They are also able to keep pace with those technologies that might alter the character of

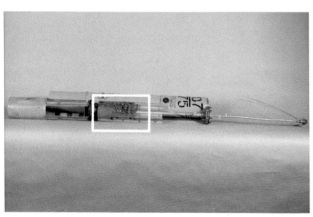

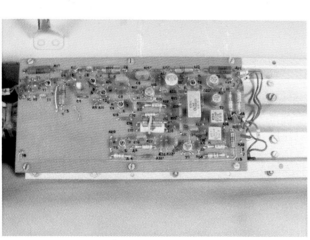

This Soviet Type-75 sonobuoy is used to detect submarines. It has many features copied from the US SSQ-41B sonobuoy.

This infrared seeker from the Soviet AA-2D/ATOLL air-to-air missile was copied from the US AIM-9D SIDEWINDER.

conflict and thereby represent a greater threat to them. For example, the illegal Soviet acquisition of sophisticated machinery for producing quiet-running propellers illustrates the impact that technology acquisition and espionage can have on the West's collective security. The Soviets spent less than $25 million to acquire this technology, a small price to pay for a capability to make their submarines much harder to detect.

Since further progress in many key areas of warfighting capability is dependent upon microelectronics and computers, the Soviets have made acquisition of this technology a high-priority target. Nearly half the illegal technology trade diversions fall into these categories. The USSR has acquired several thousand pieces of major microelectronics fabrication equipment through unscrupulous Western traders. These traders employ false licenses, deceptive equipment descriptions, dummy firms, false end-users for illegal purchasing, and smuggling of high-technology items. Their continued success in acquiring computer hardware and software technology threatens the West's lead in this critical area.

TRENDS IN KEY TECHNOLOGIES

Although the Soviet Union is narrowing the technological gap, the United States and its allies maintain the technological lead. This lead will continue to diminish, however, unless the US maintains strong safeguards against the Soviets' sophisticated efforts to acquire technology.

Selected trends in basic technology, where advances could significantly change both Soviet and American warfighting capability in the next 20 years, are presented below.

Aerodynamics — The Soviet military aircraft industry is reaping the benefits of a technological revolution. Soviet researchers are supported by large aerodynamic test facilities that are well-equipped and very sophisticated. Large investments in aerodynamics research, combined with one of the world's largest wind tunnels, have enabled the Soviets to develop aerospace systems that are increasingly competitive with Western coun-

Soviet Flight Research Institute near Moscow is the primary location for testing the BLACKJACK bomber and the Soviet space shuttle.

terparts. As a result, new Soviet military aircraft are significantly more capable and incorporate much more sophisticated electronic subsystems and armaments than their predecessors.

Although the most important aerodynamic principles were developed first in the Free World, the Soviets have demonstrated a capability to mimic Western efforts rapidly and, at times, to engineer new technology into fielded weapons before the West. The United States, however, maintains an advantage in aerodynamic computational capabilities and in state-of-the-art research as represented in the Advanced Tactical Fighter and National Aerospace Plane programs.

Biochemical Technology — The Soviets have achieved considerable progress in biological technologies such as genetic engineering. They may now be developing a new generation of chemical and biological warfare agents using this technology. The extensive Soviet

The US recently evaluated laser lethality against a ballistic missile system in a test of some SDI components. The laser used was a large chemical laser, MIRACL (Mid-Infrared Advanced Chemical Laser), which then was the most powerful continuous laser outside the Soviet Union.

fermentation capacity enables them to produce a large variety and quantity of pharmaceuticals, foods, and food supplements which had previously been imported from the West. Their R&D efforts are directed toward a wide array of biochemical disciplines, including those to solve operational and logistics problems. Current Soviet plans and policies concerning biochemical technology clearly indicate that they have short-term, mid-term, and long-term goals that have both military and civilian implications.

The United States currently has a significant biochemical technology lead over the Soviets in areas of basic research. New materials and sensors, developed as a result of biochemical exploitation, could provide significant advancements for a number of critical mission and operational needs. These include polymers for materiel applications such as new adhesives and lightweight high-strength composites, and operational applications such as antisubmarine warfare and hydrodynamic drag reduction. Other applications of biochemical technology such as non-toxic biodegradable solvents, cleaners, and detoxifiers, as well as electronic applications for optical storage devices, are possible. Detector systems capable of "all agent" detection would provide a revolutionary capability for protecting US forces from chemical and biological attack. Enhanced computer memory and optical microswitches using biochemical technology would significantly improve US weapon systems.

Computers/Software — Improvements in computing capability remain the Soviets' most pressing technological requirement. The Soviets are establishing computer studies in their schools nationwide to generate an "army of programmers." Although the Soviets have a solid understanding of basic principles, especially mathematics, they have encountered problems in applying this knowledge to computer production. Gorbachev's "perestroika" program is designed to remedy this problem and enable the accelerated production and application of computers which are critical to further breakthroughs in the military-industrial sector.

United States application of computing and information processing technologies will continue playing a pivotal role in increasing the performance of military equipment. Exploitation of advances in artificial intelligence is also expected to reduce costs, increase performance, and improve the reliability of software, thereby enhancing the overall reliability of US systems.

The United States also leads in the use of computer technology for simulation and modeling for combat-skills training. Some of the advanced technologies being developed and applied to make military training both more effective and affordable include computerized instruction systems; electroluminescent color displays; teleconferencing; fiber-optic and miniaturized cathode-ray tube, helmet-mounted displays; computer-generated imagery; and electronic networking. Exploiting new advances in these technologies could increase this lead further and provide the capability to generate high levels of combat skill, readiness, and operational expertise during peacetime.

Directed Energy — The West has a multifaceted Directed-Energy Program involving lasers, microwaves, and particle beams for both strategic and tactical missions. While the West has a lead in high average power, continuous-wave lasers, the Soviets have a lead in pulsed laser, radio-frequency, and charged particle beam directed-energy sources. Both sides are working intensively to harden space vehicles against laser attack, and the electromagnetic pulses produced by nuclear weapons.

Lasers — The Soviets have a very large, well-funded program to develop strategic and tactical laser weapons. Laser technology in the United States and the Soviet Union is generally comparable; however, the United States has emphasized development of advanced laser types for strategic defense applications.

The Soviets, on the other hand, have put greater effort into developing less complex prototype lasers and test articles that can more readily be employed in weapon applications. The Soviets have invested much more substantially in laser development and test ranges than the United States and employ more than 10,000 scientists and engineers in advanced R&D efforts.

Soviet scientists have achieved impressive results with gas-dynamic, electric discharge, and chemical lasers — and are working on several other types as well. They have built high-energy, multi-megawatt class laser devices with an emphasis on weapons application. They

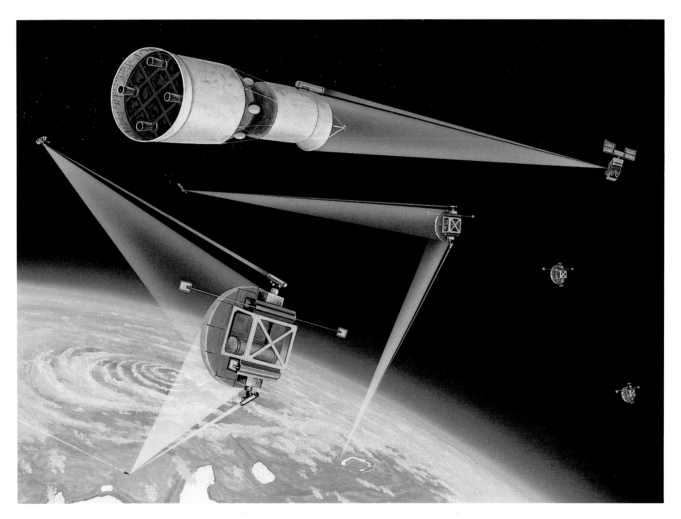

If technological developments prove successful, the Soviets might be able to deploy space-based laser systems for defense against ballistic missiles sometime after the year 2000.

have developed large pulsed lasers and have conducted numerous high-energy single-pulse materials interaction experiments.

In innovative directed-energy weapons concepts such as free-electron lasers, which have been vigorously pursued by the West, the Soviets are slightly behind. Although the Soviets lag to a degree in these rapidly changing areas, most of the advanced directed-energy weapons concepts in vogue in the West were advanced by the Soviets at least a decade earlier. In this regard, the Soviets have a broad basis for a complete understanding of directed-energy technology, both in theory and in practical military application. Accordingly, the Soviets have chosen to focus on examining electric-discharge and gas-dynamic lasers and have accumulated much more test data in order to realize actual military applications before the West.

The Soviets are using their technological capability to move toward rapid deployment of low-power laser weapons with their military forces. Their tactical laser program has progressed to where battlefield laser weapons could soon be deployed. Due to the serious nature of this threat, the United States is investigating an array of research efforts for developing defenses against Soviet lasers. Operational Soviet ground-based lasers for defense against ballistic missiles probably will not be deployed until after the year 2000.

Particle Beam — Soviet research in technologies applicable to particle beam weapons is extensive, and military support for this research has been evident since the early 1960s. Many of the accelerator technologies for particle beams were invented by the Soviets. Soviet work in certain critical technologies such as powerful accelerators is state of the art.

Radio Frequency — Many of the world's high power radio frequency (RF) and high power microwave (HPM) sources were developed by the Soviets and they lead the West in this area. The West, however, is seeking to match Soviet capabilities and is making progress on many new types of RF and HPM sources. Recent Soviet developments in the generation of radio-frequency (RF) energy could lead to fundamentally new types of weapon systems that could jam or destroy electronics equipment or be used in antipersonnel roles. The strong Soviet technology base in electromagnetic sources makes Soviet prototype short-range tactical RF weapons highly feasible.

Electronic Materials and Integrated-Circuit Manufacturing — Overall, the West enjoys a strong advantage in this area. The Soviets lag behind the West in certain solid-state component technologies such as photosensitive magnetic bubble memory, acoustic wave, and Josephson Junction devices. This situation could become more pronounced because of US advances in Very High-Speed Integrated Circuits (VHSIC). In this regard, gallium arsenide integrated-circuit chips will soon be produced, and molecular-scale electronics utilizing quantum effects are being researched.

The Soviets consistently demonstrate a sound theoretical understanding in electronics, and in some areas of circuit design and systems engineering are comparable to the West. In military electronics applications, the Soviet Union has developed strong technological capability in millimeter wave devices, as well as in over-the-horizon and phased-array radars.

The nation that effectively exploits and applies these technologies will realize remarkable increases in combat capability due to increases in computing performance and electronic design configurations that are more compact, lighter, and easier to maintain than current systems. The increased reliability resulting from these technologies will provide significant improvements in weapon systems readiness, thereby enhancing overall force capability.

Recent advances in superconducting materials offer the potential to revolutionize applications in sensors, signal processing, magnetic energy storage, and other devices. The United States is in an excellent position to exploit these recent discoveries because of its long history of research support.

Electro-Optics (Including Infrared) — As a result of considerable Soviet expenditures in electro-optic (EO) technologies in wide-ranging applications for reconnaissance, communications, navigation, and target designation, the West is only slightly ahead in this field. The West does lead in the more advanced EO technologies; however, the Soviets are fielding conventional EO equipment in numbers far greater than either the United States or its allies.

The Soviets are exceptionally strong in certain related technologies such as detector materials and solid-state lasers due to heavy R&D investments in these areas. Although based on older technology, the Soviets have fielded much larger quantities of night vision devices, laser rangefinders, and infrared search and track systems than the United States.

To preserve existing advantages over the Soviets in the future use of reconnaissance, communications, and target discrimination, tracking, and resolution, the West has programs to advance infrared, low-light, and optical technologies. Proper exploitation of these technologies will provide significantly increased capability to fight in adverse weather conditions and to operate at night. In addition, exploitation of optical data processing will improve our high-data-rate information processing.

The United States possesses a considerable lead in fiber-optics technology. Exploitation of fiber-optics technology can be of major benefit to telecommunications, large-scale computing, and other applications where wires are currently used. Fiber-optics could allow weight reduction, enable greater rates of information transfer, as well as afford better protection against electromagnetic pulse resulting from nuclear attack.

Explosives — The Soviets have made significant strides in conventional explosives. Their production of most categories of conventional high explosives is greater than that of the West. The Soviet Union, however, is slightly behind in the large-scale production of the advanced conventional high explosive (HMX). Because many Soviet weapons are inherently larger than US analogs, the difference in specific energy content is largely offset. The Soviets also produce many more types of explosive devices than does the United States, again offsetting specific performance handicaps with sheer numbers. The firepower gained through Soviet high-explosive technology is assessed to be comparable to that of the United States.

Chemical Weapons — While the United States does not seek to match the Soviets in quantity, US chemical weapons technology is comparable or better than theirs. US binary weapons technology is representative of the state of the art. Continued US research and production provide deterrence against Soviet use of their extensive chemical warfare capabilities by investigating new developments, agents, and ways to defend against chemical attack.

Materials — In certain areas, Soviet materials R&D and processing techniques lead the world. The Soviets are especially strong in metallic materials processing. They are conducting an extensive effort to improve the steels in their inventory, as well as to develop advanced processing techniques for other metals. A strong technology base, however, in metal-matrix composites will serve the United States well in such strategically important areas as the Strategic Defense Initiative. On the other hand, innovative Soviet work in light alloys based on aluminum, magnesium, and titanium gives them a major strength in the production of traditional military equipment. For example, the USSR is the only nation to fabricate titanium-hulled submarines, like the ALFA SSN.

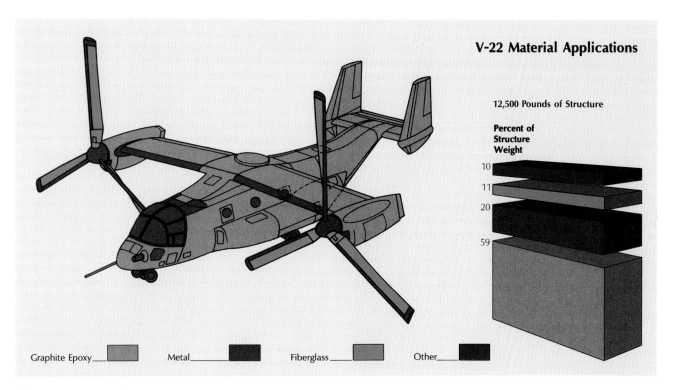

The US V-22 OSPREY contains the most extensive application of advanced composite materials in a developmental aircraft to date. Its capability to perform like a helicopter and a conventional aircraft would not be possible without the extensive use of such materials.

The exploitation of new lightweight, high-strength, high-temperature composites will lead to entirely new and highly advanced military capabilities for both the Soviet Union and the United States. In leading-edge technologies like superalloys, powder metallurgy, ceramics, and composites, Soviet R&D efforts are extensive and probably trail the West by only a small margin. In the area of advanced composites, the Soviets have had a national level program for over 10 years to develop the expertise and industrial infrastructure for production of advanced weapon systems incorporating leading-edge materials. In the United States, however, exploitation of advantages in carbon-carbon composites, plastics, ceramics, and ceramic matrix composites is already enabling production of superior military systems.

In certain fundamental science aspects such as micromechanics, the Soviets are at least equal to the West. They trail the West, however, in advanced design and construction capability.

Production/Manufacturing — The Soviets have very strong technological capabilities for transforming raw materials into final military products. The Soviets have excellent electroslag and plasma-arc remelt capabilities for producing high-quality alloys, and they match world standards in sheet metal forming and metal removal. In welding, they are international innovators in electroslag, friction, electrogas, electron beam, and pulsed arc welding. They have built the world's largest forging and extrusion presses. They are knowledgeable in computer-aided industrial production and are equal to the West on a theoretical basis. Their current major shortcoming is in computer-automated manufacturing. Accordingly, they are using the benefits of "perestroika" and national computer education programs to improve their ability to produce computers and software in line with their drive to restructure their industrial capability.

The United States leads in areas of advanced production technology which are based upon computer technology such as robotics, computer-aided design and manufacturing, and other similar based technologies. US exploitation of advanced production technologies would enable more affordable production of state-of-the-art weapon systems.

Robotics and Machine Intelligence — In the military-industrial sector, exploitation of robotics technologies in welding, structural shape processing, materials handling, and surface preparation and painting could result in increased productivity, and better quality. Operational payoffs would include improved effective-

ness, force multiplication, enhanced safety, and reduced manning. Robotics holds great potential to provide operations and maintenance support in such militarily important areas as fire fighting, ordnance and material handling, sentry and security functions, explosive ordnance disposal, mine neutralization, and undersea search and recovery.

The United States leads the USSR in basic robotics technology mainly as a result of its strength in computerization and software. The Soviets, however, are expected to concentrate on fielding quickly applications of robotics which do not require a high degree of sophistication. Although exploitation of robotics technology will lead to far-reaching improvements in US military capabilities, more extensive research and study remains to be done by the United States because problems associated with robotics are complex and include military concerns over technical feasibility, reliability, and maintainability.

Sensors — The "eyes and ears" of weapon systems consist of sensors and their associated signal processing. The Soviets have vigorously emphasized the development of a large number of sensors of different types and frequencies for a significant capability in the face of Western countermeasures. As a result of Soviet determination to exploit air defense radar-sensor technologies over the past 20 years (while the United States deemphasized its air defense radar-sensor program), new radar-sensor techniques are often first demonstrated by the Soviets.

The United States also has been slow to make extensive use of available technical countermeasures. Thus, US sensors may be unnecessarily vulnerable to a vigorous Soviet operational electronic countermeasures (ECM) program. These factors threaten the air superiority upon which the United States depends to defeat a Soviet theater offensive, and they make it imperative that the United States reestablish its resolve in meeting Soviet challenges and reverse this trend. In the application of advanced sensor technology to spacecraft, however, the United States enjoys a clear advantage.

US exploitation of new sensor technology would enable extensive advances in automatic target recognition, low-observable target detection, thermal detectors, sonar, laser and microwave arrays, countermeasure resistant sensors, laser radar seekers, and other devices. These projects collectively would provide commanders the ability to direct battles characterized by weapon systems operating too rapidly and at distances too great for human sensing and reaction.

Signature Reduction (Stealth) — The Soviets are developing reduced-signature technologies and may be testing these technologies in aircraft and other military weapon systems. They may soon begin limited operational deployment of some "stealth" technologies. The Soviets are believed to have built several test facilities to support their research and development activities.

The United States probably has a significant lead over the Soviets in the practical application of signature reduction to military systems. Due to advances in the Soviet air defense threat, reduction in the visibility of platforms is a high-priority goal for the United States. The technologies involve advanced paints, materials, and system design configurations. Exploitation of these technologies would enable development of air vehicles with the ability to evade detection; engines with low infrared emission; and antennas with low radar cross sections. Better active and passive control of electronic and acoustic signatures could significantly improve signature reduction, platform survivability, and countermeasure capabilities. Improved recognition of decoys and development of decoys are also possible.

Soviet Application of Technology in Fielded Systems

The Soviets are methodically and efficiently transitioning new technologies into their vast arsenal, oftentimes more rapidly than the West. The Soviets already hold quantitative advantages, and are now seeking better weapon system quality. Consequently, the comparative technological level of deployed Soviet systems is gradually improving. This situation is the result of their focused application of technology in shorter development cycles than are typical in the West. Consequently, the Soviets, although lagging the West in technology, frequently field systems that are sufficiently well-engineered to meet or exceed the combat capabilities of Western counterpart systems. For example, the Soviets have developed over 18 types of highly capable and flexible surface-to-air missiles (SAMs), several of which have been used in regional conflicts with devastating effectiveness. In the past 10 years alone, nine different versions of these missiles were deployed, several of which had capabilities which exceeded their Western counterparts.

The Soviets have made significant incremental improvements in the operational capabilities of their weapons as a result of their exploitation — and fielding — of technology. The following examples briefly illustrate this point:

The mobile SA-12A/GLADIATOR and the SA-X-12B/GIANT surface-to-air missiles are expected to be

Relative US/USSR Technology Level in Deployed Military Systems*

Deployed System	US Superior	US/USSR Equal	USSR Superior
STRATEGIC			
ICBMs		■	
SSBNs	■		
SLBMs	■→		
Bombers	■		
SAMs			■
Ballistic Missile Defense			■
Antisatellite			■
Cruise Missiles		←■	
TACTICAL			
Land Forces			
SAMs (Including Naval)		■→	
Tanks		■→	
Artillery		■	
Infantry Combat Vehicles		■	
Antitank Guided Missiles		■→	
Attack Helicopters	■→		
Chemical Warfare			■
Biological Warfare			■
Air Forces			
Fighter/Attack and Interceptor Aircraft	■→		
Air-to-Air Missiles	■→		
Air-to-Surface Munitions	■→		
Airlift Aircraft	■→		
Naval Forces			
SSNs	■→		
Torpedoes		■	
Sea Based Aircraft	■		
Surface Combatants	■→		
Naval Cruise Missiles		■→	
Mines			■
C³I			
Communications		■	
Electronic Countermeasure/ECCM	■→		
Early Warning	■		
Surveillance and Reconnaissance	■→		
Training Simulators	■		

*These are comparisons of system technology levels only, and are not necessarily a measure of effectiveness. The comparisons are not dependent on scenario, tactics, quantity, training or other operational factors. Systems farther than one year from IOC are not considered.

The arrows denote that the relative technology level is changing significantly in the direction indicated.

Relative comparisons of deployed technology levels shown depict overall average standing; countries may be superior, equal or inferior in subsystems of a specific technology in a deployed military system.

The Soviet T-80 tank, with reactive armor mounted around the turret, poses a challenge to Western antiarmor technology development.

The Soviet Su-27/FLANKER, in combination with the AA-10/ALAMO missile, has true look-down/shoot-down capabilities against aircraft and possibly cruise missiles penetrating at low altitudes.

attached over a tank's base armor, first appeared on Israeli tanks in 1983; by 1985 the Soviets were installing it on their tanks. As applied, the armor substantially reduces the effectiveness of Western antitank missiles by degrading a missile's shaped-charge jet. About 3,000 Soviet tanks are fitted with reactive armor mounting apparatuses.

Current Soviet aircraft such as the FULCRUM and the FLANKER exhibit sophisticated aerodynamic designs for flight in the high angle-of-attack profile. The twin vertical stabilizers, wing root leading-edge extension, and segmented wing leading-edge devices are features associated with vortex flow generation and stall alleviation. These advanced aerodynamic design characteristics provide enhanced stability and lift for increased air combat maneuvering capability approaching Western design specifications.

The radar-guided medium-range AA-10/ALAMO air-to-air missile illustrates Soviet advances in missile aerodynamics. This missile employs an advanced airframe with a unique "bow tie" set of movable wings for control. These unusually shaped wings are thought to give excellent roll control and maneuverability at high angles of attack. No Western missiles have employed this wing design.

Two modifications of the Il-76 aircraft provide major increases in warfighting capability. The MAINSTAY, an airborne warning and control aircraft, provides new capability to detect low-flying aircraft, as well as to bring forces to bear in the air battle. The MIDAS, a new aerial tanker, enables refueling-capable combat aircraft to conduct longer range operations. This refueling capability, especially for Soviet bombers equipped with advanced cruise missile systems, significantly enhances Soviet warfighting capability.

widely deployed throughout the Soviet Union in the next few years. The SA-X-12B/GIANT's long range and accuracy provide it with flexible capability for use against a range of potential targets such as interception of other missiles and attack of tactical aircraft and standoff command-and-control platforms. The missile's mobility and small size will make it difficult to verify what role it will actually play because it could be initially employed for theater air defense and then possibly pulled back for ABM defense.

The equipping of T-64B, T-72, and T-80 tanks with reactive and laminated tank armors demonstrates how effectively and rapidly the Soviets have engineered technology into their ground systems and the effect that technology can have on the military balance. Reactive armor, which consists of a series of explosive boxes

The MAINSTAY AWACS aircraft substantially improves Soviet battle management capability by providing early warning against low-altitude penetration and air battle management.

Soviet technology exploitation and modernization has resulted in an enhanced warfighting capability that includes:

- Extensive inventories of improved antiarmor weapons and highly capable attack helicopters that threaten Western armor;
- Challenges to Western air superiority as a result of new tactical aircraft for deep attack;
- Improved air defenses that reduce Western ability to achieve air superiority and to conduct deep attack;
- Extensive new capabilities in electronic combat that threaten the integrity of Western command, control, and communications;
- Improved capabilities in surveillance, reconnaissance, and target acquisition;
- Expanded capability to airlift forces and materiel;
- Expansion of naval power to include nuclear-powered surface warships and long-range cruise missiles;
- Significant advances in the ability to conduct submarine and antisubmarine warfare; and
- Significantly improved capabilities through use of new cruise missiles and tactical ballistic missiles.

In line with their modernization of conventional forces, the Soviets have developed new tactics to exploit their advantages in firepower and location so as to collapse Western defenses quickly. Western nations also have significantly improved their force capability in recent years. The central issue, however, is one of commitment toward future capability.

TECHNOLOGY'S EFFECT ON THE FUTURE BALANCE OF POWER

Warfare through the ages has evolved as a result of changes in mobility, protection, doctrine, training, size, and organization of armed forces and the tactics they employ to achieve military objectives. A major catalyst in revolutionary change, however, has been the integration of new technology within a fighting force. Changes in weapons technology can significantly enhance warfighting capability in a very short time and provide critical military advantages. As a result, in the competition between the Soviet Union and the United States, each country invests in R&D to ensure its national security is protected against technological surprise.

Soviet ALFA-Class submarines, although reaching initial operational capability in 1978, are an example of technological surprise. These titanium hull nuclear attack submarines can dive deeper and run significantly faster than existing US submarines. These abilities, as well as advances in other Soviet submarines, present uncertainties concerning future Soviet developments and what they might portend for US security.

The new AKULA-Class submarines, for example, demonstrate a level of quieting that is higher than previously anticipated. Totally new propulsion systems that result in even quieter and more capable submarines could be the goal of a number of Soviet research programs. Such systems, which would greatly reduce detectability of submarines, have obvious military significance. Therefore, the United States must invest in R&D to maintain its technological lead and protect against any new advances in Soviet capability that could affect the balance of power.

Given R&D's critical role in affecting power balances, it is imperative that constraints on US R&D activities be avoided. In this regard, the Soviet Union is demanding that arms control agreements restrict US ability to develop strategic defenses, although they have already secretly conducted extensive research far exceeding the US effort in this area. The Soviets realize fully the importance of this research, and they recognize that arms control agreements that impede Western defense technology development can prevent the US from realizing national advantages. Therefore, the Soviets, whose strategic defense research is more advanced, and whose governmental structure easily allows secret research activities, have much to gain from a limitation on US R&D — in both conventional as well as strategic defense areas. The United States and its allies must exercise great caution and avoid any agreements that may place the West at a technological and, ultimately, a strategic disadvantage.

As illustrated in the previous chapters, modernization of Soviet military forces is occurring in ways geared to accomplish longer range strategic objectives. The

The AKULA, an advanced multipurpose attack submarine, has the ability to run quietly and to launch long-range cruise missile attacks.

Soviets are taking deliberate steps to upgrade the level of technology incorporated in their military forces and to position their forces so that they may be employed more flexibly. In recognizing both their weaknesses and the future challenge, the Soviets appear to be gearing up for a more sophisticated level of competition with the West.

The Soviets realize that technology is transforming the nature of warfare and that the destructiveness, speed, and precision of new weapon systems could change the balance of power. Marshal Nikolai Ogarkov, a former Soviet Chief of General Staff has stated: "The rapid development of science and technology in recent years creates real preconditions for the emergence in the very near future of even more destructive and previously unknown types of weapons based on new physical principles."

As a result of the rapidly advancing pace of technology, battlefields of the future will be characterized by high-intensity operations; extended fields of operation; rapid shifts in points of resistance; nighttime, all-weather, and all-terrain operations; and a greater reliance on conventional capability to achieve military objectives.

Because of the Soviets' numerical force advantages and strategy of high-intensity operations, it has been US policy for some time to rely on a strategy of flexible response within the spectrum of conflict. By exploiting emerging conventional technologies, the United States, however, could reduce its reliance on nuclear capability for ultimate deterrence. In this regard, both the United States and the Soviets seek to strengthen their conventional capabilities and lessen the potential of a conflict escalating into a nuclear confrontation. These moves, however, are directed toward differing national security objectives.

The Soviet Union seeks to apply technology to meet the demands of combat they believe they will encounter on the integrated conventional battlefield. The Soviets seek to achieve victory more quickly through a conventional offensive. The United States and its allies, on the other hand, seek to exploit their technological advantages to negate the ability of the Soviets to carry out intense and rapid shock operations quickly on the conventional battlefield. The following section illustrates the potential of emerging technologies for strengthening US conventional warfighting capability and overcoming adverse trends in Soviet military power.

CONVENTIONAL US TECHNOLOGICAL OPPORTUNITIES

US and allied efforts to develop systems capable of operating on the conventional battlefield are known as Conventional Defense Improvement Initiatives (CDI). One of the major goals of these efforts is to enhance NATO's Follow-on Forces Attack (FOFA) strategy by enhancing the Alliance's capability to perform deep surveillance and subsequent air attacks in order to disrupt the advance of multiple Soviet ground force echelons and their resupply and reinforcing elements. CDI programs incorporate a number of advanced technologies, including low observables; smart munitions for long-range precision delivery; all-weather, real-time target acquisition; unmanned vehicles; and microprocessing. Advanced sensors, radar and other guidance technologies, real-time data processing, cryptology, stealth, materials processing, and directed-energy technologies individually and collectively will be keys to winning the battles of any future conflict.

In this regard, advanced US programs such as the Joint Surveillance and Target Attack Radar System, the Multiple Launch Rocket System, the Army Tactical Missile System, and the Joint Tactical Fusion Program are vitally important in the technological competition for qualitatively better weapon systems.

Command, Control, Communications, and Intelligence (C³I), and Electronic Combat

Timely collection and dissemination of information is of great importance to reduce the "fog of war." Space-based platforms, aerial and remote sensors, and computers will have a dramatic impact in the future by giving US commanders a near-instantaneous view of the battlefield.

United States superiority on the future battlefield will require application of technologically superior weapons in precise places and times. Command-and-control systems will be required to locate and confirm quickly the identity of specific enemy units; determine the proper response; direct weaponry on the target; confirm destruction; and assess battle damage.

Electronic combat, which involves mastery and control of the electromagnetic spectrum, provides the United States with a force multiplier to offset the Soviets' superior numbers in manpower and systems. C³I systems using advanced technologies must be developed in a manner to capture the "new and unusual" information hidden in the signal-rich battle environment, not only to detect and analyze such information but to disseminate it in a timely manner. These capabilities would neutralize Soviet ability to use the electronic battlefield.

Improved US battle management capabilities will be critically important in neutralizing Soviet numerical superiority. Command-and-control automation technology is a US strength that provides the capability to integrate large quantities of data from multiple sources, employ modern decision aids, and perform highly complex planning. The side that most effectively coordinates, employs, and acts upon the information provided by these technological advances will have a major advantage.

Although the battlefield of the future will be expanded, the automated battlefield management systems will make it more manageable. The commander of the future will be able to lead his forces better and manage his resources for control of the situation while reducing uncertainty. Automation will also support the role of the commander by keeping him continuously in control of the battle.

AirLand Warfare

AirLand Battle doctrine emphasizes the importance of a cohesive approach to the closer-in central battle, the deep and rear area battle, and control of the air. This expanded scope of future combat operations will require rapid shifts in US combat power to achieve decisive results. To engage the Soviets successfully, US land combat forces must be capable of engaging the enemy without lengthy preparation and of moving quickly to keep the enemy off balance. Control of forces on the highly dynamic future battlefield will necessitate increased capabilities to meet the stresses placed on C³I systems, combat support systems, and the mobility of American combat forces. Exploitation of US advantages in technology would enable the development of standoff sensor systems, unmanned reconnaissance platforms, and manned scout aircraft necessary to fight on the future battlefield.

The Air Battle — Overall, US air forces are qualitatively superior to those of the Soviet Union. The Soviets, however, are beginning to close the technological gap with their introduction of advanced aircraft with lookdown/shoot-down capability. To maintain or widen the West's lead, the United States and its allies must field applications of superior Western low-observable technology; new, more maneuverable aircraft; beyond-visual-range missiles; and fire control systems featuring multiple-target handling capability. These capabilities should be augmented by the fielding of unmanned vehicles incorporating advanced technologies.

General US technological opportunities relevant to the Air Battle include the application of low observables in manned and unmanned vehicles; advanced materials; microelectronics and VHSIC data processing; and advanced avionics systems. The ability to operate at night and in adverse weather would be enhanced as a result of advanced sensors, avionics and high-speed data-processing capability. Current US advantages in defense suppression technology should be exploited through the application of superior anti-radiation missiles, radar-warning receivers, and general electronic warfare capability. There will be applications in many lethal and nonlethal roles such as defense suppression, reconnaissance, surveillance, target acquisition, and decoys. Unmanned aerial vehicles, having a variety of combat applications, are likely to come of age in the near future. The use of unmanned vehicles would be an adjunct to, and not a replacement for, US manned forces. Western superiority in simulator technology would permit more realistic and effective training to produce superior pilots and will therefore be a crucial ingredient toward achieving air superiority.

  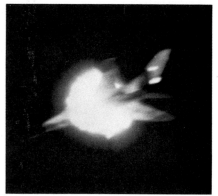

The US advanced medium-range air-to-air missile (AMRAAM) features significant improvements in operational utility, look-down/shoot-down capability, and the ability to operate in an intense electronic countermeasures environment.

The Land Battle — Soviet combat forces have a substantial numerical superiority in close-combat forces and fire support systems as compared to the United States and its allies. The need to improve this aspect to counter these robust Soviet capabilities is well recognized. To do so, the US is fielding ABRAMS tanks and BRADLEY armored fighting vehicles, which have increased firepower, speed, and mobility. The next generation — the Armored Family of Vehicles — will be developed to increase combat capability while reducing procurement and operating costs. To prevent the Soviets from interdicting the movement of Western land forces, the United States should deploy the Forward Area Air Defense System, which integrates advanced weapons, sensors, and command and control.

The current balance of forces in favor of the Soviets could perhaps be redressed by using two important advantages afforded by robotics technology. First, with fiber-optic links and teleoperation concepts, the number of weapon systems controlled by allied combat units can be increased without increasing unit size. Second, robotics would remove the weapon system operator from highly lethal environments, and thus increase

the survivability of highly trained and experienced US weapon crews.

In future close-combat battle, two technologies offer promise and complement each other very effectively. The Fiber-Optic Guided Missile, while it also will affect the conduct of air defense, can expand the high lethality engagement zone to beyond line-of-sight when used as an antitank weapon. US exploitation of hypervelocity missile technology would provide very high engagement rates and high lethality when enemy combat units come into line of sight. Balanced combinations of the antiarmor capabilities offered by these two technologies would provide the United States with significant advantages and help offset Soviet numerical superiority in armored systems.

Impact of Smart Munitions — The "fire-and-forget" nature of smart munitions provides a unique capability throughout the spectrum of combat. These weapon systems would allow the United States to attack deep targets precisely and provide capability for simultaneous engagement of multiple targets. Just as important, their longer range would enable focused integration

The Fiber-Optic Guided Missile is in development to defeat advanced helicopter and armor threats. Pictured is an early experimental firing demonstrating the potential of its antiarmor mission.

of our firepower laterally across the front, thereby serving as a force multiplier. For example, large arrays of land-mobile targets could be effectively engaged at longer ranges, thus numerically superior enemy forces would be countered before they could fire on US forces.

Recent advances in electronics and computer processing are being applied to improve seekers, sensors, and fuzes. These, coupled with new warhead technologies and doctrine, form the basis of current US thrusts in smart munitions. Smart munitions such as the Sensor Fuzed Weapon, the Search and Destroy Armor, and Smart Target Activated Fire and Forget submunitions utilize advanced directional fuze concepts and Explosively Formed Penetrator warheads that will provide significant advantages.

Maritime Warfare

An infusion of advanced technology will have a profound impact on all aspects of the maritime balance. Through the use of over-the-horizon radar technology, US and Allied nations can monitor hostile ships and aircraft. As it has in previous conflicts, the superior

exploitation and application of technology to locate, identify, and attack unfriendly forces, as well as to provide battle damage assessment, would provide an added margin of superiority.

Integrated Strike Warfare — In battles of the future, the expanded integration of maritime forces within the AirLand Battle will be crucial to successful combat operations. Military applications of technology will provide expanded capabilities for launching coordinated strikes on land targets by advanced ship-launched (surface and submarine) cruise missiles and carrier-based aviation such as the Advanced Tactical Aircraft. These advanced weapon systems will strengthen integration of naval deep-strike capabilities with land-based aviation and could significantly affect the ground campaign in NATO and in other areas of the world.

Antiair Warfare (AAW) — As a result of the tremendous capability inherent in US carrier aviation and extensive shipboard AAW systems, the capability exists to defend against enemy airstrikes on carrier battle forces, convoys, and some land areas. The development of the Advanced Tactical Fighter aircraft will significantly enhance this robust capability. Battle force survivability, to continue both the war at sea and strikes inland, will depend on US ability to neutralize the Soviet air threat. In this regard, applications of technology that strengthen US ability to negate air threats posed by the Soviets are vitally important.

Submarine Warfare — As a result of the numerical superiority of Soviet submarines, and Moscow's likely strategies for employing them, a high, favorable combat exchange rate with the Soviets would be crucial in any future conflict. A new US attack submarine under development, the SSN-21/SEAWOLF, will improve greatly US ability to combine firepower, mobility, speed, endurance, survivability, and stealth to combat Soviet submarines. Detection is the key to successful antisubmarine warfare; inadvertent emissions will be a primary source of detection as submarines become quieter. Exploitation of the acoustic and nonacoustic environment — for both offensive and defensive purposes — will become increasingly important for US, allied, and Soviet forces in submarine warfare. US exploitation of technology for the innovative use of submerged launch platforms against air- and land-based targets such as tactical ballistic and cruise missiles would go a long way in redressing existing imbalances in overall force structure.

Exploitation of technology in areas of active sonar and nonacoustic means of detection can enable the United States to maintain its lead in antisubmarine

Smart munitions use shoot-to-kill technology to attack more vulnerable areas of armored targets.

portend a new age in warfare as new concepts, new doctrine, and new force structures are developed. As strategic defenses mature, there will be a need to rethink conventional deterrence in a world reshaped by the reduced numbers and values of nuclear weapons. Other shifts in the balances of power may result from technology's inevitable advance. The military implications of technology's influence will not be limited to land, sea, and air because revolutionary advances in both the United States and Soviet Union are making space the last frontier and high ground for strategic influence.

In spite of the US desire to reduce the level of international tension through arms control agreements, the inevitable advance of technology will have a profound effect upon the world balance of power. The US must be careful not to underestimate Soviet intent or technological capability nor to negotiate away advantages. Were they integrated with a force that is already quantitatively superior, seemingly innocuous applications of advanced technology could provide the Soviets with qualitative advantages as well. This deadly combination could provide the Soviets significant strategic and tactical advantages in wartime and have a corrosive effect on the deterrent posture of Western alliances in peacetime.

The West's current technological lead is threatened by an extensive Soviet commitment to surpass the United States and its allies. Given their levels of investment, the Soviets could eventually deploy numerous high-technology weapons in those areas where they do not have them now. The challenge for the United States and its allies is to maintain technological superiority in an era of declining defense budgets and a more sophisticated level of Soviet competition. This challenge requires a reenergized US and allied commitment to field highly capable military forces by translating current technology advantages into actual defense capabilities. As a critical element of collective security, the United States and its allies must rethink how best to marshal the potential of superior national resources to exploit their technological advantages while the West still has a commanding lead.

The opportunities to use this technological edge to improve the West's conventional capabilities significantly are almost unlimited; but if the science and technology programs that present options for the future are to be realized, the Alliance must invest wisely in them now. To do otherwise risks conceding the technological initiative to the Soviet Union, which will have serious implications for the future balance of world power. Regardless of Western actions, the Soviets can be counted upon to be relentless in pursuing the technology that will support their ultimate goals.

warfare. Because of the Soviets' dedicated acoustical quieting efforts, there is a major need to exploit current US advantages in acoustics to improve surface ship, airborne and submarine sonar arrays and signal processing.

CHALLENGES AND CONSTRAINTS

New surveillance systems, high-speed semiconductors, artificial intelligence, optical devices, stealth, advanced propulsion systems, and a host of other advances

156

The Vertical Launch System is capable of firing antiair or antisurface missiles. Combined with the AEGIS radar, VLS provides the US Navy with quick-reaction, high-firepower, and improved electronic countermeasures.

CHAPTER IX

Collective Security: Our Risks and Responsibilities

The preceding chapters clearly demonstrate the basis for President Reagan's statement, "we are safer, but not yet safe." Since 1981, America has moved away from the dangerous trends of the 1970s, which were characterized by consistent real cuts in defense spending and an unrealistic attitude about the threats we and our allies faced in the world. The effect of these trends was to create great risks for the West and greater intransigence and opportunities for the Soviet Union. The Soviets' intransigence was shown in their walking out of arms negotiations. Their opportunism was seen in Ethiopia, South Yemen, Angola, and Afghanistan, to note just a few cases.

As *Soviet Military Power 1988* shows, Soviet behavior and the character of their military buildup have changed very little in the decade of the 1980s, but America's response to that behavior has changed significantly. The strength of our collective response has resulted in the Soviets' return to serious and realistic negotiations.

One point, however, must be stressed with respect to our posture toward the Soviet Union, and that concerns the requirement imposed to reduce our defense spending substantially. Penury, as former Defense Secretary Caspar W. Weinberger often said, has its price; that price is the increased risks America and its allies will confront as a result of the dramatic cuts being made in military spending.

Admiral William J. Crowe, Jr., Chairman of the Joint Chiefs of Staff, has emphasized that such risks seldom present themselves immediately. Rather, they accrue over years as a consequence of reduced investment in the equipment, research, and manpower that are needed to deter or fight a war. The threats we face today will not abate. In the years ahead, however, we may simply be less capable of meeting those threats.

The trend toward reduced defense funding that began in 1985 is beginning to mirror the ruinous decade of the 1970s. There is no reason to believe that the consequences of our adversaries' perception of an American withdrawal from its global commitments will be any different than it was in those years. Indeed, as this report demonstrates, the Soviets have made such substantial improvements in their military power since the 1970s that any unwillingness on our part to maintain a global balance of power could have potentially disastrous consequences.

Since the publication of *Soviet Military Power 1987*, the Soviets have intensified their public relations campaign designed to portray a new Soviet commitment to peace and to persuade the West that Moscow's intentions are benign. In this respect, Soviet General Secretary Gorbachev's initiatives, such as democratization of the Communist Party and Soviet society, "perestroika" of the Soviet economy and society, and "glasnost" have had a significant impact in both Soviet domestic and foreign policy. These themes strike a concordant note in Western democracies, but prudence dictates caution to see whether the Soviet leadership is willing and able to translate its rhetoric into reality. Thus, the significance and durability of these themes remain unclear; but what is clear is that, thus far, they have had no perceptible impact on Soviet global goals, as indicated by their actions, or the continuing buildup of Soviet military power far in excess of any legitimate defense needs.

We know that General Secretary Gorbachev is dissatisfied with the performance of the Soviet economy. However, the resources to rebuild and reinvigorate the civilian economy will not be taken at the expense of military capabilities. Indeed, we expect that sector to continue its steady growth. While growth in the domestic economy is one aim of General Secretary Gorbachev's reforms, it is also true that a major motivation for these reforms is to develop the capability to compete more effectively in the military arena over the long term. Moreover, even if the Soviets were to decide to make no new investments in their military weapons production capacity, the enormous investment already made means that Soviet defense production will not be reduced significantly — at least through 1990.

Thus, regardless of the General Secretary's much publicized proposals for reform and the possibility of meaningful changes, actual Soviet military capabilities are continuing to improve and expand. Our defense policy cannot be based on Soviet pronouncements, or

While the Soviet Union remains the most dangerous threat to our collective security, there are many other diverse threats and challenges, like those in the Persian Gulf, for which we must also be adequately prepared.

on hopes for a moderation in the Kremlin's behavior. Rather, we must ensure that we have the means to meet the Soviet threat as manifested by their actions and their capabilities, not their words.

We believe that the strategic balance today is essentially stable. This balance, however, must be understood in broad terms and not merely through weapons counts and simple exchange models. Such factors as the asymmetries in US and Soviet passive and active defenses would have a major influence on the ability of our retaliatory forces to perform their missions. America's ability to deter aggression is based, in large measure, on how the Soviets perceive their ability to achieve their political and military goals from a nuclear exchange. Thus, the continued modernization of Soviet strategic offensive forces combined with Moscow's robust strategic defense program could erode our strategic deterrent's credibility.

Therefore, it remains our responsibility to continue to modernize our offensive and defensive strategic capabilities to demonstrate to the Soviets that they do not possess an exploitable military advantage at the strategic nuclear level.

The major regional and functional balances are complex and interdependent. In Europe, we remain concerned with the advantages the Warsaw Pact holds over NATO in most categories of forces. These advantages stem, in part, from the continuing pace of Warsaw Pact weapons production that has outstripped NATO's efforts over the past decade. As a result, the Warsaw Pact has been able to expand and modernize its forces at a faster rate than has the NATO Alliance. This situation is particularly worrisome because NATO's strategy of "flexible response" calls for a credible deterrent across the entire spectrum of conflict. If we are to remain capable of deterring Soviet aggression in Europe, these adverse trends must be reversed.

The Middle East/Southwest Asia remains an area of great concern to the United States for a number of very critical political, military, and economic reasons. There, as elsewhere, the local military balances — notably the Iran-Iraq, Arab-Israeli, and India-Pakistan balances — play a very important part in assessing the potential for conflict in the region.

For example, the Soviet Union's proximity to the Persian Gulf region provides it with significant military advantages, but these are offset by the clear determination of the region's states to maintain their independence from Soviet domination. Were the Soviets to attempt to seize the region's oil fields with military force, they would have to sustain long lines of communications over extremely difficult terrain, which would be vulnerable to air attack and interdiction.

Further, since the establishment of the US Central Command, we have improved our capability to project military force rapidly into the region. This improved capability, together with the fact that we would require far fewer forces to defend the region than the Soviets would to conquer it, act as a powerful deterrent to Soviet aggression.

In the Far East, we continue to observe the Soviets upgrading their military forces. Although Moscow and its clients, the North Koreans and the Vietnamese, retain some clear advantages, several theater-wide factors favor the United States and our allies in the region. Most notably, close allies such as Japan provide bases and infrastructure to support our forward-deployed forces. Japan's key location, modernization of its self-defense forces, and assumption of new missions also enable it to provide for a major part of its own defense. Japan's continued economic growth, and the economic dynamism of the entire Pacific Basin as exemplified by South Korea, serve to broaden the basis for developing the self-defense capabilities of friendly regional countries. These very positive economic developments make the long-term regional trends in the military balance appear very favorable.

As was pointed out in the assessment of the maritime balance, the United States and the Soviet Union have entirely different requirements for naval power. For instance, the United States and its allies are critically dependent on the world's oceans for resupply, reinforcement, and power projection. Thus, maritime superiority is essential for us to satisfy our collective security requirements. The Soviets, on the other hand, need

only deny certain key areas to us and our allies for their maritime strategy to be effective. As this report points out, the trends in the naval balance are not entirely favorable and the margin of superiority that we enjoy is being reduced. Nevertheless, we and our allies maintain a substantial lead over the Soviets in many important areas of naval warfare.

We also enjoy significant advantages over the Soviets in our comparative abilities to project military power at great distances. The Soviets, however, are gradually expanding their capability in this area by developing very useful military assets — airlift forces, the merchant marine, arms sales, and military assistance programs — which would assist them greatly in projecting military power.

Both the United States and the Soviet Union look to technology as a means to enhance their military capabilities. While the United States and our European and Japanese allies enjoy significant advantages, particularly in our combined abilities to innovate, the Soviets have demonstrated their ability to acquire, develop, and field militarily relevant technologies, often before we do.

As we assess the results of our investment in enhancing our own military capabilities over the last seven years, it is clear that we can look with pride to the great progress we have made. By any measure, our forces are better equipped, better compensated and better trained, and far more ready than they have been at any time since the end of the Vietnam War. We and our allies have maintained our lead in some areas of the military balance — such as the maritime balance — and narrowed the gap in others.

But what about the future?

Major new weapon systems incorporating new technologies require long lead times to perfect, produce, and field in sufficient quantity to have a significant effect on our defense capabilities. But actual military capabilities, and the resultant military balances, tend to change gradually. Thus, we must prepare now to counter threats that will emerge in 10 to 15 years. Both the United States and the Soviet Union face a number of potentially revolutionary new technologies that may dramatically alter the characteristics of future conflict. Both sides face economic pressures that will constrain the development and deployment of these new systems. Given the tremendous Soviet investment in current military technology and equipment, it should not be surprising that the Soviets may be searching for ways to limit, or at least delay, the development and deployment of new weapon systems, for example those concerned with SDI, that may make currently fielded systems obsolete.

Soviet military analysts appear generally satisfied with their current and near-term (five years) military capabilities. They appear to be increasingly concerned, however, about their mid- to long-term prospects (five to 10 years and beyond). They have been impressed by strong signs of a renewed Western willingness to compete militarily. They have always been concerned about Western technological competence, and they fear provoking the West into making a sustained commitment to translate technological superiority into a superior fielded military capability. This concern is reinforced by a growing doubt that the overall performance of the Soviet economy will support a full range of options to resolve mid- and long-term military requirements.

There are a number of new conventional weapons technologies that could substantially alter any future military balance. NATO countries are working on advanced sensors and targeting technologies that could significantly improve conventional defense against Warsaw Pact tank armies.

Improved accuracy and a variety of conventional munitions warheads for Soviet short-range missiles could make these systems an important factor, particularly if integrated into a massive Soviet air operation timed to coincide with the initiation of hostilities. On the other hand, NATO deployment of a tactical ballistic missile defense could neutralize this threat. Soviet submarine quieting will make US antisubmarine warfare more difficult. This increased Soviet capability could free additional naval assets from defensive orientations and allow them to focus on other missions, to include an increased threat to critical sea lines of communication.

While the Soviets are actively exploring a host of new technologies, they remain concerned about their ability to compete over the long term. They believe that their economic efficiency and general economic competence must be improved substantially. Gorbachev's drive to implement "perestroika" and "glasnost" are highly visible signs of a major new effort to revitalize the Soviet economy, an effort which they see as vital for the support of their long-range goals.

The Soviet effort to restructure their economy will not be easy, nor can it be accomplished without risk. Since the economy of the Soviet Union is totally controlled by the central political apparatus, economic reform can have major political implications. Efforts to decentralize economic decisionmaking (and thus improve economic performance) may result in reduced political control. This concern is a major reason that past efforts have been strongly resisted, and why there is considerable current opposition to reform. Gorbachev wants improved economic performance, but he does not want to reduce Communist Party control. The goals are antithetical. Gorbachev may be searching for an equilibrium that is unattainable. If he is too cautious, there may be no improvement in the economy. He has already provoked considerable opposition from Communist Party and state bureaucrats who are strongly opposed to constraints on their personal power and influence. If Gorbachev is too ambitious in implementing reform, a backlash might produce unanticipated political and social results. Yet from a strictly military perspective, the ultimate measures of true reform will be measurably reduced military spending and decreased force structure.

Whatever the ultimate consequences of "glasnost" or the hopes for meaningful change in the Soviet Union, the security responsibilities of the West rest, as always, in our own hands. Moreover, threats inherent in the international system and hostile powers quite independent of the Soviet Union will continue to require that America, as the Free World's leading power, bear a significant defense burden. But this is not, as some might argue, a message of pessimism and despair. True, the challenge posed by the Kremlin and others compels us to spend more for defense than we would prefer. Yet as more than 40 years of experience has demonstrated, if we do what is required to build and modernize the defense forces needed and offer political and moral leadership to the world, we can avoid tempting our adversaries into dangerous confrontations, while offering hope to those struggling to free themselves from the bonds of tyranny and oppression. The point is that there is no mystery as to what America should do in the face of Soviet military power, or indeed the host of other threats that challenge our security. The question turns on our collective willingness to remain true to our heritage as a free people.

SOVIET
MILITARY
POWER

First Edition	September 1981
Second Edition	March 1983
Third Edition	April 1984
Fourth Edition	April 1985
Fifth Edition	March 1986
Sixth Edition	March 1987
Seventh Edition	April 1988

ILLUSTRATIONS

INDEX

ILLUSTRATIONS

V

VI

VII

VIII

■ ■ ■

IX

INDEX

A

AA-9/AMOS missile, 82

AA-10/ALAMO, 82, 150

AAW. *See* Antiair warfare

Abe, Shintaro, 27

ABM Treaty, 56, 58, 103. *See also* Ballistic missile defense

ABRAMS tank, 154

Advanced cruise missile (ACM), 100, 102

Advanced Tactical Fighter, 144

AEGIS cruiser, 123, 130, 131

Aerial refueling, 51, 107, 110, 121, 137, 150

Aerodynamics, 143-144, 150

Aeroflot, 29, 30, 93

Afghanistan, 8, 18, 158

  Arab states and, 24

  Geneva Accords, 24-25

  Soviet occupation of, 9, 23-25, 119, 120

  US and, 23-25, 138

Africa, 9, 30-31, 138

Air battle, future, 153

Air cushion vehicles (ACVs), 108, 131

Air defense, 68, 71-73, 80-82, 85-86, 102-103, 107-108. *See also* Surface-to-air missiles

Air Defense Forces, Soviet, 13, 16, 38, 68, 80-82, 89

Air Defense Initiative (ADI), 102

Air Forces, Soviet

  Commander in Chief of, 13, 16

  conventional, 68, 71, 78-82, 93

  logistics and readiness of, 89, 91-92

  maritime role of, 128

  military balance in Europe and, 108, 110, 117

  radioelectronic combat and, 89

  strategic aviation and, 38, 40, 44, 50-53, 102

Air Forces of the Military Districts and Groups of Forces (AF MD/GOF), 78, 79-80

Aircraft carriers

  current Soviet, 68, 83, 84, 87

  new generation of Soviet, 38, 84-85, 130, 131, 134

  US, 130-131, 155

Aircraft production, 36, 37, 38-39

AirLand Battle (NATO), 12, 153-155

Airlift capabilities

  Soviet, 93, 121, 136-137

  US, 121, 131, 136-137

Air-launched cruise missile (ALCM), 40, 44, 50, 51, 53, 67, 100, 102, 123

Air-superiority fighter (ASF), 82

Air-to-air missiles, 81-82, 150

Akhromeyev, Sergey, 13

AKULA-Class submarine (SSN), 38, 51, 53, 85, 151

ALCM. *See* Air-launched cruise missiles

ALEXANDER BRYKIN missile support ship, 50

Alfonsin, Raul, 28

Algeria, 23

Alloys technology, 148

ALFA-Class submarine (SSN), 147, 151

Amphibious warfare, 86, 87, 107, 108, 124, 130, 131, 136

Andropov, Yuri, 9

Angola, 30, 31, 83, 138-139, 158

Antiair warfare (AAW) US capabilities in, 155

Antiaircraft weapons, 75, 76-77

Antisatellite (ASAT) capabilities, 59, 64-65, 66

Antiship cruise missiles (ASCM), 28, 83, 86, 87, 130-131

Antisubmarine warfare (ASW)

  Soviet capabilities in, 82, 83, 86, 87, 123, 124

  technology and future of, 155-156

  US capabilities in, 102, 123, 124, 126, 128-129, 155-156, 161

Antisurface warfare forces, (ASUW), 82, 83, 84-85, 86

An-12/CUB transport, 93, 136

An-22/COCK transport, 93

AN-26/CURL transport, 28

An-32/CLINE transport, 26

An-72/COALER transport, 39

An-124/CONDOR transport, 39, 93, 131, 136

Arab League, 23

Arab states, 22-23, 123

Arab-Israeli War (1973), 121

Arctic, 48

Argentina, 28

Arkhipov, Ivan, 27

Armor, 37, 38

Armored Family of Vehicles, 154

Armored Personnel Carrier (APC), 28, 74, 75, 119

Arms control

  INF Treaty and, 53, 54, 109, 118

  Soviet objectives in, 12, 19, 20, 22, 105, 151

Arms sales, 23, 25-26, 29, 138, 160

Army Tactical Missile System (ATACMS), 68

ARS-12U decontamination apparatus, 78

ARS-14 decontamination apparatus, 78

Artillery, 37, 55, 68, 74, 75-76, 109

ASAT. *See* Antisatellite capabilities

ASCM. *See* Antiship cruise missiles

ASEAN (Association of Southeast Asian Nations), 28

ASUW. *See* Antisurface warfare

ASW. *See* Antisubmarine warfare

AS-4/KITCHEN ALCM, 51, 123

AS-6/KINGFISH ALCM, 123

AS-15/KENT ALCM, 40, 44, 50, 51, 53

Austria, 108

AWACS aircraft, 82, 107, 110, 150

B

Bab el Mandeb strait, 118

BACKFIRE bomber. *See* Tu-22M/BACKFIRE

BADGER bomber. *See* Tu-16/BADGER

Ballistic missile defense. *See also* Strategic Defense Initiative

  Soviet active, 55-58, 102, 103-104, 149-150.

  Soviet passive, 58-62

  Soviet space program and, 64, 66

  US neglect of, 98, 103

BALZAM-Class auxiliary intelligence collection ship (AGI), 89

Bases

  Soviet access to foreign, 28, 83, 124, 139

  US access to foreign, 123, 124, 139

BEAR bomber. *See* Tu-95/BEAR

BELUGA-Class submarine, 85

Biochemical technology, 144

BISON tanker, 51

Black Sea, 108, 131

Black Sea Fleet, 86

BLACKJACK bomber, 38, 44, 50, 51, 102

BLINDER bomber. *See* Tu-22/BLINDER

BMP infantry fighting vehicle (IFV), 74, 75, 119

BM-21 rocket launcher, 29

F

Economy, Soviet
  military dimensions of, 32-36, 43
  military implications of reforming, 33, 34-35, 40, 43, 141-142, 158, 161
  problems of, 8-9, 17, 32, 33
  reforms proposed for, 10, 33-34, 161
Egypt, 23, 139
El Salvador, 138
Electromagnetic pulses (EMP), 145
Electronic countermeasures (ECM), 79, 86, 89, 148
Electronic intelligence ocean reconnaissance satellite (EORSAT), 62, 63
Electronic materials and integrated circuit manufacturing technology, 146
Electro-optic (EO) technology, 146-147
ELF (extremely low frequency) communications system, 48
"Energiya", 65
EORSAT (electronic intelligence ocean reconnaissance satellite), 62, 63
Ethiopia, 30-31, 119, 138, 139, 158
Ethnic groups, 40-42
Europe, military balance in, 106-118
  air forces and, 108, 110, 117
  command and control and, 113
  defense capabilities and strategies and, 117
  deterrence and, 113, 116-117, 118
  Follow on Forces Attack (FOFA) and, 12, 68, 113, 117, 152
  ground forces and, 108, 110-111, 117
  logistics, 91, 112, 113
  maritime operations and, 107, 108
  NATO strategy and, 96-97, 106, 113, 117, 118, 152
  nonstrategic nuclear forces and, 108-110
  nuclear escalation and, 106, 116, 117, 118
  outside of Central Region (Western TVD) of, 106-108
  overview of, 106, 159-160
  sustainability of forces and, 111, 113, 117
  Theater Strategic Operation and, 69-74, 90-91, 117
  Warsaw Pact strategy and, 106, 107, 108, 113, 117
Explosively Formed Penetrator (EFP), 155
Explosives technology, 147

Falkland Islands war, 137
Far East. *See* East Asia/Pacific
Far Eastern Theater of Military Operations (TVD), 13, 71, 75, 91
FENCER aircraft, 53, 123.
Fiber-Optic Guided Missile (FOG-M), 154
Fiber-optics technology, 147
FIDDLER, 82
Fighter and fighter/bomber aircraft. *See also* specific aircraft
  capabilities of, 81-82
  mission and deployment of, 79-80, 86, 107-108, 110
  production of, 37, 38-39, 68
FIREBAR aircraft, 82
FISHBED aircraft, 29
FITTER aircraft, 39
FITTER C aircraft, 86
Five Year Plans, 34, 40
FLAGON aircraft, 82
FLANKER aircraft, 39, 107
FLANKER B aircraft, 82
"Flexible response," 11, 96-97, 106, 116, 117, 118, 152
FLOGGER aircraft, 29
Follow on Forces Attack (FOFA), 12, 68, 113, 117, 152
Foreign Ministry, 18
Foreign policy, Soviet
  maritime elements supporting, 82, 83, 87
  orientation, under Gorbachev, 18-20, 31
  toward Afghanistan, 8, 9, 18, 23-25, 119, 120, 158
  toward Africa/Indian Ocean, 29-31, 119
  toward East Asia, 26-28
  toward Eastern Europe, 20-22
  toward India, 25-26
  toward Latin America, 28-29, 138
  toward the Middle East, 22-23, 119, 122
  toward North Korea, 27
  toward Pakistan, 25
  toward the South Pacific, 28
  toward Vietnam, 27-28, 126
  toward Western Europe, 20, 158
Foreign trade, 21, 27, 29, 31
FORGER aircraft, 39, 86, 137
Forging technology, 148
Forward Area Air Defense System, 154

FOXHOUND aircraft, 107. *See Also* MiG-31/FOXHOUND
FOXTROT-Class submarines, 26, 29
FROG (free-rocket-over-ground) missile, 55, 76, 78, 109
FROGFOOT, 39
Frontal aviation, 79-80
FULCRUM. *See* MiG-29
F-14, 123
F/A-18, 123, 130

G

GALOSH ABM missiles, 44, 55-56, 65
Gandhi, Rajiv, 25
Gareyev, M. A., 12
GAZELLE ABM missiles, 44, 55-56
General Staff, 13, 16, 17
Geneva Accords. *See also* Afghanistan
German Democratic, Republic. *See* East Germany
Germany, Federal Republic of. *See* West Germany
"Glasnost," 10, 158, 161
GLCM. *See* Ground-launched cruise missiles
Global navigation satellite system (GLONASS), 63
GOA SAM, 29
Goals and objectives, Soviet. *See also* specific areas and issues
  determinants of, 8
  general foreign policy, 8, 17, 18
  unchanging nature of, 7, 9, 17, 18, 31, 158
GOLF II submarine, 53
Gorbachev, Mikhail
  approach to Eastern Europe of, 20-22
  and China, 26-27
  on chemical weapons, 77
  on defense spending, 35
  economic goals and policies of, 10, 33-35, 141, 158, 161
  emphasis on Asia by, 26
  general foreign policy approach under, 18-20
  military doctrine under, 12
  on Soviet strategic defense effort, 55
  on space activities, 62
  statement on Afghanistan, 24

M   ■   ■ N   ■